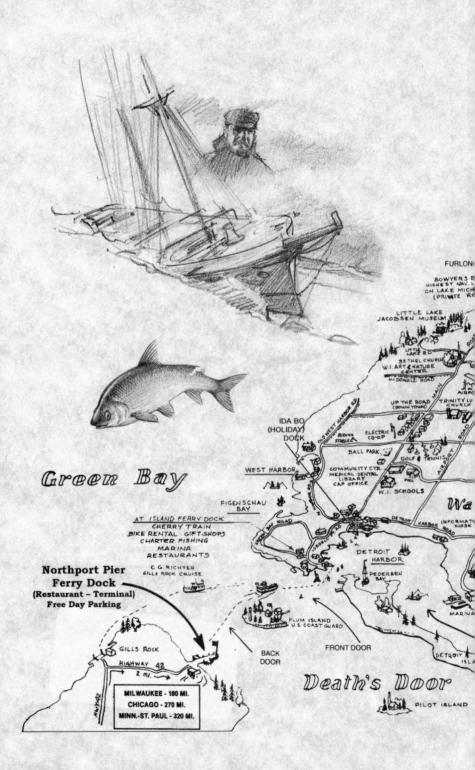

FURLON

BOWYER'S
HIGHEST NAV. L.
ON LAKE MICH
(PRIVATE RO

LITTLE LAKE
JACOBSEN MUSEUM

LITTLE
LAKE RD
BETHEL CHURCH
W.I. ART & NATURE
CENTER
McDONALD ROAD

UP THE ROAD
(DOWN TOWN)

TRINITY LU
CHURCH

IDA BO
(HOLIDAY)
DOCK

RIDING
STABLE

ELECTRIC
CO-OP

BALL PARK

GOLF & TENNIS

WEST HARBOR

COMMUNITY CTR.
MEDICAL-DENTAL
LIBRARY
CAP OFFICE

POOL

W.I. SCHOOLS

Green Bay

FIGENSCHAU
BAY

DETROIT

Wa

AT ISLAND FERRY DOCK
CHERRY TRAIN
BIKE RENTAL GIFT SHOPS
CHARTER FISHING
MARINA
RESTAURANTS

INFORMATI
KIOSK

DETROIT
HARBOR

C.G. RICHTER
GILLS ROCK CRUISE

PEDERSEN
BAY

**Northport Pier
Ferry Dock**
(Restaurant – Terminal)
Free Day Parking

MARINA

PLUM ISLAND
U.S. COAST GUARD

GILLS ROCK

HIGHWAY 42
2 mi.

BACK
DOOR

FRONT DOOR

DETROIT
ISL

MILWAUKEE - 180 MI.
CHICAGO - 270 MI.
MINN.-ST. PAUL - 320 MI.

Death's Door

PILOT ISLAND

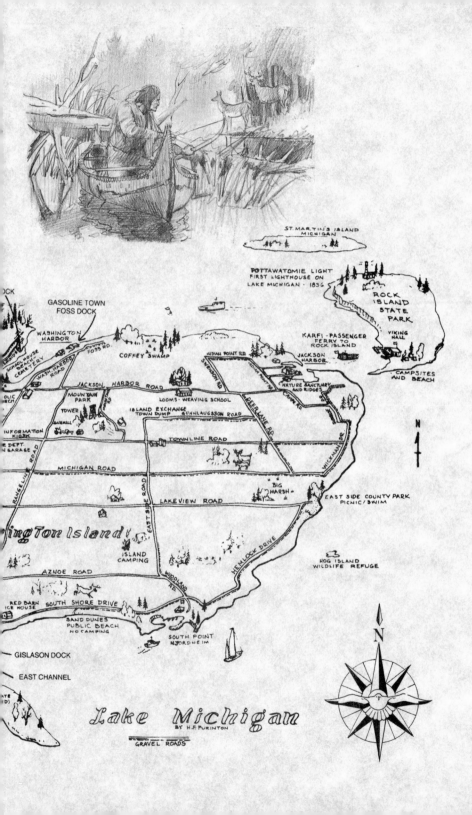

St. Martin's Island Michigan

Pottawatomie Light
First Lighthouse on
Lake Michigan · 1836

Rock
Island
State
Park

Viking
Hall

Gasoline Town
Foss Dock

Washington Harbor

Karfi · Passenger
Ferry to Rock Island

Jackson Harbor

Campsites
and Beach

School House Beach Cemetery

Foss Rd.

Coffey Swamp

Indian Point Rd.

Wash. Harbor Road

Nature Sanctuary
and Ridges

Jackson Harbor Road

Sheldon Rd.

Deer Lane Rd.

Chip Rd.

Mountain Park

Looms · Weaving School

Tower

Sawmill

Island Exchange
Town Dump

Gunnlaugsson Road

Information Kiosk

Fire Dept.
Town Garage

Range Line Road

Townline Road

Wickman Dr.

Michigan Road

East Side Road

Lakeview Road

Big
Marsh

East Side County Park
Picnic / Swim

...ington Island

Island
Camping

Hemlock Drive

Hog Island
Wildlife Refuge

Aznoe Road

Woodland Rd.

Red Barn
Ice House

South Shore Drive

Sand Dunes
Public Beach
No Camping

South Point
N. Jordheim

Gislason Dock

East Channel

Lake Michigan
By H.P. Purinton

N

Gravel Roads

WORDS ON WATER

A Ferryman's Journal
Washington Island, WI
2007

by

Richard Purinton

About the Author

Richard Purinton was born in Sturgeon Bay September 22, 1947. He graduated from Sturgeon Bay High School in 1965, and UW-Madison in 1970 with a BA in journalism. He served four years in the U.S. Navy as quartermaster and married Mary Jo Richter in 1972. They raised three children in their island home. Richard has worked for Washington Island Ferry Line since 1974, first as deckhand, then ferry captain, general manager, and most recently as company president.

Richard has written for several marine periodicals (*Work Boat, Foghorn*), contributed a chapter in the Land Trust book *The Nature of Door,* and edited and published the 1990 photographic essay *Over and Back: A Picture History of Transportation to Washington Island,* which received a Wisconsin State Historical Society Award of Merit. In March 2007 he began blog postings at **www.ferrycabinnews.blogspot.com,** News and Opinion from Washington Island, the Surrounding Islands and the Island Community — From a Ferry Operator's Point of View.

Acknowledgements

Thanks to Norbert Blei for his challenge to begin a daily journal from a ferry operator's perspective, and for his continuing encouragement.

Selected entries from *Words On Water* appeared in a chapter of *Other Voices* published in May 2007 by Cross + Roads Press, edited by Norbert Blei. The tribute to J.J. Ehlenfeldt appeared in the *Island Observer.*

Publisher/Editor N. Blei
Layout Editor: Jan Mielke
Cover and text page photos: Richard Purinton
Map: H. F. Purinton
Map drawings: Charles Peterson
Copyright: © 2009 CROSS+ROADS PRESS
ISBN: 978-1-889460-22-2

10 9 8 7 6 5 4 3 2
Second Printing

Printed in Canada.

CROSS ✚ ROADS PRESS
Door County Editions
P.O. Box 33
Ellison Bay, WI 54210
www.norbertblei.com
www.bleidoorcountytimes.com

to
Mary Jo

To the Island
an Introduction
by
Norbert Blei

It was around 1956. My first visit. I was a guest of my future in-laws who had access to a house in Ephraim one week each summer. I remember taking a ride with them by car one afternoon all the way to Gills Rock—a considerable distance in those days. The plan was to buy some smoked fish for dinner at the small store on the dock, take in the view, watch the ferry from Washington Island arrive or depart, if you were lucky to be there at the time. Simple pleasures.

I remember the *Griffin* or the *C.G.Richter* (two small ferry boats which carried about 8 or 9 cars and a number of passengers) sidling up to the dock, the mooring line tossed, made fast, the engine powering down, the steel-plate, side ramp slowly lowered by a winch ...steel banging on concrete, voices of the crew, the line of waiting automobiles up the hill, starting up, ready to be driven on-board ...the small ferry rocking a little with the weight of each car leaving the dock for the deck, skillfully parked, slipped into the smallest space by a crew member.

A quiet excitement in the air. A journey over the water to who-knows-where about to begin.

It was not the *Queen Mary* arriving or departing, nor a Carnival cruise ship. But it *was* a picture postcard setting. Old-time Wisconsin. A man and a boy fishing from the dock. White gulls squawking, winging against a blue sky, setting down on roofs, on fishing tugs, sprinkling themselves upon the bobbing water...waiting for *something* to engage their nature...only to ascend suddenly against the bluff, the panorama in the distance. There was the feel of a lake breeze. The smell of fish. And the gentle warmth of the sun, destined to set hours away above, slipping into the waters and clouds...setting off a light-show you could never capture with a Brownie camera, though you kept trying. It all made for the wonder of travel. Being there...elsewhere. A certain calm.

A study of engagement, disengagement. Reflection. All from a small ferry dock. Something you could not quite find at the edge-of-nowhere, anywhere else in the Midwest, if you hailed from the city, came north each summer to find yourself on a Wisconsin peninsula surrounded by blue water and air so fresh air you could taste. Something to take back, to keep—the way it was, the way you were.

And at that point, just around the harbor where the ferry docked...the 'Top o' the Thumb,' the 'Tip of the Peninsula'... at the very end of the Door peninsula, where on a clear day you could see all the way to Escanaba, Michigan, there was *that* strait folks talked about, separating the mainland from the Island, that dangerous passageway connecting Lake Michigan to Green Bay, steeped in local history, printed on maps as *Porte Des Mortes*. A watery graveyard of old sailing vessels. Memories of Indians, canoes, the French, schooners, white sails, storms, drowned sailors, lighthouses...foghorns singing mournfully over the depths.

A stretch of water the Island ferry continues to cross every day, every season, in all kinds of weather.

If you looked very hard north, north-east from the tip of the peninsula, scanned the islands in the distance, the water meeting the horizon, there...maybe you caught just a glimpse of if it, the Island ferry about to enter, cross the haunted Death's Door again...all of the back-and forth business of time and passengers, everything caught in such beautiful falling, lifting, innocent summer light.

Just to witness this part of the end of the peninsula, the beginning of something else, got you thinking. Took you back, took you elsewhere—be it Gills Rock in the early days, or the dock at Northport where the ferries began running in 1984.

Who is the ferryman in the wheelhouse?

What must his life be like?

What's over there, anyway?

How could anyone live on an island?

There must be some real stories there.

JANUARY

Tuesday, January 2 –

I live on Washington Island, Wisconsin, off the tip of the Door Peninsula. The island is surrounded by the waters of Lake Michigan to the east and Green Bay to the west.

This island seems a mystery to many, including myself some days. How people find Washington Island, or how it finds them, must be as varied as the people themselves. What moves people to live on or visit this island?

Some arrive for recreation and never care to leave. They plan and even scheme for the day when they retire or change jobs, for the day fate will intervene and present them with an opportunity to live here or visit more frequently. Marriage and divorce can also be great motivators.

In my case, it was marriage to an island girl, Mary Jo Richter, and her shared interest in returning to Wisconsin to live and raise our one year old son, Hoyt. I was on the down slope of a four year enlistment in the U.S. Navy, and we lived in San Diego. Navy life, the ships, going to sea, the bustle of San Diego — all of that held great appeal for us. But, we missed the seasons, the waters of Lake Michigan, and the familiarity of friends, family and places.

This morning we awaken to a light frost. The sun arises with clear, blue skies. It's a morning with the feel of early fall, not early new year. There's not a snow bank in sight. The several days of heavy rain have long since soaked in and the pavement is dry.

It's a great day — and a great drive to work — all four minutes of it spent in my truck, barely enough time to let the coffee cool or the heater get warm. With the low gas warning light flashing, I pulled off at the Hansen Amoco station.

Contractor and Islander baseball coach, Ted Jorgenson, on the other side of the pumps, and I exchanged greetings and information on the bowl games of the night before. Gas cap snapped in place, half tank "fill" in my truck, and on to the ferry dock.

The drive is just two miles from home — from the golf course where home juts between the eighth green and number nine fairway — a drive I make twice or more a day, nearly every day of the year.

Like many mornings, I pass only one or two cars. Today none, except Ted's truck at the filling station. Some days a deer or several turkeys might cross the road, but on this second day of January traffic is nil. The first ferry of the day is 8 a.m. And today's the last day of multiple ferry trips before the scant winter ferry schedule begins.

Not but a few years earlier, before the powerful *Arni J. Richter* icebreaker began winter service, we ran four or five round trips after Year's Day to get the waiting crowd back to the mainland after a long holiday weekend. It was an all day affair, then, back-to-back trips with the *C.G. Richter* and its 9-car capacity. Sometimes the crew squeezed on an extra car or two, so that by the last crossing only three or four cars were left to be loaded. With the *C.G.*, if ice blocked the route — and there was ice on January 1st about 40 percent of the time — then trips took longer.

Altogether different results emanate from the *Arni J. Richter*. We make four trips through the New Year's holiday, each one on schedule whether there is ice enroute or not. Customers and crew know where they stand, that trips will be made in a timely manner. Traffic flows without a hitch.

The morning ferry this 2nd of January, this first real work day of the new year, is filled with people and cars heading across the Door, southward to homes in Green Bay, Chicago, Milwaukee. On the return trip the ferry is mostly empty. Maybe a few retirees or islanders who shopped on the mainland travel today, perhaps a furnace repairman coming to the island for a house call. Today school resumes, so young families with children are already here, children in school, parents at work or in their homes.

Mid-morning, the 2006 Harley Davidson calendar is taken down and the 2007 version tacked to my bulletin board.

This is where I work, my office. One eye is on the clock, another on the ferry's progress, and my mind is floating between the Federal Register proposal for Voyage Data Recorders, company end-of-year reports, and the tidying-up of Christmas correspondence.

This first day of the new year feels good. It's sunny, bright and the days ahead are going to be exciting.

Wednesday, January 3 –

Thirty-two years ago I asked Arni Richter, my father-in-law, if I could work for him. This inquiry came with about 16 months left to complete my Navy enlistment. I was a quartermaster, meaning I worked in ship navigation with bridge record keeping. I was a wheelsman at times, and I maintained navigational charts and publications.

But prior to that, I had a love of sailing. Operating mechanically propelled vessels wasn't my greatest interest, but working on and around the water was. Mary Jo and I decided to move back to Wisconsin, to Washington Island, and I would begin work for Arni on the Ferry Line.

This is still what I do. Daily I check the ferries, observe the current weather and try to look ahead at tomorrow's conditions. Day's end is marked by a line of autos with headlights on streaming past our home on Main Road, sign of the last ferry of the day mooring, discharging its load, and the crew securing it for the evening.

We have great times as a couple and as a family with our three grown children — two of them married with children of their own. But I am always conscious of living on an island where what we do — ferrying people, cars and freight — is of the greatest importance to the island community. There are few activities in which my work is not brought to mind. Most of the time my thoughts are a relaxing reference to my work, but occasionally they contain all the stress, discontent and decision-making inherent in any business environment.

So this morning while sitting at my desk in the SW corner of the Ferry Terminal building, sun streams through the windows as the office phones ring with calls for making or changing ferry reservations.

My tasks these days are mostly administrative, with only occasional days spent outdoors or onboard the ferry as captain or crew. Here is a sampling of today's activities:

- Letter to Carl Nolen, president of Capital Brewing Company, producer of Island Wheat Beer.
- Register for on-line Random Drug Test program with employee names for our company DOT drug testing program.
- Check the ads listing our interest in finding a new lessee at our Northport Restaurant. This one is a tough one, potentially!
- Correspond with Ellen Hooker, biologist with the Wisconsin Division of Animal Health, about cormorant disease on Pilot Island.
- Review and edit — next to final edit — our Ferry Line 2007 brochure with schedule.
- Send comment letter to the docket for Federal Register notice on Voyage Data Recorders — small black boxes our government is considering placing aboard passenger vessels. So far, our size vessels are not included, but in the future, who knows what ideas catch the fancy of the people in Washington, D.C.?

— and so on. Much of what I do seems peripheral and far away from the daily routine of putting people on the ferry and getting them safely across the Door. But these other activities, sometimes side tours, can often take interesting turns that benefit this business and our ability to provide service at a profit.

With traffic slowly declining over the past three years, we're more conscious than ever of operating efficiently and profitably.

I may break up today's work outline with a hair cut at Jeannie Gunnlaugsson's hair shop, and with tree-cutting, chain sawing at Arni's home. Something very enjoyable about my day is that it's never dull, and never too repetitive.

It's nearly 10 a.m. when the *Arni J. Richter*, on time, rounds the tripod, the three-legged harbor entrance marker, on its return trip. Today is the first day of our winter ferry schedule, with the ferry making one morning round trip, and one in the afternoon.

Mail, freight and traffic will discharge at our island dock in just a few minutes.

Thursday, January 4 –

Record high temperatures are predicted today across NE Wisconsin. It wasn't even cold enough for frost last night.

An early, special ferry brought in two liquid propane tankers for Hansen Oil for off-loading at the tank storage facility near Townline and Gunnlaugsson Roads. Tomorrow, a special ferry is again scheduled, this time for a single bulk gasoline tanker for Keith Mann's Citgo pumps.

LP has been the fuel of choice for most new construction and for retrofitting island homes because of the compact, efficient gas furnaces. For years, a few homeowners used bottled gas for stoves and small cottage heating systems. Around 1990 the trend shifted to LP from wood, fuel oil, or kerosene, and the generally more expensive electric heat.

Do we want to carry potentially hazardous cargo at times of the year when roads, docks and ferry decks may be icy? We're not eager to haul that sort of commodity in winter, but there is both the public service aspect and the emergency re-supply that is now possible with a new and larger winter ferry.

In order to compensate for the expense and difficulty of carrying large trucks and heavy cargo in winter, we raise our rates from December 21st through March 31st. In winter, costs are greater per trip. The cost of docks and shore ramps, the expense of a winter ferry, and other supporting infrastructure, not to mention insurance and administrative costs, all require a significant return in revenue. Only a portion of the service provided is offset by winter income.

The "call" to load trucks with products such as LP is ours, and it's based on marine forecasts. We often consult our website weather link at www.wisferry.com and our seasoned judgment based on experiences of the past. Wind speed, wind direction, wave height and air temperature can each be critical factors in deciding whether to haul those tankers or not.

All LP or gasoline loads must be special ferry transports without any passengers or other vehicles. Only the tankers and their drivers are permitted. Fuel oil, with a lower flammability rating, can be carried with a mixed load of passengers, vehicles and cargo.

Friday, January 5 –

An article I read in the *Door County Advocate* marine column reminded me of Sir Ernest Shackleton, who died and was buried on South Georgia Island. A book I read in seventh grade about Shackleton had great impact on me. It gave me a notion of what willful and prepared men can do when facing adventure and tough conditions.

The Advocate ran a frontpage story, as they always do, with photos on the Jacksonport annual New Year's Day Polar Bear Swim. Great theater. Good photo ops. Lots of people. Is it a media event? If no one came to cover it — no cameras, no TV, no press, no onlookers — would it still be fun? Admirably, profits earned on concessions go to non-profit organizations, and the focus is to have fun, which people of all ages seem to do.

Washington Island has its own small gathering on January 1st. On that day, Jens Hansen, Bill Schutz, Paul Swanson and friends have sampled the waters of Washington Harbor's Schoolhouse Beach.

Bill's comment: "I think we're doing it the right way. They (the Jacksonport dippers) only get wet to the chest, or neck. We put our heads under!"

So, without cheering crowds or TV cameras, Bill, Jens and friends do their annual dip in cold lake waters, freezing no matter where you go this time of year. One island advantage is that the water at Schoolhouse is deep and clear. You can easily get your whole body wet, head to toe, just 25 feet off shore.

This was one island activity of many this New Year's Day.

At the Sportsman's Club (and there are sports women, too!) anyone interested and capable of shooting clay birds can compete for a Loot Shoot, by age category, by gender, and for the "Champion of Champions." This tradition begins at 12 noon, an event begun at least 30 years ago by avid outdoorsman Dick VerHalen and his wife,

Marilyn. Marilyn made up a pot of chili and towed the spread by sled to their tennis court at the edge of their meadow where dozens of islanders competed in the cold against each other, clay birds flying through the air.

Saturday, January 6 –

Today I'm back in the office for a five-hour Saturday after making three trips as part of crew yesterday. Once again, calm seas and warm temperatures today.

A funeral for Ann Greenfeldt brings members of an old island fishing family back for the burial at Schoolhouse Beach Cemetery.

This is the last ferry ride, the ride home to the island for burial.

Typically, Casperson Funeral Home of Sister Bay handles nearly every island funeral service. Casperson stockpiles concrete vaults at the Town Shop in December for such winter eventualities, eliminating the difficulty of arranging for a heavy vault truck to cross to the island in mid-winter.

Undertaking is one service not available on the island, but we have been most fortunate to have a reliable and flexible service in Sister Bay. Greg, his father Clyde, and Clyde's father before him, knew the faces and names of many island families. That familiarity alone is a measure of comfort to grieving families.

There are many interesting angles and stories regarding funerals. We laugh nervously when making light of grave matters.

Arni likes to tell the story of a casket slipping into the lake as he and his father, Carl, transferred a box with body from a rowing skiff to the open fantail of the fish tug-freight boat *Welcome*. They had anchored off the ice banks near Europe Bay, awaiting the delivery of the casket from Mr. Casperson, Clyde's father. From shore it was transferred to a small rowboat, and from there to the awaiting *Welcome*. It was at that point when the box slipped from their grip. Imagine several hundred pounds of wooden casket and dead weight teetering between small skiff and fish tug, perhaps a small swell still running from the previous night. The casket was partially submerged.

Mr. Casperson opened and reached into the retrieved box and "straightened up the gentleman's clothes and tie." No water had entered the casket. Arni raised anchor for the homeward trip to Detroit Harbor. One imagines the casket inside the small fish tug, jammed alongside the engine box, stove, mail and other assorted freight in the hold of the fish tug.

Clyde Casperson's undertaking services to islanders were well known. Years ago Ella Carlson was transported by ambulance through Sister Bay, having just been transferred from the island ambulance at Northport after a winter ferry ride across the Door. Ella said to the ambulance crew, sensing this ferry ride might be her next-to-last, "Step on it when you go past Clyde's."

Sense of humor? Or sense of the future tinged with superstition? Ella was buried several weeks later at the island cemetery alongside her husband of many years.

Tuesday, January 9 –

"Do you haul the ferries out of water in winter?" we're sometimes asked. The only time we haul them out of water is when they are dry docked, and then generally for special work or for a Coast Guard hull inspection, required every five years.

For typical winter lay up, all water systems are drained and the hulls are allowed to freeze in the ice. Of course, this winter there is no ice yet, and so the ferries bob freely at the piers.

We expect a new generator to be delivered in a day or two for the ferry *Robert Noble*. The existing 120v ship's service will be changed to 220v, and that will require new electrical panels and rewiring. The electrical panel order will require the longest lead time.

Once this job is accomplished, our ferry should be in good shape for many years except for the replacement of the main engines, which are original equipment and were rebuilt two years ago.

Winter can be beautiful, and it can also be productive. Besides our ferry project, in various parts of the island carpenters and tradesmen are building new homes. Several of these homes, I'm told, are post-and-beam construction, substantial second homes.

Marsten Anderson, Sister Bay, was just in to the office and said, "Hello." He's looking at a masonry job near Jackson Harbor. Bill Llwellyn had started the work, but he was tragically killed in an accident behind his home Christmas eve morning. A limb broke from a tree and struck him in the head. He was found on the ground, saw still idling alongside him. The emergency page for the Island Rescue Squad came in while church was in progress, and at least two island paramedics got up to leave for the call.

Bill could not be revived. He had recently retired to the island and lived in the former home of his parents, Jim and Vi, both deceased. Jim owned and operated Jim's Up the Road for many years, also known as Nelsen's Hall. Vi drove taxi, and she provided a true service. For many hours each summer day, Vi would wait patiently in her taxi near the Ferry Dock for customers. Vi spent almost as many hours at the dock as any ferry employee. She was upbeat, always smiling, and she gave a tour loaded with local insight. Some of her customers requested her tour services year after year, like visiting yachtsman George Kress of Green Bay who sailed into Detroit Harbor every summer for decades aboard his sailboat *Aria*.

After Vi's passing, friends planted a small maple with an engraved plaque at the base near the ferry dock.

Thursday, January 11 –

Blackbirds at daybreak are specks in treetops, backlit by a red morning sun, scattering as independent flyers, then regrouping, swooping, a black floating banner that settles in the next grove of hardwoods.

They remind me this morning of shoppers at Mann's Store, on independent missions for cheese, bread, eggs, their carts blocking the narrow aisles by the fruit and vegetable section, the last turn just before flocking to the checkout. Their chattering is also hard to avoid from one or two aisles over and at times you wish you weren't there to overhear. If you want gossip and news while gathering your dinner, follow the flock.

Friday, January 12 –
Uff Da Marbles

This board game, generally for two or four players, uses a couple of card decks with jokers, a board with holes around the perimeter, and five marbles for each player. The object is to move from Start Gate to Home Gate before your opponent does the same. It's mostly card luck, with a little skill, and it moves quickly.

Barry and Grace Ann Carpenter brought it to the island and then taught it to 50 or so others over a several year period of time. This Friday evening at KK Fiske, we will participate in the first Uff Da Marble Tourney. Actually, it's a social event, not a competition.

Kenny Koyen, ever the entrepreneur and magnet for media coverage, was the recent subject of Mark DeCarlo's "Taste of America" on the Travel Channel last Tuesday evening. Kenny took DeCarlo and his snappy humor out on the lake aboard the *Sea Diver*, along with Kenny's son, Jesse. They lifted nets with enough whitefish to stock a pot for a fish-boil. DeCarlo clowned while the kettle boiled. The show offered viewers a look at a fishboil in its edited form, and an even hastier showing of a select crowd at KK tasting the results. DeCarlo's friendly enthusiasm for the whitefish boil faded as cameras were turned off, and he seemed to have one foot already out the door, on to another community and another local American delicacy. He left with a new fedora on his head, a gift from Kenny.

But who can fault even a small sandwich of airtime between booyah in Brussels and liver mush in North Carolina? It was national publicity for this island and for Door County. Kenny, with his homespun appearance, multiple interests and skills, and a heart for his home on Washington Island, has the ability to attract a camera lens. That is a commendable island success story, and it runs to his lawyer baskets, Island Wheat Beer, and the latest, Death's Door vodka.

Saturday, January 13 –

Overcast has given way to sun and blue skies. Ice now covers three-quarters of the harbor during the last 24 hours. It's cold — typical, January cold — but still very easy to get out and enjoy the fresh air and outdoors.

I was in a reverie of sorts on the internet, reading about Sedona, AZ, and vortexes, an interest of Mary Jo's. Sedona is a possible destination for us in April. My wish is to ride a Harley through the mountainous landscapes. Hers is to seek greater inner peace and knowledge. I think we will both succeed!

But, as I was lost in thought on the descriptive text about vortexes, geographic places where spiritual connections with the past, present and future can be easily found, I drifted to thoughts of vortexes I've found special in my own backyard:

- The quiet of a deep swamp in November after being led by tracks or the sight of white tails or birds.
- The immensity and power of ice fields in February off the island's west side. The snaps and pops as fields of ice grind and expand. The pinkish glow of the late afternoon winter sun, with Door Bluff headlands seven or more miles in the distance. The notion that I could set off on foot for Marinette, Cedar River, or Escanaba if I chose, a crossing to the far-off mainland commonly made years ago by islanders. I imagine spending a week in a shack out on the ice, miles off shore, fishing through the ice for a living.

An island experience can be solitary, allowing the mind to enfold friends and voices from the past.

I think of my grandparents' farm on Old Stage Road near Sister Bay,

Richard and Emma Kalms and their nine children, raised in the absence of electricity, the miles of stone fences, a kitchen wood stove for cooking and heat, and the large stone at the base of the granary steps with a foot groove worn in over time from ascending to chores. I know it was much the same for island farmers, too—the toughness of the East Siders who tamed swamp and rock-strewn fields by hand or with horse.

I can feel that strength and energy in certain locations when I'm patient and able to listen. I'm guessing there is other energy out there, too, from the early French explorers and trappers, and from the various native tribes that lived along the island shores.

A strong energy flows from the waters of Death's Door, and for me, at least, this energy is positive, reassuring, comforting. I once said to an island preacher, naively leaping to a marketing conclusion based on strong personal influences, that our job here, or at least one of our main tasks as residents and providers of services to island guests, is to help put them in touch with their spirit.

Is this what a vortex is? Is that what Sedona is all about? I feel inadequate and unqualified to delve any deeper than that, and for most of us, the expression of one's interest in "recharging batteries of life" may be just that simple — no need to hear the tree or rock talk to us, but just enjoy the experience and observe enough quiet to hear our own thoughts.

"What's so special about the island?" is a frequently asked question. There is no short or simple answer. It is the rock here, the tree there, the ice field or the bird. It's also the people, and the memory of humankind, the connection with the universe — and God.

There is no Island connection with God more special than another spot on earth, but maybe the island's location and sense of community provide an easier way to get to the core of being, here more easily than at other earthly locations.

Connecting must be balanced with food, clothing, family harmony and a supportive, nurturing community. This isn't always easy to achieve or sustain. For a few, isolation overwhelms and the familiar — wherever and whatever that is — calls. And there is also the distasteful manipulation by a few personalities, or by government, or by society itself, even in so small a setting. Even on Washington Island, at times life may seem unbearable.

There is a dark and unpleasant side to life in any community, no matter the pull of the vortex.

Wednesday, January 17 –

Our coldest day of the winter thus far, 17 degrees F this morning, with a sharp 25-plus mph wind out of the NW.

These conditions influence tactics used by our captains to avoid taking on spray or solid water over the bow or dipping the rail far enough in a trough to take slop on deck. In these cold temperatures, spray freezes to the steel decks almost instantly and begins to layer in ever greater thickness.

Aside from chipping off ice with wooden mallets or chisels, or having the luxury to allow ice to melt or evaporate, another option is to apply chemical products.

We found, thanks to a conversation with Madeline Island Ferry Line folks, a limestone-based product in either liquid or pellet form. It turns ice to slush which can then be shoveled off the decks. It can also be applied while in port, pre-treating decks or steps prior to heading into seas.

At this time of year, when high winds and seas are common, it's possible to baby the boat along, gently nudging the bow into the larger swells rather than bashing against them, to avoid icing down.

This Wednesday morning our crew went over "light" with no traffic at 6:30 a.m. and returned at 7:15 from Northport with a gasoline and an LP tanker — one each. Despite the avoidance of heavy seas by rolling in the troughs, not ideal with such a load, the decks became icy.

That first trip of the day was followed by the regular 8 a.m. departure from the island, put 15 minutes behind schedule, and then later by a third round trip to return the empty tankers.

On Wednesdays in winter we schedule only one round trip. The afternoon is held aside for a special round trip, like today, or for maintenance. Today, Rich Ellefson is arranging with FABCO/CAT to do work on a small exhaust leak on the port engine. So far, it's a small leak, but it can create a mess if ignored. On the other hand, it's a big job to correct the defect. First the engine needs to cool. Then many parts are dismantled before the culprit part can be found and changed out.

It appears now the work may be done next Wednesday at the Northport pier. That way, if work is in any way halted for lack of parts, we can make a trip to Green Bay to get them. During the time the ferry is down, our only ferry available these winter days for service, the island will be without emergency ferry service for eight hours or more. It's not a good time to have a heart attack if you are an islander.

That's the nature of such an engine repair and a sampling of the considerations it creates. We hope repairs can be accomplished in as short a time frame as possible.

Thursday, January 18 –

School isn't in session Friday, so there was a flurry of phone calls and a scramble to get the remaining spots on the ferry for the great exodus. Our vehicle will be among them as we head for Sturgeon Bay and Oshkosh for errands and to spend two nights with our four year old grandson while his parents travel to Iowa.

For islanders, this act of leaving home has become known as going "off-island." Of late, it has become popular, with expanded use through books and articles, to refer to Door County as simply, "Door." Examples: I'm headed to Door. Welcome to Door. We're having a great time in Door, wish you were here in Door, etc.

Islanders have a few colloquialisms, too. We cross the Door, referring to that body of water, the passage known as Death's Door. Otherwise, it's nearly always THE Door. Then, there is also the term "Back Door," the part of the Door less easily seen from Washington Island, that strait lying between Plum Island and Northport. The other part more familiar to us, between Plum and Detroit Islands, is the "Front Door."

Whether speaking or writing it I live and work in Door County, but more specifically on Washington Island. For islanders there is a tendency to refer to home as "The Island," and when they leave it to head south, they are going to "Door County" rather than the peninsula or the mainland. This perspective is balanced by callers in summer who ask for directions to leave Door County and catch a ferry to the Island.

The separation by water creates differences in attitude, illusions of place. We're in Door County, a part of the State of Wisconsin. For the most part, we're happy in our distanced relationship on Washington Island.

Friday, January 19 –

Mary Jo and I toss our bags in the Nissan along with seemingly ever-present bags of goods for St. Vincent DePaul's in Green Bay, and we head to the ferry and a weekend with our grandson, Atlas, in Oshkosh.

During the night there were 25 mph winds. We could hear it in the bare-branched trees around our home. As a consequence, the ferry captain chooses the south route through the "Front Door." We glide past the old Plum Island Coast Guard station buildings, past buoy #2, a red nun marking the middle ground, working our way between Plum and Detroit Islands. Our course is first toward Pilot, and then we swing back around the south tip of Plum Island toward Northport. The captain pulls the throttles back on several occasions to let the steeper seas roll past without sending a cascade of water onto the foredeck, and to avoid slamming the bow. There are bright, blue skies above. It's a beautiful winter's day, despite the 18-degree temperature. We have a full load of vehicles on board, including numerous commercial vans, two box trucks (Mann's Store and Mann's Mercantile), and a contingency of islanders headed for points south.

The trip across takes slightly longer on this southern route, but not much longer. Despite the care of the captain, many auto windshields, especially those in the forward half of the car deck, are covered with frozen spray. The crew motions cars ahead, but many drivers can't see, and the crew assists with scrapers to clear the thin, hard film of ice.

It reminded me of a trip on a Christmas morning when the ferry departed the island in 10-degree temperatures, winds howling from the west, right "on the nose" as the ferry headed out the channel and toward Plum Island. There was no opportunity to slow, no choice in routes to avoid the seas. Seas were steep and the spray flew, covering the entire car deck and the windows of the *Robert Noble*. One crew member had to work with a scraper on the pilot house windows to keep an open hole through which the pilot could see to steer. Under the slight lee of the reef on Plum Island, a decision was made to return to Washington Island and forgo the effort already made. It was Christmas...there would be disappointment. But the alternative wasn't a good one. I met the ferry as it pulled back in to the island with several inches of hardened spray on deck. Carol, my sister-in-law, was among those in her car parked about mid-way down the deck. She assumed the ferry had arrived at Northport. Her windshield was so ice covered she hadn't realized the ferry had turned back to the island.

Tuesday, January 23 –

Winter Tuesdays used to be among my favorite days.

With only one round trip per day, and with only one day during the week Dr. Tom Wilson visited the island — Tuesdays — I looked forward to his visit as did Mary Jo and the rest of our family. Except for his first winter of island dentistry, Tom has stayed with us at our home on his island overnights. We both loved sports and were both class of '65 high school graduates, Tom from Nicolet High, me from Sturgeon Bay.

Tom's understanding of island life and his interest in his patients here made for great visits and memorable times. Tom and Gunilla, his Swedish born wife, visited us from time to time. They stayed with our children in 1979 when we left on a trip to Mexico. The day Mary Jo and I returned was the annual island Men's Day, where snowmobilers and card players gathered at Fred Young's shed for fun and cards and a fish boil. Tom rode on the back of my snowmobile.

The next morning, a Friday, the ferry broke down at the southern end of Plum Island. A broken reduction gear, coupled with heavy ice of 10 or more inches, meant a long wait for the Coast Guard icebreaker to appear on scene from Sturgeon Bay. By nightfall, the cutter *Acacia* appeared off Pilot Island. By nine p.m. the cutter had broken a track from the south end of Plum to the Potato Dock, where heavy weights were swung by foredeck boom to smack the thick, virgin ice. Then, with a cable strung for towing, forward being the only direction the ferry propeller could rotate, the *C.G. Richter* and its compliment of passengers was escorted toward the Potato Dock. After 10 that evening, with temperatures on their way down to minus 28 F, the coldest night that winter, I met the ferry off shore with my snowmobile and carried passengers one-by-one to waiting cars and families on shore.

Tom and Gunilla weren't among them, however. A sailor on the *Acacia* had severe cramps, kidney stones perhaps, and the Coast Guard skipper asked if there was a doctor on board. Tom said he was only a dentist, but that didn't matter. He and Gunilla boarded by means of the Jacob's ladder thrown over the side and scrambled up to the warmth and good smells of the cutter's galley. The *Acacia* then turned toward Northport to discharge the sick sailor and Tom and Gunilla before returning to finish the escort of the *C.G.* By midnight, Nathan Gunnlaugsson and Alvin Cornell had lines over to the old Potato Dock's rough pilings, unused since the early '70s when the potato boat carferries, old Mackinac Straits railroad carferries, were moored there.

Then the *Acacia* sailed for home, and in the hours of the night that remained I slept aboard the ferry, tending the single-cylinder Nordberg generator from time to time until the REA crew arrived at dawn to string a wire from the nearest electric pole to power the ferry. Tom and Gunilla's car was one of nine parked on board the ferry, and there it would remain for the next two and a half weeks until the ferry was repaired and the track to Northport was opened once again. Actually, it required two more visits from the *Acacia* to open up the track to where the ferry could make its own headway, safely. During prior weeks we drove snowmobiles across the Door to carry mail and freight, taking an occasional passenger over the ice. That winter was only one of two times I snowmobiled across Plum Island, taking a short cut to Northport.

But, back to Tom Wilson and our friendship.

We both enjoyed getting up early. I'd put on the coffee pot, and then we'd ride around the island "shooting the breeze," commenting on new homes under construction, sports, politics. One of those early mornings, a year when there had been excellent brown trout fishing off the west side of the island, on a whim I drove Tom on a shoreline tour by ice in the company pickup. We entered the ice near Figenschau Bay and then drove around little islands toward West Harbor.

For reasons I can't explain today, I drove a new route back to shore, dead center through the entrance to West Harbor where currents were generally strongest. That weekend, a warming trend and current opened a hole in the ice, and now after refreezing the ice was only three inches thick.

But, of course, I ignored that possibility as we drove along, chattering away about some topic or another. Our jeep pickup's bow was pointed perfectly toward the inner harbor when the back wheels dropped. I barely had time to utter "Oh s_ _ t" before the front set dropped through. The force of water and oncoming ice cracked the windshield. In no time, lake water began to fill the cab. Uncertain of my next move — I clumsily tried to open the door against ice and water pressure — I looked over at Tom, and he neatly rolled down his window and scrambled up onto the ice with his canvas briefcase. I followed his example. With water now covering my knees in the cab, I rolled down my window. I took the cardboard box from the seat that held both the Ferry Line's outgoing mail and my 35 mm Nikon camera and slid it onto the truck roof overhead. Then I pulled myself out the window, slipping into the icy water up to my armpits. I stood on bottom!

Using the pickup truck as a step, I rolled onto solid, flat ice and grabbed my camera from the cardboard box and photographed Tom, glowing with adrenaline, standing in front of the semi-submerged truck. We had the good fortune to be safely on the ice, not under it, and it showed in Tom's smile. Tom, incredibly, hadn't even gotten wet feet or clothing. His briefcase that held patient dental records and sets of dentures in various stages of construction, was also dry and safe.

We hiked a short distance to Herb and Marianna Gibson's, and they offered us hot coffee and use of their phone. I called the Ferry Dock and asked for someone else to get the mail (it wasn't even yet

7:45!). Herb drove Tom out to catch the 8 a.m. ferry home. That morning was probably our most memorable, that and the fact it was Valentine's Day and we found our wives most appreciative for our return.

Monday, January 29 –

Ten degrees. Clear, pale blue skies.

If customers — prospective island visitors — would ride our ferry on such a morning as this, they would describe it as "incredibly beautiful."

The ferry runs easily through the channel ice as we depart the island dock. The noise of the engines, a deep metallic rumble, is soon drowned out by the noise of the hull splitting window pane ice.

Overnight, in open water outside the tripod, the ice formed in one to three inches of "flat ice." This new ice splits easily and shatters into shards, tossed upward and outward across the flat, glassy surface. The effect of the skating ice shards is mesmerizing.

This flat ice extends to Plum Island and beyond. Except for a few holes caused by upwelling currents and warmer water and the several navigational buoys, the icy surface is flat all the way.

There are dozens of different types of ice.

This morning there is no lake swell, and the ice, if it could be trusted, would make a perfect skating surface. But other days, even when the ice cover is 10 inches thick, the surface undulates like a rubber sheet, a giant waterbed. The *AJR* has no problem breaking through this ice, but how much does the ice slow us down?

The global positioning device (GPS) in the wheel house reads 8.6 mph while we are in the 10-inch ice. Then, when we enter an open stretch of water near the south tip of Plum Island, our speed-over-bottom increases gradually: 8.5; 8.9; 9.0; and finally, we read 9.1 mph.

The trend reverses as we again enter an ice field.

This difference in speed is imperceptible, almost, but it indicates what ice, or ice and snow combined in thick layers, can do to create friction on the hull.

Sounds of ice against the hull are like the rattling of a large garbage drum, the crunching of very heavy glass, or the distant echoes of gunshots, repeated. But the sound is not annoying, not so loud that it's irritating. Such noise means forward progress through the ice. Not hearing that sound in winter means the ferry is in open water, or it's stopped.

Tuesday, January 30 –

Lawyers are a preferred meal to islanders. We like them many different ways: boiled, fried, and deep fried, often lightly battered.

Called eelpout or burbot, this fish, considered trash fish by many, is a great treat when properly prepared. Lawyers must be fresh. Holding them for days deteriorates the flavor and for this reason they don't do well frozen or shipped on ice.

Commercial fishermen catch them in their nets. Most of the time such a catch is a nuisance because it means the nets aren't catching the more valuable whitefish.

Lawyers can also be caught with hook and line. Bobbing for lawyers, they call it. Cut a hole through the west side ice in about 40 feet of water anytime from mid-January through March. That's the time lawyers swim to shallow water to spawn. Use a big hook and stinky bait or maybe, tinfoil and no bait at all. It's a matter of preference and what's handy. Let the heavy lead weight go down first and hit bottom. Above that is the large hook, wrapped with an old smelt or other fish chunk. Smart lawyer fishermen keep smelt in their freezer and use rubber bands to hold the ripe bait onto their hook for repeated bobbing. They're fun to catch, like pulling up a large boot. Just hand-over-hand the line.

Preparing lawyers is another matter. All the meat is back aft, where the heart is also located. It's the position of the heart in the posterior from which the name "lawyer" is given. Cut around the head and skin it like a bullhead with a pair of pliers. The majority of the fish is head and guts. Filleted from the bone, the flesh is white and resembles cod, and it's referred to locally as the poor-man's lobster, or the poor-man's codfish.

KK Fiske is the place to go on the island for the best basket of lawyers around. Even better with Island Wheat Beer.

FEBRUARY

Thursday, February 1 –

Location: Appleton airport
Our travel from Washington Island, the beginning of a two-week trip, was typical of winter ferry travel. The morning temperature was 10 degrees F. We cruised through an ice field near the tripod. Ray Hansen had ordered two LP tankers, and for some reason either Ray or the drivers miscued on the Northport departure time, 8:15 a.m. at Northport, rather than the 7:15 a.m. pick-up time commonly used in the past. As a result, our ferry crew arrived at the mainland dock at 7 a.m. and waited, waited. A call placed by Rich found the truckers running on a different time schedule.

The *Arni J.* left Northport finally with the two tankers at 8:15 a.m., and for that reason, the ferry was nearly an hour late in leaving the island for its regular trip. I heard no complaints, but I'm confident there were some from people who had to adjust their tight appointment schedule. The ferry will make a third trip around 11 a.m. to return the empty tankers.

Tuesday, February 8 –
From Charleston, SC, thinking of home

Winter Woes – Our old ferry office holding tank froze up frequently in zero degree weather. The steel holding tank, connected by underground piping to a single commode, was installed in July of 1975. Because it was at or near lake level, and potentially buoyant, a metal strap and a concrete saddle poured over the top held it down. The holding tank was buried beneath blacktop not fifteen feet from the front door of the office building. Piped to it was a single commode in a 40" x 40" toilet space with a tiny corner sink.

Because the pavement was plowed in winter for cars that parked in front of the office, frost worked downward and hastened freeze-up of the piping and tank contents. It was on the coldest of days, it seemed, when the toilet would not flush and the backed-up system indicated a full tank. Then we began the process of heating the black top with a torpedo heater under canvas tarps, so that six to eight hours later we could chip out the three inch layer of black top, and the foot of gravel and stone, finally gaining access to the tank cover.

Following hours, and maybe several days of heat application, we could at last put a suction hose through the tank opening and pump the tank dry. Thawing pipes and effluent so that we could pump waste was an unpleasant diversion from the normal winter work routine. During this time the office reeked of unpleasant odors.

Many positive attributes were built into our new 1996 office, but the improved sanitation system ranked near the top. This facility has both public toilets and an employee toilet, with good ventilation, adequate sink space, and fixtures that are plumbed into a system that accepts effluent flawlessly. The system also accepts liquid waste from ferry holding tanks.

Office effluent first flows to an ejector pit, and from there it is pumped uphill to a concrete septic tank where the solids settle. Then the liquid flows by gravity to a steel dosing tank. Two dosing pumps alternately push the liquid effluent through nearly 400 feet of piping to a concrete tank behind the town Welcome Center. There, effluent from the Welcome Center and the Ferry Line is combined and distributed into an above-ground mound system.

It seems to be a rather complicated system in a rural setting, but it has worked well.

Friday, February 9 –

Home News – February has turned out to be a cold, cold month. Often we experience a mid-February thaw in which snow and ice melt, with occasional rainfall, and standing water on top of the ice. Avid ice fishermen will jig their bait through the ice for lawyers while standing in 10 inches of water on top of ice, which in turn floats upon 30 or more feet of water.

A warming trend in February isn't usually welcomed. Snowmobilers, cross-country skiers, and makers of snowmen must either play quickly or wait another day, perhaps another winter.

Around this same date in 2001 I accepted the Passenger Vessel Association (PVA) presidency in Savannah, GA, at the Savannah Convention Center. During my acceptance speech, I introduced myself and Washington Island to several hundred Association members and friends. It was a milestone memory.

The 365 days as president of that organization went very quickly, and I passed the gavel to incoming president Fred Hall of the Port Jefferson Steamboat Company, Port Jefferson, Long Island at the convention in Biloxi, MS. During my year in office I received daily communications and I participated in meetings, conference calls, and attended the funeral of a former PVA president in San Francisco.

When I was first presented with the opportunity to ascend the PVA officer chairs in 1999, I posed the opportunity to Arni Richter, who was my superior and company president. I wanted Arni to know that if I accepted, there would be considerable travel, with more of my time allocated to association business.

Arni's response: "So, they're having trouble finding candidates?"

I had expected support from one who was a founder of a similar organization on the Great Lakes in 1975. Our personal communication, already intermittent and sometimes strained, continued slowly down hill thereafter.

Saturday, February 10 – Savannah, GA
Arni's Retirement

February 5th, 2002 was Arni's 92nd birthday. As it happened, this day was also Arni's official retirement day.

Mary Jo prepared a birthday party. Besides Arni and his caretaker Chris, also present were his daughters Carol and Estelle, our son, Hoyt, and his wife, Kirsten.

At noon, WDOR broadcast the news release I had prepared that described Arni's long and noted career and his announced retirement. Hard of hearing, Arni heard only part of the radio news item, but friends soon called our home to congratulate him.

We sat politely around the dining table in our living room. What should have been cause to celebrate was a somber moment for Arni who wore dark glasses, fit-overs to protect his eyes from bright sunlight. They also covered his eyes, and tears occasionally trickled down his cheeks from beneath the sunglasses. He faced his day with quiet pride.

After lunch, we had cake and ice cream. Then, an hour or so later, we had cake and ice cream once again, this time at the ferry dock. Prior to the close of the workday, following arrival of the afternoon ferry, crewmembers joined Arni in the lunch room to wish him happy birthday.

A slight tension tinged the air. This was only the second of two visits Arni had made since our crew voted in an official National Labor Relations Board election a few weeks earlier. It was a thumbs-up or thumbs-down vote on whether or not a union would represent employees of Washington Island Ferry Line. Two months of tension, meetings, and private consultations preceeded that vote, a vote that could have gone either way and changed our company's destiny.

We were most fortunate, as it happened, to gain a majority of votes favoring the company management over the union. Arni never understood how we arrived at the point we did, a legally binding labor vote. He never saw it coming, or chose not to recognize the shift. He was angry at the way it happened, and when it was over he didn't possess the same sense of relief I did. Toledo's union representatives left the island ferry dock promptly that same afternoon, disappointed not to have recorded a single vote in their favor. In the final count, there were seven votes for the company, with the remaining five votes not cast.

Several times during this process, Arni expressed the notion he could gather everyone into a room, sit them down and ask them, "What's the problem?" The problem was, no one wanted to meet with him because they were beyond lecturing. Resentment had crept in and there was no way to close the gap.

So, for Arni's birthday I prepared a press release, approved days earlier by Arni, sent to radio and newspaper before Arni reversed his decision. Despite congratulations from friends and acquaintances on 62 years of a job well done as head of the island's ferry company, and despite a well-deserved retirement, he was bitter and frustrated.

As for the cake and ice cream that day, our crew warmly welcomed Arni and wished him well. Arni responded warmly, too. Erik Foss, a captain of many years with a gift of quick wit, said, "Arni, when you turn 100, I'll buy you a steak dinner."

With equal wit and quickness that has always been his trademark, Arni smiled, "What? No cigar?"

With that, ice had been broken. In some ways that afternoon was a new beginning for the crew, for me, for the Ferry Line. On the other hand, what took place was simply a logical step in life and in business as well as a necessary change in Ferry Line dynamics.

Arni's retirement had been announced that day, but it would not yet be an accomplished fact.

Sunday, February 11 – Jeykll Island, GA
Island School Transition

When we stayed two nights on Hilton Head Island and signed up for the timeshare sales pitch, our salesman was a young man in his late twenties who graduated from Hilton Head Island High School. He was one of nearly 1100 in his class.

We asked him questions about his school, making comparisons

with Washington Island's school system. Our youngest son, Thordur, was one of 13 island graduates in 1997. Mary Jo went to grade school at Detroit Harbor, then transferred to the Washington Harbor School, now the Art & Nature Center, for high school. However, a new one-floor addition with several classrooms was completed at the Detroit Harbor School in time for her senior year. With Washington Harbor School then closed, she graduated in 1965 from the Detroit Harbor School, a single school building that held the entire K-12 Washington Island School District.

As Washington Island School Board president for approximately six years, I participated in the planning and design of the present day Washington Island School, and I also oversaw demolition of the old school located closer to Main Road, on the same property as the present day school.

Razing of the old Detroit Harbor School structure was bid out in July of 1986. Local contractor Lonnie Jorgenson and Norb Novak from Denmark teamed up for the dismantling project. Many components such as the maple flooring, were sold to island residents. Other salvageable materials were sold off-island. The remainder of demolition materials went to the island landfill.

The old bell tower was purchased by Chick and Sharon Stults, but the bell was kept by the School District. Ken Koyen rode the bell tower down to the ground on the end of crane operater Norb Novak's cable.

Wooden maple classroom flooring strips can be seen at Ken Koyen's Granary, reassembled as the top surface of his Main Road bar. The steel fire escape and stair tower were purchased by M & L Concrete for use at the cement plant (owned then by brothers-in-law Martin Andersen and Lou Small)

Lonnie Jorgenson filled the hole in the ground, covering the below grade foundation that once housed the old school office. Norb Novak returned several days after grading was completed with a hacksaw to remove a piece of rebar that protruded from the soil.

The old school building walls were distinctive, made of cement blocks molded in a form resembling cut stone, produced by Adolph Moe. Although there was opposition to tearing down the old school building, had it remained it would have been a liability to the Town and it would have blocked the foreground view of the new school and the Community Center. Cost to the School District for demolition was in the range of $6000 to $7000.

Monday, February 12 – Jeykll Island, GA

At home, I'm told the ice is getting thicker. The bay ice is set, and residents are ice fishing and snowmobiling along the island's west side as well as in Detroit Harbor, Jackson Harbor, and between Jackson Harbor and Rock Island. There's nothing like a trip around Rock Island or Detroit Island in mid-winter, when there are no other souls around.

Home temperatures today rose into the teens, Hoyt reported by phone, making for a considerably more bearable climate than single digits or minus temperatures.

Yet, cold weather is stimulating and makes me feel alive. Back inside from outdoor activity, I appreciate sources of heat that much more, such as the wood stove in our basement. A wood stove can be a joyous centerpiece for a winter workshop.

***

What sets Washington Island uniquely apart from the rest of Door County? Or Wisconsin?

- Water on all sides
- Isolation — if only partial or psychological
- A strong sense of community- even when there's great divergence of opinion
- Few large developments
- A relatively low number of visitors, and therefore, slow tourism economy, which promotes sameness, a slow-to-change infrastructure and economic base.

A few years ago several island coffee shop minds saw a need to brainstorm economic development as a way to jumpstart the island economy, diversify it, and improve job opportunities for the young people of the island. Have any of those ideas come to fruition yet? Are young people today more inclined or less inclined to stay on the island? Is moving off the island to find employment and opportunity a new trend, or just a continuation of long standing-behavior?

Is it a bad thing to move away from a small community for work opportunity, to raise a family, to get an education, or to accumulate job skills? Some leave, marry, raise a family, and then return upon retirement, with financial security in place.

For most, money is the primary motivator. For those who want higher earnings and maybe better benefits, it is almost imperative to seek employment elsewhere. But there are plusses for staying on Washington Island and being part of a small community, too, advantages that overshadow earnings and are balanced with fiscally conservative living.

Friday, February 16 – Oshkosh

Zero degrees in Oshkosh and sunny. Today it warmed to 21 degrees at Northport.

When we pulled up to the Northport Pier, Friday afternoon, passengers waited on the pier to board the ferry for the Fishing Derby Weekend which also featured the Island Players production of "*Diary of Anne Frank*."

The last vehicle off the ferry when it arrived at Northport was the island hearse, a steel blue Chrysler owned by Casperson Funeral Home, stored on the island in a heated garage. Who passed away? It was Floyd Koyen, an island plumber retired these past 25 years.

Mary Jo and I left our two vehicles on the pier. Both would be loaded another trip, when space was available. We sat in the lower, main deck cabin and visited with Melanie Koyen and Cathy Meader. Also on board were several Van Rites from Green Bay. About 10-12 years ago during a NE snowstorm, the older men of this family lost their 3-wheel ATV as water levels rose and lifted the field of ice. A large section on which they had been fishing split from West Harbor's beach and floated to sea in the blizzard. The men just managed to jump the widening crack, getting themselves safely to shore.

***

Our return home is a welcoming experience. We were pleased to see our ferry crew and the faces of familiar passengers.

We couldn't wait to see our little grandson after two weeks' absence. That evening we poured through a large box of catalogs and newspapers and one paper sack of letter mail.

Saturday, February 17 –

Home again. It's a beautiful winter morning — 21 degrees at 7 a.m. A dusting of snow rests on my truck.

Across from the ferry dock, snowmobiles and cars zipped across the ice of Detroit Harbor, cruising back and forth from shore to fish shanties, and occasionally to Detroit Island. Largest fish caught so far during the week were hung from hooks in front of Nelsen's Hall. They would be weighed and joined by more fish this weekend, awaiting the award of cash prizes Sunday afternoon.

Mother Nature has a way of evening the score with fishermen who take from the lake. Two trucks have reportedly gone through the ice: Jim Jorgenson's pickup and one owned by Mike Van Rite of Green Bay.

Mike had been on the ferry yesterday when we returned, planning to ice fish with his sons, and I spoke with him about his incident years ago when he lost the three-wheeler off the west side.

Sunday, February 18 –

Another cold, clear, crisp morning with winds from the NW. A dozen ice fishermen can be seen on the ice beyond West Harbor at sunrise, a pocket of frozen water partially enclosed by the Little Islands. We can see them from West Harbor Road as we take an early Sunday morning ride.

Since returning home I've fired our basement woodstove, and the house is toasty. My wood supply needs to be replenished, however.

The island fishing derby ends officially at noon, today, and when I returned from church cars lined both sides of Main Road near Nelsen's Hall for chili, the awarding of prizes, and later, bingo.

It should come as no surprise, given local interest in fishing for and eating lawyers, that the greatest prize money awarded by the Island Lions, sponsors of the event, goes to the largest lawyer. The winning lawyer is often 10 pounds or greater. A young island fisherman, Richard Bjarnarson, once caught a 13 1/2-pound lawyer, a new state record.

We spent our late Sunday afternoon in a favorite winter pastime, Scrabble and popcorn.

Monday, February 19 –

The morning is windy with a southerly draft and a warming trend is in the making.

I toured the *Robert Noble* after the departure of the 8 a.m. ferry. Sailing out the channel on the decks of the *Arni J. Richter* were dozens of people returning home following the island winter holiday weekend. All will be quiet again for several weeks until Spring Fever gets people moving, or a fresh snowfall brings them back for more outdoor activities.

The ice cutter *Mackinaw* is due in Green Bay waters this afternoon to conduct ice breaking exercises. Captain John Little reported by marine radio the cutter *Mackinaw* intends to run the charted ore boat track from Rock Island Passage to Chambers Island. Instruments and technicians ride on board to measure icebreaking capabilities and to record ice thickness. This is a newly commissioned, untested vessel.

***

Flu has hit locally. Hoyt went home this PM after toughing it out for a weekend as a crew on the ferry. Mary Jo never got out of bed today and she has a fever, cough, and sore joints. It is far better to be home with such ailments than in a motel or at someone else's home. I'm hoping this skips past me.

Tuesday, February 20, 2007 –

A stunning, beautiful day, with temperatures approaching 47 degrees in the sun.

Floyd Koyen, age 94, was buried today and received a final salute from our American Legion rifle squad members.

He was the son of Volney and Kate Koyen, an island pioneer family that drilled wells and ran sawmills. They were very clever mechanics, practical people who knew how to get things done. Floyd became a licensed Master Plumber in time. He also worked as caretaker for Chester Thordarson on Rock Island. Floyd once told me of the job he and his wife had keeping the Thordarson greenhouse plants from freezing by stoking a wood boiler through the winter. Floyd said many cords of wood were burned to keep the heat up, an exercise that Thordarson after a time gave up on.

Floyd loved jokes, told with a deadpan face. He also raised pigeons and chinchillas. His obituary stated, "Floyd's favorite day of the week was loading up his dog and going to the dump."

Wednesday, February 21 –

It is son Thor's birthday, his 27th.

The night Mary Jo went into labor with Thor happened to be a Tuesday, and dentist Tom Wilson had just come to our home to stay the evening, his normal routine. Typical of Tom's easy going nature, he had no qualms about staying with our two children, Hoyt (seven) and Evy (four), while Mary Jo and I rode the *C.G. Richter* to Northport that evening with captains Alvin Cornell and Dave Johnson.

Thor now builds beautiful wooden boats in an epoxy, cold-molded style with Van Dam Woodcraft of Boyne City, MI. He's an accomplished craftsman and enjoys his work.

Friday, February 23 –

Another cool, crisp, glorious morning, with blue skies and only a puff of cumulus floating here or there.

The ferry had a slower crossing. Yesterday's NNW winds did not bring ice into the passages until early afternoon, but this morning the bay ice was still there and under some pressure. By 8:30 a.m., normally the time the ferry would be entering the breakwater at Northport, the *AJR* had just cleared the south end of Plum Island.

Several men are working each day on the *Robert Noble* electrical project, a task that has grown into a larger job than just wiring. Bill Crance is picking up wires, steel, bits of odds and ends including tools, from the car deck in anticipation of the impending snow storm. Anywhere from a few inches to a foot is possible across northern Wisconsin, although at present, brown grass shows through hardened patches of snow everywhere on lawn and in woods. A fresh covering would be welcomed. Besides, we still have more than six weeks of official winter, and we may as well enjoy it.

Saturday, February 24 –

An item from my nautical calendar: "In 2003 a speed record for ice boats was achieved on Lake Monona of 155.84 MPH."

This would be excellent iceboating weather in Detroit Harbor. Earlier snows melted and the ice surfaces are glassy-smooth. Except for the ice shanties, there are few obstacles to worry about. But, no one iceboats here. Because conditions are so variable, to enjoy that sport to the fullest you would need to be mobile and travel to the best lake surfaces from weekend to weekend. Old timers on the island used "wind sleds," heavy work sleds fitted with runners and sails, about the closest thing to iceboats these harbors have seen. These were practical, working craft designed to take island fishermen offshore in the search for trout or other fish, fish that could be caught through the ice and later shipped for income. A few such wind sleds may exist in barns or sheds, but in my 32 years here I've never seen one used.

The temperature today is 21 degrees, with a NE wind. The ice broke up with yesterday's ferry track slicing toward Plum Island, and as a result, large pieces, one field at least half a mile across, filled the Front Door. The *Arni J.* sailed between cakes of ice that only recently refroze overnight, and the going was easy. Most of the ice encountered on the way to the South end of Plum Island consisted of large, heavier pieces, but the ferry always parted the ice. Plates varied from 12 to about 16 inches. Every so often a hunk of ice lay on top of the rest of the glassy field, making it easy to judge thickness, the result of three prior weeks of cold temperatures and no snow.

After our ferry reached the south end of Plum Island, our course swung to starboard and we emerged from the heavier, broken cakes to lighter overnight ice. Our hull speed increased with lessened hull friction, and as we ran more freely, captain Bill Jorgenson added RPMs to the engines.

The previous day, I was told by our crew, they had made only 3 1/2 kts. at 1400 rpms through the 16-inch thick flat ice field. While slow going, this was still twice the thickness the old *C.G.* was capable of breaking, period. Progress on the *C.G. Richter* would have been halted, and we might have had to turn back. The old, single diesel V-8 Murphy was prone to overheat after lugging for a period of minutes. When that happened, the operator would need to back down to cool the engine temperature, and get water flowing freely beneath the engine keel coolers before reentering deep ice.

Icebreaking trips on the *C.G. Richter* took a long time and required patience on the part of crew and passengers. We worried long term about taking life out of the engine and marine gear with the heating issues.

I stood on deck for 10 minutes and visited with Dan Kaniff, Chicago, whose family owns Njord Heim Marina. Dan is a scuba diver who's spent many hours searching for shipwrecks and diving in Lake Michigan. During our visits we joke about Dan someday finding the "Poverty Island gold" or La Salle's *Griffin*, a romantic quest held by more than one diver over the years.

Mary Jo and I were enroute to Sturgeon Bay to help celebrate my mother's 90th birthday this coming Sunday. Later, we met with my two sisters, Helen and Martha, to prepare for table settings and food service at Bay View Lutheran Church on Maple Street.

The Saturday night forecast predicted heavy snowfall Sunday.

Sunday, February 25 –
At the Maritime Inn

Although it hadn't snowed when we went to bed at 10:30 p.m., the TV meteorologist updated his winter storm warning by increasing it to a possible 18-inch blizzard by Monday. Awakened at 7 a.m. by a plow outside our room, we saw swirling snow and a good 6-inch accumulation on the ground in the motel parking lot.

This day was to be mother's 90th birthday celebration. We would attend church, then have a party in the Fellowship Hall for around 75 people. Most of the food was already prepared, and most of it was stored in the church refrigerator. Could party plans continue?

One couple flew from Philadelphia for the event, a naval architect who worked his first years following graduation with the R.A. Stearn firm in Sturgeon Bay where my father also worked. Youngest sister, Martha, flew from Jupiter, FL, and helped with food preparations. Nephews Ben and Jesse came from New York City and New Jersey. Niece Jenny came from Connecticut, and brother Jim and his wife, Chris, had driven from Chicago.

By late morning, with church cancelled, doors locked, and parking lot unplowed, we opted for Plan B, an offer from Leathem Smith Lodge to use their facility, a short drive from Mom's home.

We had a wonderful time. Owner and Manager Mary Buccola was most gracious and offered us use of the bar and lounge area. We also had access to the kitchen for coffee, ovens, and other food preparations. It was a most cozy and comfortable setting where approximately 50 people gathered while outdoors the snow accumulation approached twelve inches.

We wished Mom a Happy Birthday – and visited – and ate food – until nearly 4:30 p.m.

Tuesday, February 27 –

We're back on the island again. The morning is quiet. Temperatures are in the upper 20s, and there is still snow to clean up. Hoyt and I shoveled Arni's sidewalk and in front of his garage, and I raked snow from his roof. Inside, Arni was in his pajamas and had discomfort. He seems unable to get up and walk around, with similar symptoms now for several days. The island's temporary medical doctor, Dr. Whitenack, was called because Arni wasn't physically able to get to the island clinic. So the Doc made a house call with clinic assistant Pete Andersen.

While the doctor examined Arni, Hoyt and I checked Arni's front living room window. It had cracked down the center during high winds over the weekend. We surmised that gusts of wind from the east swept across the harbor ice with enough force and wet snow to bow the glass. Upon close examination, only the inside pane of the thermal window split. I applied a clear caulk to temporarily cover the crack. The window itself should be OK until a warm spring day when it can be replaced.

Meanwhile, Dr. Whitenack recommended Arni be transported in an ambulance, for comfort sake, to the Door County Memorial Hospital in Sturgeon Bay. The 1 p.m. ferry departed with Arni onboard in the ambulance.

Around 2 p.m., a fire call brought fire engines and the island's volunteer firemen to John Hanlin's home. His car had caught fire in the driveway, cause unknown, and it was completely consumed within minutes by flames, even the tires. No one was in the car and no one was hurt, fortunately.

During the late afternoon, I had a conversation with Carol, a representative of an outdoor advertising company concerning our interest in a new signboard:

Carol: "We have a southbound reader that's available."

Me: "Well, that's not really what we're looking for. We prefer they see it coming up the county, not heading home."

Carol: " Well, they go, they gotta come."

Me: "Pardon?"

Carol: " They go, they gotta come."

Me: "I suppose you're right."

Wednesday, February 28 –

It's 32 degrees by early morning, a most beautiful morning with exquisite snow cover on trees and roadsides, thick white pelts on evergreen limbs. The soft lighting of early morning, too weak for shadows, makes the snow appear to glow. An ideal winter morning.

Mid-morning, however, brought unpleasant news. Our recent application for a permit from the Wisconsin DNR to expand the south ramp and ramp approach at Northport, under review by the State for the past 60 days, may be in jeopardy. This bit of information comes after inquiring as to the status of our permit application, now three months since it was initially mailed for review.

MARCH

Saturday, March 1 –

Twenty-eight degrees. Windy. Forecast: lots of snow and wind. Prior to 8 a.m. winds were moderate at 20 kts. from the east. The morning ferry had left on time.

About 9:30 a.m., time of departure from Northport, the winds picked up sharply and it began to snow heavily. The *AJR* got away from the Northport pier OK, turned around in the slush ice inside the breakwall, and then headed home.

By 11 a.m., it was "blowing a gagger," a slang sailor term for high, stormy winds. We cancelled the p.m. trip.

We spent our afternoon in the lunchroom discussing various training topics, a good time to check in with everyone and to discuss safety issues. The midday weather was wild. Whitecaps built over a very short fetch of 200 feet, and snow clouds swirled and twisted across the harbor ice. Not making a trip becomes an easier call when the conditions are extreme, as they are now.

***

We went to Hoyt and Kirsten's for supper in the snowstorm. Their house is perched on a snow-swept ridge with open fields on all sides. Their drive was clear except for one, large drift. Hoyt stuck the plow truck in that one deep drift and called Rich. Several minutes later, Rich had arrived and punched through with his plow. We followed his cleared path to the garage.

Hoyt and Kirsten's house windows shuddered and air whistled and screeched through tiny openings in the 50-plus mph winds as we ate supper and visited.

Around 6:30 p.m., thunder clapped and a bolt of lightning shot across the sky. As I read Aidan a book before his bedtime, the rain changed back to huge snowflakes. Later, with Aidan tucked in bed, we drove home in a blinding snowfall. The flakes, now large and wet, were in our headlights and covered the road. Headlamp reflections from the banks of plowed snow at the roadsides were our guide.

Friday, March 2 –

The morning temperature was 28 degrees, and the atmosphere was clear but overcast. We awoke to a near calm following the night's storm. Wet, wind-driven snow stuck to the trunks of trees. Perhaps only 4-5 inches of snow had fallen, but it was heavy snow, drifted into rows.

The crew had arrived early at the ferry dock. The dock and deck surfaces had been plowed, shoveled and prepared for the 8 a.m. departure. While awaiting the arrival of one last car, we noted the lake level had risen nearly one foot in the push of strong easterly winds. That level will ebb as the day progresses.

Arni will return home today from the hospital. He's received help and should be fine at home once again, perhaps less mobile than before.

We received our septic bill in the mail for installation work done at Northport. It is a horrendously costly system with multiple pumps and chambers. There must be better, lower cost solutions. The bill was nearly $90,000.

By noon, patches of blue appear over the line of cedars. Skis may slide swiftly through wood trails, when snow shovels are rested.

Saturday, March 3 –

Twenty-two degrees. Sunny, then overcast. Large snowflakes fall, then sunny once more. The winds have swung to the NW, and with colder air and a shift in wind direction, bay ice will slide through the Door. The ferry makes its trip without incident, but the ice is deep, and snow has filled in the voids. The going will be harder still if more ice comes through the Door.

Mary Jo and I departed on the 1 p.m. ferry for Oshkosh. I would be attending the 2007 Governor's Conference on Tourism in Appleton, starting Sunday afternoon, and we would stay with our daughter and her family.

***

Snow lays in the ferry's route, sticky, deep and slushy. It grabs the hull and the increased friction slows the ferry down. Hulls are designed for liquids. Water is necessary for steerage and for engine cooling. Snow lays on water in deep bands and grabs like dry cotton on rough skin.

It became apparent on our trip to Northport that this snow-covered ice was difficult to break. Although we pushed hard against it, bow into ice, we moved forward only slightly for our efforts. We then backed away and Bill Jorgenson, captain, found an easier, open lead. The ferry encountered a much different set of conditions upon its return, we later learned.

A large ice field had moved into the Door while the crew loaded for the return trip at Northport, and after nearly 1 1/2 hours with no possibility of getting through the ice fields, the crew turned back to Northport for safe harbor. Passengers and their vehicles were unloaded, and their drivers headed south down Highway 42 to find food and nearby lodging for the night.

Rich Ellefson, our Operations Manager who was on board as a crewmember, Jim Hanson and Bill Jorgenson found their night's rest at an Ellison Bay motel, while back at the island ferry office, Hoyt fielded phone calls throughout the afternoon. Calls came from the public, from passenger family members, from the crew on the ferry, and from the U.S. Coast Guard.

The ferry crew would try again Sunday morning with the assistance of a Coast Guard ice cutter. When a call for assistance is made, Coast Guard Sector Sault Ste. Marie in Upper Michigan determines what ice breaking "vessel assets" may be used. The *Mobile Bay*, home ported five hours away from our location in Sturgeon Bay, was in a repair status. The *Biscayne Bay*, a sister vessel of the 135-foot cutter class, was dispatched instead from St. Ignace, MI, about a seven hour sail to Death's Door.

Sunday, March 4 –

The *Biscayne Bay's* skipper, despite recommendations from Hoyt, entered Green Bay waters through the Rock Island passage to the north of Washington Island. He immediately encountered bay ice. By the time the cutter had made Denny's Bluff on the west side of Washington Island, its progress was only a few yards with each buck against the ice.

This course, into stacked and layered bay ice, was also the long way around. It was mid-to-late morning when the cutter reversed course and retraced its route through Rock Island Passage, back into the open lake, and southward to Death's Door and Plum Island where the overdue, loaded ferry lay waiting assistance.

Although the main part of the Door passage was clear of ice where the ferry awaited the cutter, the Front Door between Plum Island and the Detroit Harbor entrance was choked with ice, heavy ice that was driven and pressed to the bottom in certain areas.

It took the *Biscayne Bay* hours to make a track from the south end of Plum Island to the Detroit Harbor tripod, where, nearing shore, both heavy ice and sufficient water for navigation ran thin. For a good share of this five-hour exercise, the *Arni J. Richter* broke ice alongside the *Biscayne Bay*, "team-breaking" as it were, to improve progress in the heavy going. By mid-afternoon, the *AJR* had moored at the island dock, discharged, reloaded, and was ready for the day's second run.

Thursday, March 8 –

Sunny and beautiful. A light layer of ice 4-6 inches thick now encompasses the entire route to Northport, the result of several nights' freeze.

In light of our ferry's difficulties four days ago and how handy today's portable phones can be, I am thinking of technology and my dislike for carrying a cell phone. I do carry one, but only when I'm off the island. Hoyt and Rich carry theirs and use them frequently, a good thing for connections with emergency services. And for me when I want to call them.

Friday, March 9 –

Weak sunshine, but a clear morning. Temperature slightly below 32 degrees and predicted to rise throughout the day.

I rode the ferry to Northport to meet a prospect for the restaurant. The *Arni J. Richter* rode against a slight southerly wind. Ice lay ahead to the south end of Plum Island. When we made open water there, the ferry pitched in lively fashion.

Other than a few errant, thick, aqua blue ice chunks washed over by waves, the Back Door was clear of ice. Rounding the south point of Plum Island, we noticed black objects on the ice banks near shore. These objects turned out to be an immature eagle and several crows. The eagle dwarfed the crows in size.

I spent time that morning at Northport removing snow and ice from the restaurant eaves and widening paths to the doors. I discussed restaurant operations with a prospective lessee.

My trip homeward was on a ferry deck filled with vehicles and freight, a relatively routine and quick crossing except for rolling seas from the southeast.

Later, after we arrived in port, I learned that a freight cart shed its wheel chocks and was in danger of hitting the last car in the stern, near the centerline of the ferry. The owner, concerned for her car, held the cart for the remainder of the trip, not an acceptable duty for a passenger. It needs to be addressed for her satisfaction and future occasions.

Saturday, March 10 –

Frost last night, but the morning is sunny and bright, and we are to experience temperatures warming into the 40's, perhaps 50's within a few days.

The ice situation is stable, that is, there has been little to no change. With bay ice staying put, our ferry route between the middle ground buoy, Plum Island #2, and the old Plum Island Coast Guard Station is easy going.

We continue to have discussions here amongst ourselves as to what the best options might have been last Saturday. Could our crew have saved time by heading west of Plum Island? Would they have made it safely home or been set in ice until help arrived?

My estimation, not having personally been on the ferry during that portion of the trip, was that the decision to turn back to Northport and await further assistance, was proper and best under the circumstances. Breaking a track west of Plum Island, given the large fields that lay for miles to the west, likely all the way to Cedar River, MI, may have resulted in exposure to pressures within the fields. Even a slight shift of ice fields driven by NW winds, or currents, or pressures built up within the fields, would be impossible to overcome if the ferry were pressed by them.

The public may misconstrue our mission and our decision making at times as too conservative. However, loss of mechanical power, damage to rudders, overheated engines, or any one of the myriad of things that can go wrong, including simply being stuck (or stuck in ice after dark), are always possibilities. For those reasons, being moored to a pier, even when it's the side of the route we'd rather not be on, at least puts us in a position to go another day. Coupled with help from the Coast Guard, our ferry was better off to wait a few hours than to go it alone in hopes of a more rapid crossing.

This is the nature of winter travel: decisions, obstacles, and difficulties.

I'm proud of the job our crew did on shore and underway in assessing and meeting the challenges that weekend. The public's perception, I hope, reflects a healthy respect for our work to keep them safe and moving.

Small exceptions to routine crossings can be understood as part of the deal for an island surrounded by water and ice.

Sunday, March 11 –

Warm. Melting. Well above freezing.

So, if island life is connected by a tenuous lifeline, with ice, harsh weather and the uncertainty of ferry travel influencing all aspects of island life, why live on Washington Island?

First, the days with on-time reliability far outnumber the very few when the outcome may be in question.

Second, medical emergencies aside, island life is extremely safe and the stress levels are low. The big questions tend to be: Is the mail in yet? Has the ferry landed yet? Who will be the next island medical provider? Has Mann's gotten their weekly grocery shipment (which translates to bread, fresh fruits, vegetables and meats)?

Third, not advertised but a part of island life, is low crime. People know and trust their neighbors. Assaults, robberies and rapes are rare to non-existent. Despite close-quarters living, and possibilities for crime, people are trusting. If there is a fault, it may lie in too much trust. The ferry serves as a filter against troublemakers. He who wishes to commit a crime on a small island will soon be found out.

Fourth, young and old come together in community activities. There is a mutual respect, support, and kind recognition with blended age groups.

Fifth, problems — and there are a variety of them as there are in any community — are usually tackled with consensus. Sometimes the debate and answers cause figurative blood letting, but when busy days, starry nights and beautiful colors surround us, wounds in friendships, in business relationships, and even with family, slowly begin to heal.

When inner tension becomes impossible to contain, then the only fresh alternative is to move away, always a difficult decision to make. Such a move can also be taken hard by those who stay, who might feel as though they are the ones being left behind. In losing a neighbor resident, a feeling of personal blame or community inadequacy can creep in.

One observation of a personal nature to add to the above is that once a passenger traveling to Washington Island crosses the Door — perhaps after a long ride from the city after having left home, work, and the stresses of those places behind — the traveler finds elation in the open blue horizons with an edge of green in the distance. A mystery of what awaits on Washington Island intensifies as the ferry slowly makes its way into harbor. The anticipation may be heightened if the ferry ride has been through ice or through rough seas. There is exhilaration, finally, the relief to be safely on dry land — a comfortable island.

I believe these experiences repeated by islanders and frequent visitors time and again inspire each of us to find out more about this island community. Despite the difficulties of getting here, including the challenge of working around the ferry schedule, good citizens who appreciate Washington Island evolve.

Tuesday, March 13 –

Word came of the death of two former islanders, Erv Smith and Tom Cook. Neither man had lived on the island as a resident for many years, but both remained closely connected with the island from their youth, and both still held island property. Tom and his wife, Beverly, own a summer home not far down the beach from the Potato Dock, besides a home in Sturgeon Bay and another in Naples, FL. Tom and Bev have been generous to the Town, to the island's churches and other organizations.

Looking out my office window, the harbor is still. Loose cakes of ice float lazily, more open surface than ice. A slight current encourages them, first in one direction, then the other. A few swans bob in the open water, heads down as they search for weeds or other edible matter.

Of any day thus far, the channel looks like the beginning of spring, the start of the long process of break up. In two weeks and a few days, we start the busier April ferry schedule. People anticipate more travel options. And yet, if temperatures get cold once again, we could as easily experience heavy bay ice into the middle of April. It all depends on weather patterns. Wind. Temperature. Sunshine. Rain. All contribute to the grinding, melting, and reduction of ice from Green Bay waters.

Wednesday, March 14 –

Calm morning once more. Loose ice in the channel and the route to Plum Island, but not enough ice and not packed tight enough to cause any problem with our ferry.

Kenny Koyen stood on the pier next to his fish tug, *See Diver*. Boxes of frozen "glop," nets filled with algae, are dumped in a frozen heap. They resemble blocks of frozen spinach, except for their lighter color. I couldn't smell the algae with my head cold (and maybe, too, because they were frozen) but once thawed, these green cakes will emanate a putrid, musty smell.

Kenny continues to fish through the winter despite the odds of having his nets raked over the bottom by currents or filled with unwanted algae. In years past, slime or weeds could sometimes be removed by leaving the nets to be washed again by currents. Not this algae, though, so fine and hair-like that it clumps and won't wash from the nets. Great amounts of this algae must be either suspended or tumbling along the lake bottom, because algae has caused major expense for commercial fishermen.

Kenny estimates is costs him $300 per box of nets to cut away the old junk, save the leads and floats, and restring new netting. Fortunately, one old fisherman, Harold Greenfeldt, enjoys stringing nets. He works in the heated entry of Kenny's restaurant, KK Fiske, where the floor is smooth. Customers come and go, and some look over Harold's shoulder, making small talk and passing the time.

Kenny and his brother, Tom, or his son, Jesse, whoever is available, fish their rig pretty much year around. The only other licensed Washington Island commercial fisherman remaining is Jeff McDonald, who is also a carpenter and architect. One of Jeff's fishing partners is Jake Ellefson, a wizened, retired commercial fisherman with a lifetime of experience on the lake.

The *See Diver* and the *C & R* are what remain of a 35- to 40-boat island fishing fleet. In the 1930s multiple families and crewmembers made their living from each fish tug. A man or two worked ashore for the larger operations, boiling or repairing nets. The boiling was necessary when the twine was all cotton, so that the netting wouldn't rot. The twine since WWII has been nylon or other synthetic material.

Thursday, March 15 –

Cold once more this morning, about 15 degrees at 7:30 a.m., warming up to 21 degrees by 1 p.m. There was skim ice in the channel this morning, broken up by the ferry. Crossing continues to be good, with little to no ice interference to slow the trip down.

The funeral of Tom Cook will be held Saturday, which will necessitate careful scheduling of ferry reservations and a couple of extra trips to get everyone back and forth.

The funeral will begin at 11 a.m. at Bethel Church, about the same time Tim Jessen starts the annual St. Patrick's Day Parade from the REA to Karly's Bar, complete with bagpipers, flutist, and an assortment of people ready to have a good time. The Legion Post 402 has been asked to provide a color guard for Tom's funeral, and the squad will be firing about the time the parade ends.

***

Streaks of snowmelt on the roadway were frozen into slick puddles along the curves of Lobdell Point Road. Harbor ice still offers a solid road for ice fishermen now that the temperatures have solidified the melted snow. For the few fishermen who have yet to get their shacks off the ice, today is the DNR's deadline.

We saw a few snowmobiles headed to Detroit Island shortly after 8 a.m., most likely contractor Martin Andersen and a co-worker headed to a house on Rabbit Point. Martin seems to enjoy taking on construction projects there, and he's built most of the 15 or so homes on Detroit Island, including his own cabin. Martin's latest project is at the base of Rabbit Point, where coincidentally an eagle built a nest about the time the foundation went in. By late June the large stick nest had two fledglings in it, even while workers added flooring, walls and rafters. By mid-July the two juvenile eaglets were up and about, making attempts to fly, remaining close to the nest while one or both parents circled overhead.

A visitor here at the office yesterday, Mack Gunnlaugsson, thinks there may be as many as eight or nine eagles in the area between Plum Island and Rock Island, given the number he and others have seen this winter. Or, perhaps he's seen the same eagles again and again.

***

One major challenge will be to find someone for the Northport restaurant, and we may have gotten a step closer today. We met here in our island offices with a candidate from Sturgeon Bay who appears sincere, honest, experienced in restaurant business, and is most willing to get the job started. The next couple of weeks will tell us if we can move ahead, or keep looking for another candidate.

The middle of the month of March — the Ides of March — is here, and the time remaining before the real tourism season is upon us will go by quickly. Placing the right someone in the restaurant is important from a public relations standpoint, for the need to have the building managed, and for the income we will get from the building and facility.

Friday, March 16 –

Low 20s this morning with a light breeze.

The West Channel is again covered with thin "window pane" ice, smooth and clear like glass, and the few large, errant chunks of heavier ice floating around are locked in place until the ferry goes through, winds pick up, or currents push them around.

The low light from the east this morning highlighted the rugged pile of ice where a field scraped over the middle ground, a nine-foot shoal between Detroit and Plum Islands marked by the red nun, the Plum Island #2 buoy on the nautical chart.

This ice pile might be termed a "shove" because it was pushed onto this reef under pressure of a moving field. This occurred two weeks ago when we had strong winds, the bay ice broke up, and there were ensuing ice problems. With the exception of the middle ground shove, most of the ice in our route has now broken up and moved through toward the lake.

About this time of year ice characteristics change, caused by the changes in temperatures, and the melt and freeze cycles.

Water on top of ice, either from melting snow or rain, seeps through small cracks, gradually enlarging them. Eventually, aided by sunlight and warming, the standing moisture finds its way through the hard blue ice and drains to the lake below. Or, it might be absorbed by the porous ice surface and refrozen on cold nights. This takes place many times as break up of the bay approaches. The resultant ice is never quite as hard as when first frozen.

January ice may be a hard, rubbery sheet, as observed with undulation of an ice field when a ground swell runs underneath. By March, this ice begins to break more easily upon impact of the ferry's bow. Such conditions signal the near-end of winter and the true start of open water. Eventually, the grinding and bumping from wave and wind action breaks down big pieces into ever-smaller chunks, and finally, there are several weeks of icy mush before the bay is entirely liquid once again.

The whiteness of ice locked in Detroit Harbor also changes as the snow and surface ice melt. As standing water on top of ice sinks completely through the ice, it turns dark, a warning to stop driving pickups or snowmobiles across the harbor. From several major thaws the ice composition becomes needled or honeycombed, rotten in the sense there is little to hold the vertical shards together.

A miraculous thing, I think, that in early April there can still be huge fields of ice on the bay and Detroit Harbor still frozen and locked tight. Along Washington Island's western shore, ice shoves powered by storms sometimes reach as high as the tops of shoreline cedars. Remnant piles may remain in late April, about the time potatoes might be ambitiously planted.

Yet, just two months later, in mid-June, youngsters are seen swimming at Schoolhouse Beach. But until then, cold water and cool breezes create a very long, extended spring.

Saturday, March 17 – St. Pat's Day

Today the island hosted a parade and a funeral, two separate events, but with a stretch of imagination, they might have been tastefully linked.

Thomas G. Cook, 79, buried today, was an island boy with a great talent for numbers and accounting. He put his talents to good purpose as he rose through the ranks of Tenneco's Walker Muffler in Racine. On his watch, Tom steered the merger of Walker Muffler and J. I. Case, and he wound up heading the Tenneco Automotive Division shortly afterward.

A huge man with a huge heart, Tom also had a large group of friends. He gave generously to island churches, and he supported the Island Ball Team and other island institutions.

On my way to attend Tom Cook's funeral on the north end of Main Road at Bethel Church, I looked upon the scene at Karly's where parade-goers were assembling alongside snow banks at 10:30 a.m. Intense sunlight had followed heavy frost each of the previous days, and it cleared the pavement, perfect footing Tim Jessen and friends, dressed in kilts, waiting to parade down Main Road.

One mile north on Main Road, also at 11a.m., the Tom Cook funeral was scheduled to begin. Over 100 people jammed into Bethel Church, "The little church with the big mission...." in Washington Harbor. As American Legion Members there to pay tribute, we stood in uniform as people filed into church. I visited with two of Tom's sons and I referred to the parade about to begin. Tom's middle son, Greg, remarked, "Dad would have liked that, heading up the parade, an Old Fashioned in his hand."

As the service was about to begin, there were hugs and handshakes exchanged between family and friends. Our Legion squad was led past Tom's casket by Greg Casperson, who escorted us to the front pews, next to the organ and the side door.

Both piano and an organ were played while Pastor Greene in strong voice led hymn singing. He delivered a sermon message, describing Tom and his life of giving to others. Another hymn, a prayer, and the service concluded. We filed out the side door and took up our rifles, assembled in formation, at attention. A sharp series of commands; three volleys fired in unison and the ping of empty brass casings as they struck the shoveled concrete walk.

Pall bearers hoisted the casket and walked it slowly toward the hearse, followed by a final prayer, and then a spontaneous request from the minister: "Let's all sing, *'Take Me Out To The Ball Game*,' one more time for Tom." And we did. There were tears, certainly, but also many smiles from those who remembered Tom's love for island baseball.

Tom followed the Islanders team each Sunday in summer and he knew the players, the sons and grandsons and nephews of players and friends when he grew up — Hansens, Jorgensons, Gunnlaugssons, Johnsons, Hagens, Bjarnarsons, and other long-standing island family names.

Later, we joined family and friends in the social hall for a lunch prepared by the ladies of the church. This was not the same size crowd that had been in church, for several had already slipped into their cars and headed south to Karly's for green beer, corned beef and cabbage. It was St. Patrick's Day, after all. Had Tom still been with us, that's where he would have been.

Sunday, March 18 –

During the night, temperatures dipped into the mid-20s. Frost greeted the morning sun and the day turned bright and beautiful once again.

Rich Ellefson says its great maple syrup weather. Cold nights with warm sunshine during the day moves sap up the trunks of maple trees. A matter of hydraulics, according to the experts, but it's still hard to understand the rising of sap from roots beneath frozen soil. On a good day each maple tree tap can yield one-half gallon of sap.

Rich, his wife, Kerstin, and two young boys, Mack and Jed, collect sap in buckets and store it overnight in large drums. Then, Grampa Dick Ellefson, back from Florida early this year, keeps an eye on the fire. It takes many hours to boil down a single batch and that translates into lots of firewood. The first batch of syrup is usually the clearest, the lightest, and therefore, the most highly prized.

***

I arose at 5:15 this morning and worked in my basement on a carving project, a St. Andrew's cross for the Stav church.

Later, on my way home from church, I made a quick visit to see Aidan before his nap. His smiles are infectious, and he looks different, older now, with new teeth in his smile rather than just gums. He's putting out more sounds, most of them recognizable for the objects or activities he intends to describe.

***

A print of an Icelandic family sitting in their one-room farmhouse or hillside cavern is on our home office desk. There are at least three family generations along with farm animals. This sketch depicts a scene by candlelight, perhaps in the 1800s or a time earlier than that. The artist focused on the one person reading aloud to the others. Iceland is, or was, the nation with the highest literacy rate of any nation in the world. True, not a large population, but Iceland is quite rural with many miles between towns and villages and farms. The emphasis on learning to read has always been great despite the distances and isolated farms.

I'd like to think not all learning of importance takes place in major cities or universities. They are centers for learning, teaching, for research and experimentation, but basic reading and writing can take place almost anywhere. "Truth has no bounds" best describes this, and in some cases, the opportunities to retreat to silence and inner thought might actually encourage original ideas and concepts.

Tuesday, March 20 –

The evening turned cold, dropping to 18 degrees by morning, and a stiff wind blew much of the night. Fortunately, the Door didn't have much ice. Loose pieces of bay ice blew out the passage during the night or fetched up on headlands west of the Door. Ferry crossing was good today.

During the noon hour, between trips, Hoyt put on his air tank and dove under the *Arni J.'s* stern to inspect the rudders, propellers and the stern bearings. Other than a few nicks on the outer edges of the blades, apparently received when reversing in loose stones, the underbody looked good. Vibration has increased on the starboard shaft, quite noticeably since the hours spent churning heavy ice cakes several weeks back. The port shaft has always been good, absolutely smooth and vibration-free, but the starboard shaft from the very first winter season has shown vibration.

During an elective drydocking in 2004 to discern vibration problems, Bay Ship's machinists shot a sight down the stern tube to determine straightness of the bore, using the center of the output flange on the Twin Disc marine gear. Results were reported to us as perfect.

However, the stuffing box alignment still appears to be a problem. The stern tube through which the shaft rotates is off enough in alignment (improper bore is our guess) that it aggravates other problems when the shaft and propeller are working hard. At that same time we also found a damaged rudder pintle bearing from dragging over rocks. That was our doing and not the shipyard's fault, but it was a possible contributor to the vibration problem. Once fixed and re-floated, the ferry performed quite well, but the demanding test of rugged ice still awaited.

Hoyt's dry suit kept him reasonably warm. He was probably warmer in the water than standing in the cold air.

***

A new employee, Tully Ellefson, joined us Monday. Tully is an uncle to Rich, our Operations Manager, and he's had extensive experience at Snap-On Tool company, Bay Ship, and Hi-Tech in Sturgeon Bay before coming to the island.

***

Swans across the harbor are swimming among the ice floes. WDNR shoots them to keep their adult numbers in check, a rather violent action designed to keep mother nature in man's balance.

Wednesday, Mar. 21 –

We drove to Sturgeon Bay in the mist and fog. Later in the day we experienced loud claps of thunder and bolts of lightening. I visited Uncle Harold Knutson, 89, in the hospital, where he is recuperating from a broken hip socket.

At the Maritime Inn, half a dozen islanders met in the lobby and cafeteria area. We meet more island acquaintances in the stores later. It's a local fact of life: leave the island to meet your neighbors.

Friday, March 23 –

A glorious morning, again. Worries of the world seem far away on this most pleasant of mornings. There is more to do than feed the birds, but that is how I started out my day, right after taking out the trash. Then, on to work at the ferry dock with a sore left leg from medical treatment the day before.

The ferry trip today is once again smooth and our route is glassy-calm, ice-free. We discuss getting another ferry refitted and ready for operation early next week, so that by the time early April arrives we'll have two functioning vessels to help keep the schedule. If only the ice further west in the bay will soften and break up. The temperature predictions are for 50-degree days very soon.

***

The *Robert Noble* electrical project is coming along quite well. Ed Hutchins is winding up the wiring part of this job by connecting switches in the engine room entry. But there is other work going on as the scope of the project has enlarged. Bill Crance ground new steel plates for replacement of decks in the two heads. After 28 years of corrosion around the deck drains and toilets, it was time to trim out the rusted portions and weld in new plate. That need became evident only after running new wiring, which in turn led to piping new water lines, all of which brought closer examination of the spaces neglected for too long. In replacing deck plating, wall panels in the heads were found to be soggy from leaking rainwater, wicked up into insulation. This is the optimum time to fix those items and return the cabin and heads to top condition.

Overall, our project is still on track, but there is much cleaning and painting once the metal work, electrical, and piping is finished. New epoxy flooring will be applied in the bathrooms after a plan has been conceived for remounting the toilets.

All or nearly all of these remodeling jobs are beyond the observation, or appreciation, of the typical passenger.

***

Grandson Atlas, after eating Gramma's pancakes with maple syrup again for breakfast, put on a puppet show. He made the tickets from strips of adding machine paper, promptly collected our tickets, and then put on the show. His "stage" was a cloth with pockets made to resemble castle windows, draped inside a doorway. The audience sits on one side while the puppeteer works from the other. This is the same stage used by his mother, Evy, 25 years ago. Atlas loves science, too, and so this morning after the puppet show we watched a science video on energy. It's fun to observe the open, absorptive mind of a 4-year-old who wants to "learn and do" all day long.

We drove with Atlas to Jackson Harbor where we walked the trail and stood in puddles along the shallow shoreline on Carlin's Point. In the short time we were there we saw sand hill cranes, swans, an eagle, and we heard a woodpecker drumming against a rotten birch. Fog hung heavily off Rock Island's shore in the distance. Momentarily, the sun popped through, giving us added warmth. Just as quickly it disappeared, and the fog rolled back in thicker than before, and the air immediately cooled.

We learned later of record high temperatures near 60 F in Green

Bay and southern Wisconsin, but here cold lake waters and fog kept us cool. That will be the expected pattern until the lake warms up sufficiently...like, maybe, mid-June.

Tuesday, March 27 –

A day of business off the island. Thick fog in the Door, but no ice enroute. The atmosphere first became thicker toward Sturgeon Bay, then burned off to a clear, blue sky by 10:30.

A long list of appointments are scheduled for Hoyt and me: doctor, lawyer, accountant, financial advisor and shipyard. These meetings kept us busy all day long and into early evening, and again the next morning, before heading north on Highway 57 to catch the ferry home. As with other overnights, we met islanders at the Maritime Inn, and we saw many more familiar faces about town. Our late morning lunch meeting at Cedar Crossing was at a table adjacent to Kay and Gordon Jaeger. Our hostess was Kathy Jorgenson, formerly of the island, and the waitress at the next table was Vicki (Gunnlaugsson) Burke, also formerly of Washington Island.

Wednesday, March 28 –

Work steadily progresses on shore projects. We are but a few days away from the start of April's ferry schedule of five trips per day, with an added trip beginning April 6th.

A long semi unit with an enclosed trailer for hauling cars, from SAS of Luxemburg, WI, came on the ferry to pick up John Hanlin's car, the one that was burned up in a fire a few weeks ago. It will be examined by investigators to determine the cause.

Tuesday of next week, local elections will be held for Town Board and School Board, and for a referendum to increase the allowable amount the school can add to the tax levy. The difference is about $48,000, not a large dollar figure by any means, and it's pretty hard to argue that it isn't needed. The island school system has little "fluff" in it now, and state laws dictate only so many percentage points of increase each year in levy amount.

Friday, March 30 –

Gray and overcast with moderate NE winds. Temperatures are in the mid-30s by early morning.

This is the second-to-last day of the month and also second-to-last day on the winter schedule. It follows that we are nearing the end of the reservation book with a return to "first-come-first-served" for vehicles.

There is no ice enroute. Detroit Harbor's ice has broken away from the northern shore and drifted toward Pedersen Bay. It's dark and rotten, and where it struck Richter's Point and Dead Horse Island it raised into ruffles, white like a line of breakers, the needled ice piled several feet into the air. In a few more days this winter's harbor ice will be entirely chewed and ready to disappear.

Saturday, March 31 –

Once again the sky is gray and overcast, but it's not raining...yet.

The patch of dark harbor ice is still wedged at the upper end of the ferry channel, with small pieces broken off during the night filling our slip. I saw a small fishing boat trolling the channel as I was ready to leave the office late yesterday afternoon, trolling for brown trout or northern pike. Just days ago the last of the ice fishermen were seen on 4-wheelers out on the ice.

Years ago, in the late '50s, the spring perch run was a major island activity. There was no limit on perch caught then, and there were so many perch the Detroit Harbor docks were lined with fishermen. According to old-timer ferry captains, by turning over the ferry wheel first thing in the morning, perch that schooled under the hull were killed and floated to the surface. Last year, too, we saw thick schools of young perch, like clouds, all within our ferry slip for some reason. They were all of similar class, about five inches in length with maybe one or two females nearby guarding them from predators.

Not entirely coincidental to the disappearance of harbor ice and the arrival of perch is the arrival of the first cormorant from wherever it winters. Hoyt spotted the first one early in the week. The year before, he said, March 15th was the first cormorant arrival.

APRIL

Sunday, April 1 –

April Fool's Day. April is poetry month. Heavy fog early after thunderstorms during night. Thirty-eight degrees.

The ferry's radar and GPS must be warmed up and working this morning for the early trip, to be employed with the compass and wits of the pilot. The sky overhead seems bright at 9 a.m. The sun may burn through the thin veil later this morning.

***

Yesterday afternoon, I began yard work by picking up sticks fallen during heavy snows and wild winter winds. Our home has 30 or more large maple trees and 10 or more oaks in addition to long rows of mature cedars along the north and south lot lines. Seeds, leaves and bits of vegetation are everywhere. Even though I spent hours cleaning up our yard last fall, there are always more leaves in spring, windblown from flower beds and hedges, and stubborn leaves that hung on limbs beyond Christmas.

As I raked I listened to music on headphones, a CD player strapped to my waist. The work is tedious, but only if I let it become so. Each leaf — and there are thousands — is a reminder of the green spring to come — the pale greens of summer, and vibrant colors of fall — all within the next five months. Some leaf remains are only stems and veins at this point, while others are as crisp as the day they fell from the tree. I am fortunate to have a yard full of leaves and the health to enjoy this spring raking ritual.

A pull of the rake at a stubborn pile of matted, wet vegetation revealed tender shoots of daffodils and tulips, resting beauty about to spring forth. And 'spring' is not too strong a word. Along our north lot line where the sun warms the soil, daffodils pierce the mat of leaves and lift them from the ground when they emerge. There, flowers with a leaf necklace are testament to the strength of regeneration.

***

Mary Jo and I visited Arni. Although he was in bed, he was in recuperation as much for a back problem as for a possible stroke. He looked good, joked, and he found humor in the fact he was diagnosed having a small stroke. He looked forward to a visit from his Green Bay doctor Monday, who promised to travel to the island to Arni's home. Arni's recall was excellent, and he seemed not only interested, but also well informed about the weather, the swans swimming in the harbor not far from shore, and daughter Stel's arrival back on the island after a winter in Sturgeon Bay.

Monday, April 2 –

High in the 30s to start with, and by mid afternoon skies cleared, then turned a beautiful blue. We enjoyed the mid-50s and a very pleasant afternoon without wind.

Eric Brodersen began work today at the Ferry Line after approximately four years working for Lampert's Home Center stocking and delivering lumber and construction materials. We welcomed big Eric and his steady, quiet approach to things.

***

Our ferry traffic seems brisk, but without comparing numbers it's always hard to tell, because our schedule has also increased. Part of the current traffic surge is from pent up island shoppers who can now get to major stores and back in one day with increased ferry travel options.

At noon a green WDNR tank truck drove off the island ferry dock carrying brown trout fingerlings from the Wild Rose State Hatchery, west of Oshkosh. Each spring, for many years, the Island Sportsman's Club and the Ferry Line have sponsored this trout planting in hopes these fish might return for improved fishing opportunities in adjacent waters. We give a complimentary ride for the truck, driver and fish, and we offer use of the Potato Dock as a site to unload the trout. This year, though, the new driver got mixed up with directions and drove out on Kap's Marina dock instead. The fish won't know the difference.

The term "Potato Dock" is unusual, I suppose, to anyone not familiar with Washington Island's history of potato farming, especially the efforts of Ed Anderson who planted many acres here in the 1950s and 1960s. At the height of production, in order to get his potatoes cleaned, sorted, bagged and to market, he set up equipment on the old Straits of Mackinac carferry hulls, the *City of Cheboygan* and the *City of Munising*.

These carferries, once rendered obsolete by construction of the bridge across the straits, were purchased by Anderson. He used them for potato storage until late fall when they were towed to Benton

Harbor and Chicago markets. Anderson constructed his dock from stone rubble using every island stone fence he could find, plus other odds and ends that added bulk to the pier. Walt Jorgenson, a foreman for the Anderson farm, claims they buried several old cars in the pier. The outer end of the pier was formed from two sections of old wooden dry dock towed from a Sturgeon Bay shipyard.

Anderson's potato operation went bankrupt in the early 1970s. His property was auctioned by the Continental Mortgage Company. An extended Lithuanian family from Chicago named Slenys bought the dock property and held it for nearly 20 years. During this time the vacant dock slumped back into the lake, overgrown with brush and weeds and undermined by high water of the late 1980s. In 1995 the Ferry Line made an offer accepted by the Slenys' family.

Over the past twelve years we've cut brush, filled wash-outs, dredged, drove sheet steel to protect the face of the pier, placed large stones along the west edge for protection from breaking seas, and graveled the surface. Today, we use it to moor idled ferries, particularly in winter. The natural depth in that location is about 15 feet, enough to allows deeper draft vessels such as research vessels and Coast Guard cutters to moor there on occasion.

Tuesday, April 3 –

Thirty-eight degrees and overcast, with fog and haze. There is a moderate breeze from ENE.

I boarded the early ferry for a trip to Green Bay. Others had the same idea. Mack Gunnlaugsson's truck filled out the ferry foredeck. A good number of island restaurant owners, I learned, were headed to Green Bay to attend the annual Dierks-Waukesha Food Show at Shopko Hall near Lambeau Stadium. The purpose of this show is to offer schools, restaurants, and other food institutions ideas for menus, introduce products, and establish supplier-client contact.

Mack Gunnlaugsson drives his 25-foot straight truck almost weekly to Green Bay and Sturgeon Bay, picking up supplies for island businesses, for his own Brothers Too business, and assorted orders for others. His loads typically include kegs of beer for island taverns, bottled and canned beverages, mattresses, furniture, appliances, and so on. It's a great service, with delivery to the island customer's door.

But a trucking business is only one of Mack's interests. He hauls beverages for the partnership he and brother Jim operate, called "Brothers Too." Their store sells packaged liquor, ice, shoes (Minnetonka Moccasins) and appliances, cigars, and other supporting items.

In the back shop Mack repairs television sets, in addition to making house calls to fix home appliances. He received electronics training in the Navy and he's able to fix just about anything, one of those rare individuals in a community you can count on to fix something when it breaks, at a very reasonable rate. A typical homeowner may call to say, "My washing machine is thumping and sounds like it will run away." Mack responds, "Isn't that the Whirlpool top-loading model, etc., maybe15 years old?" The homeowner says, "I think so. You put it in when you replaced my Sears." Mack: "Geez. I'm awfully busy...booked up for the next two weeks. I suppose you need it right away?" Homeowner: "Well, I've got wash in it right now." Mack: "I'll see what I can do. No promises until next week."

By that afternoon, Mack has repaired the appliance and left a note describing what he's done. A bill follows a month later for the cost of parts plus modest labor. That's a real service, at an unreal price. It's also one reason why, if you live on Washington Island, it only makes sense to buy your appliances from Mack. He not only sells, he installs, and he carts the old one away for you.

What does Mack's brother, Jim, do when he's not tending the liquor store? Jim has a construction business. He and Mack have also built a mini-storage business. Together, these two brothers get lots done in a week. Service is their mission.

For many years there was a good reason to stop at their store early in the morning. It held a bakery operated by their mother, Joy, and Jim's wife, Marsha. The aroma of cinnamon rolls, cookies and breads filled the store. At a certain point, the early hours and work became too much for Grandma Joy, and the bakery was dismantled to make room for liquor and other products.

If no one is at the counter when you walk in, just holler and Mack, Jim or one of their employees will soon appear to help you.

Wednesday, April 4 –

The weather forecast predicted high winds and possible snow. It didn't disappoint. The early morning 5 a.m. winds were moderate, but velocities increased at daybreak. Joel Gunnlaugsson ran the *Eyrarbakki* to Northport on the early trip, but with 6-to-8-footers in the Door he recommend shutting down.

We called off the rest of the day's trips based on Joel's experienced eye and a forecast for winds to continue in the range of 30-40 kts. Rich and our office staff, Kim and Bill, had already begun rescheduling semi trucks and other traffic the previous day, based on today's high winds forecast. We hope to reschedule them for Thursday morning and get back on track by mid-day. If all goes well, we might run two early boats to pick up extra trucks and the traffic backlog. At least we didn't have snow accumulation like the northwestern part of the state where 8 inches was reported.

Our crew has found plenty of work to do in the steel storage building and down in the bilges of the ferries, cleaning out grease, rust, and whatever else may have accumulated there during the course of a season. If not tended to regularly, rust soon gets out of hand, and in the extreme, plates might need replacement. We gain peace of mind that all surfaces and corners are inspected and cared for.

Thursday, April 5 –

Winds blew hard during the entire night, tearing through the trees surrounding our home. The heavier gusts sounded like a freight train. The Channel 2 TV meteorologist reported NW winds with speeds to 59 kts in Gills Rock. I think he meant Northport where the National Oceanic and Atmospheric Administration (NOAA) tower is located, that measures wind speed and wind direction in the Door.

Rich Ellefson was at the Ferry Line office by 6:15 a.m. to assess conditions. Based on the history file accessed on our computer link to NOAA weather tower information, and with telltale signs of breaking seas, he called off the early ferry trip. We had hoped to get in the early ferry followed shortly thereafter by a second trip. From our office windows, looking down the backsides of the waves, we can see foam on breaking waves.

Seldom do wind speeds sustain for 24 hours or more. More often, we observe a declining trend in wind speeds within 12 to 16 hours as the high pressure fills in, skies begin to clear, and the day warms up. Today, however, none of this has happened. We are experiencing 30 to 40-plus kt wind speeds, verified by the ore carrier *Joseph Block* northbound through the Door around 10:45 a.m., headed for the ore docks in Escanaba. The *Block's* captain reported winds in the upper 30s, and choppy seas west of Plum Island were at 8 to 10 feet as his ship slugged against them through the Door.

The fact that it was only 18 degrees early this morning, and has risen only slightly to 23 degrees by 11a.m., is another factor against making a ferry trip. Airborne spray at this air temperature freezes instantly on cold steel, and the bow of the *Joseph Block* looked white because of it.

Our ferry office phones have been ringing constantly with

questions about whether or not we are running. When will we run? When do we think we might run? Will the wind die down? How much must it settle down before we try? Is the mail in yet?... and so on ... from callers on both sides of the Door. It's always easier when the forecast calls for winds to lay down in the afternoon, but that's not today's forecast. No real let up is predicted in the next 24 hours.

In the meantime, anyone can view the Northport dock through our web cam located on the NOAA tower, via our website. On Washington Island, a half-dozen cars are parked in line, the owners saving a spot, eager to get off the island. Many others have ridden out to the dock to see us in person, for reassurance, hoping for a chance yet today to get across, back to work, to appointments, and so on.

We are considered the island lifeline, but today we're unable to make connection with the mainland. Once we get running again, we'll have between two and three loads of backlogged traffic. Our Northport terminal freight garage is filling up, too, and the freight carts there already hold as much as they can, with more freight deliveries before the afternoon is out consisting of parcels, food, auto parts, and hardware. Our flatbed stake truck, Lil' Atlas, already has two pallets of goods on it. The U.S. Mail, a priority item, will also be carried, with two days' worth of mail squeezed in the minivan.

✳✳✳

"Stranded" is a relative term, and most of the time we hear it used by persons who believe they are stranded on Washington Island.

Island residents Hoyt and Kirsten and little Aidan are among the "stranded" on the mainland, unable to get home. But they're quite comfortable in Sturgeon Bay at Kirsten's mother's home, waiting for word when we're running again. Other travelers may not be so fortunate, having driven long distances from a motel or relatives' home, or wherever they were staying. They have little choice other than to stay in touch, an inconvenience beyond the simple delay, an unexpected night's lodging.

Friday, April 6 –

The ferry *Eyrarbakki* is returning now from the early run, the going still slowed by the winds and seas, winds now in the 25-30 mph range. To provide the most comfortable ride, our captains tack their way across Door waters. As soon as the ferry clears the entrance light their course edges under the lee of Lobdell's Point, west of the Potato Dock and past the Tom Cook and Minnow Emmerson homes, past the

Rutledge home...and on to the northwest. As the ferry works out from under Willow Point, away from flat water, passengers begin to experience swells that work along Washington Island's west shore. The skipper pulls back on the throttles when a large sea presents itself, then motors ahead to gain as much sea room as possible on Plum Island. Once the seas begin to throw spray over the bow and the ride becomes clearly uncomfortable, the skipper puts the wheel over to port and his course swings downwind for a point somewhere between Northport and Ellstrom's Bluff on the Peninsula. He works to gain windward searoom on Plum Island every chance he gets, putting the ferry in position to run downhill with the larger swells that roll from the direction of Minneapolis Shoals, some 20 miles to the north. Once squared away for Northport, the ferry should run more easily with swells astern, "riding like a duck."

The *Eyrarbakki* handles very well in such seas. It has a high bow and a quick, responsive helm. In my opinion, with its cable steering, this is the most responsive of all our ferries. The *Eyrarbakki* was built in 1970, among the first hulls Bay Shipbuilding launched after moving their shipyard from the banks of the Manitowoc River to a location on Sturgeon Bay's waterfront. The ship's wheel takes just 2 1/2 turns hard-over to hard-over, and with cable steering you can feel rudder pressure on the helm, which helps you to know when your rudders are on centerline. No rudder angle indicator is necessary. One drawback to this system comes when backing. You need to jam the wheel hard over with a spoke against your thigh. If you don't maintain a firm grip, water pressure can flip the rudders, spinning the wheel and rapping your knuckles or wrist before the steering quadrants hit the stops. Slamming against the rudder stops can also result in broken quadrant bolts, dropping the frame piece that connects the steering for each rudder, an event you don't want to experience underway.

The ferry is now in and has unloaded, depositing still more freight at our island terminal. Yesterday the crew brought in four carts heaped with freight. This time of year many of the gift stores are receiving stock for summer retail, and dozens of parcels, large and small, jam the UPS cart. Most of these boxes stacked on our island shelves or piled in our terminal garage will be picked up before noon, making room for this day's shipments later on.

Saturday, April 7 –

My first move this morning was for my long johns. They've hung on the closet hook for the past several weeks, but it's time to put them back on. The thermometer must be broken. It hasn't varied more than four degrees, night or day, in the past four days.

The difference this morning as I looked outdoors was a fresh cover of snow on the ground, with more snow falling.

My second move was to build a fire in the wood stove that supplements our oil furnace and provides even heating. Later on, I intend to do some wood carving, a perfect morning for that, and a comfortable place to work once the stove has warmed up the two-foot thick stone walls. Our home is on a laid foundation, built around 1915.

Out at the ferry dock, we're now running six trips daily. This morning, for the fourth day in a row, our temperatures are below 26 degrees and ice has reformed on Detroit Harbor, extending toward the ferry channel. By tomorrow morning ice may encompass the ferry slips.

Last night we ran the first Friday night ferry of the new season, a trip designed to accommodate visitors who can't make an afternoon ferry. At five o'clock, as Rich departed the island on the *Arni J.*, a snow squall blew through the Door, and with it winds 10-15 kts above the steady 30 kts already experienced. For about twenty minutes, he reported, it whipped up seas and blocked visibility with near whiteout.

I rode out to the dock at 8:20 p.m. to check in with the crew. It was blustery, still blowing 30 kts with snow flurries in the air. The ferry deck had a thick layer of ice on it from rolling in the seas earlier, taking on spray. Coming out of the breakwall on their last trip at 6:30 p.m., 12-ft. seas ran parallel with the outer stone breakwall, and the *Arni J.* took several vicious rolls before Rich squared away toward Pilot Island. The result of their efforts had been the transport of a total of six cars with their passengers. Now, with winds still gusting at 30 from the NW, I wondered how this evening ferry's revenues would balance with the effort expended. Normally, for Easter weekend we anticipate extra traffic to the island, relatives and cottage owners.

An Easter egg hunt, with some 800 eggs painted and ready to go for the little egg hunters at the Rec Center, may have to be held indoors. Or, maybe, just hide them in the snow and hope for the best!

Tonight at 9 p.m. is the Easter Vigil Service at the Stavkirke. Electric baseboard heaters have been turned on to preheat the Stav for worshippers. At 6:15 a.m. Sunday morning, keeping a tradition begun many years back, an Easter Sunrise Service will be held at Percy Johnson Park. Attendees may wish to wear their snowmobiling outfits instead of Easter Hats. Maybe, bring their snowmobiles, too. A temporary wooden cross has been erected in the beach sand, and an invitation is open to all worshippers. For tomorrow morning's service,

Pastors Phil Green of Bethel and Frank Maxwell of Trinity Lutheran will share the sunrise worship duties. St. Michael's Catholic parish of Washington Island will hold their formal Easter service this Saturday afternoon at Trinity Lutheran Church. In one fashion or another, and regardless of weather, Easter will be observed here on Washington Island.

Our crew and our customers are eager for a return to warm weather, clean decks, thawed pipes.

Sunday, April 8 –

The fifty or so worshippers who arose early to attend the Easter Morning Sunrise service at Percy Johnson County Park had to bundle up to stay warm.

Winds had diminished during the night to maybe 15-20 mph but were still cold.

At this location, about 25 years ago at the east end of Town Line Road, a motorist drove into the lake, having arrived on the late Friday night ferry looking for a cottage in the dark. Their car wound up in the lake, water above the floorboards. Fortunately, the east side beach at that location is gradually receding shelf rock, covered with only a few feet of water. Following that incident, a "Dead End" barricade and sign were erected there. The Easter cross is erected on the beach each year just beyond this barricade.

Easter Sunday typically draws one of the largest crowds of Christians of the calendar year. Hoyt and Kirsten's Aidan, 1 1/2 years old now, was the appointed toddler who carried an egg to the altar. He followed the candles and various adornments reset following their Maundy Thursday removal. Soon candles were lit and hymns were sung, and the congregation was in a happy, joyous mood, with smiles all around. Easter was in the air, and Aidan swayed with the music, standing on the church pew, his first church experience.

Mary Jo prepared a late afternoon picnic-style dinner rather than the traditional Easter ham. We elected to do pork in the form of Mann's Store bratwurst, grilled outdoors, steeped afterward in beer and onions. Mary Jo prepared plates of food for Arni.

In late afternoon Aidan, Hoyt and Kirsten joined us for supper. Hoyt had been captain on the early ferry that morning with Ken Berggren, and the two remained on standby for what we term 'overload' trips the rest of the day. Overloads are extra, unscheduled ferries run to catch up with traffic between or after the regular ferry.

Mann's Store brats are the best around, by far. Their ingredients contain fresh pork, well-trimmed, minus gristle or other surprises found in lesser quality products. Flavorful spices are added to these custom-made sausages by Jerry Mann. Jerry learned his trade in sausage making from Werner "Butch" Pearson, who knew the meat cutting trade well. We often took our venison to Butch, partly because we enjoyed seeing his excitement over the chance to process meat. He couldn't wait to get his hands on a deer carcass to butcher and process. He would instruct me to "...let it hang for at least t'ree days." But as soon as he heard I'd shot a deer, he'd call to inquire when I was going to bring it over so he could begin cutting it up.

In between butchering chores, he told us about his younger days as a bouncer for a Chicago speakeasy.

Monday, April 9 –

Sunny, blue skies and slightly above freezing this morning.

Our crew made an early trip with the *Arni J.*, then doubled back to Northport for two tankers, LP and gas, for Hansen Oil. The *Eyrarbakki* made the 8 o'clock island departure. Winds are near calm and it's a beautiful day on the water even if temperatures are nearly 20 degrees below normal.

The thin patches of snow are fewer and fewer, shrinking as the day warms. Yet more snow is in the forecast for Wednesday. In the meantime, before snow has a chance to cover the grass, there may be an opportunity to do some raking around the ferry office grounds.

***

This day has gone by quickly at the office with the completion of several letters of correspondence, the April Passenger Cabin News, a reworking of a draft for the Birding Festival, and various phone calls. I checked in with the crew and hustled freight carts, unloading contents in our terminal as the carts were rolled up the dock from the ferry.

Today has remained sunny, but in other parts of the state there is another winter storm warning. When will winter end and spring demonstrate it is here to stay?

Thursday, April 12 –

A few snowflakes, then by 4 p.m. a near-blizzard on Wednesday afternoon. The last trip went OK, but with lots of wind and poor visibility. Mary Jo and I rode out to the Potato Dock just prior to dark to observe the conditions. Snow blew horizontally and white caps smacked the end of the pier. A short distance offshore, rafts of ducks, possibly a hundred or more birds, treaded water in an effort to stay together, avoiding flight in the low visibility and oncoming darkness. This morning, we had six inches of heavy, wet snow, with a temperature of 30 degrees. The bottom layer of snow dripped with slush when shoveling. All hands shoveled for the first hour or so. The 8 o'clock ferry loaded and departed, then more shoveling. The 7 a.m. early ferry crew had shoveled without assistance before they loaded vehicles and people. After cleaning up at the ferry dock, I drove to church and shoveled some more.

***

Back at the ferry dock in the passenger lobby at 4 p.m., we hosted a discussion group on the first Washington Island Birding Festival. Broad details have already been made public, but further detail is needed, with support from a committee. The people who participated were keenly interested in birding, and they were helpful and energetic with their suggestions. Among our group of adults was Con McDonald, already a knowledgeable birder at age fourteen. His interaction with the adults was impressive as he made suggestions based on his local knowledge and birding observations. Our meeting retired at 6 p.m.

***

At 7:30 p.m. the American Legion members met, our first gathering of 2007. Discussion topics ranged from dues to the new Door County War Memorial dedication. Will anyone represent the post? I volunteered along with several other members. Were new uniforms needed? Who would be the Memorial Day program speaker? Would we again ask high school students to participate in writing patriotic essays, and if so, what will the essay theme be? A nomination committee was appointed for new officers.

After coffee and dessert with the members, I drove home in the dark with snow still blowing.

Friday, April 13 –

It's sunny this morning with the feeling it will finally get warmer today. The overnight temperature fell below 32 degrees, but that won't last long. By 9 a.m. melting begins, and by noon there are more brown patches than white on the ferry dock lawn. Perhaps spring is here! I've said before:"Spring is here!" Perhaps repetitious recitation will make it so.

***

I chaired the Stavkirke Committee meeting, and our main business was to prioritize several projects that have lapsed, such as a boardwalk from road to the church. This Stavkirke, replica of a centuries-old Norwegian church with twelve main pine pillars, or stavs, is one of the most frequently visited sites on the island, and visitors from all over the world sign the guest register. A ledger on the altar is available to those who wish to leave a prayer or personal reflection.

Saturday, April 14 –

Bright and sunny today with early morning frost, very little wind. The main event Saturday was a marathon, six-hour, Ferry Line Board of Director's meeting, held at our home. Directors discussed many topics, and we broke new ground with several decisions that impact shareholders.

I had hoped to get outdoors and burn a pile of brush in the backyard — I even had a burning permit — but our meeting lasted too long, and meanwhile a southerly breeze sprang up. Another day.

That evening at Karly's hall I attended the Washington Island Sportsman's Club annual banquet. It's been a great event in the past, with dinner, door prizes (nearly 30 of them), raffles for guns or a bow, a silent auction of products donated by community businesses and individuals, and a program. This year, island teacher and naturalist, Steve Waldron, gave a slide program, beautiful island shots taken with his digital camera.

A unique thing about this event is that nearly one-third of the attendees are ladies or young people, demonstrating that there's wide public interest in outdoor activities. A number of island women are now avid turkey and deer hunters. To help attract young people, the club hosts a BB gun target shooting contest before dinner, a turkey call event, and a youth nature photography contest.

While this event wound down, further south on Main Road the Trueblood Performing Arts Center (TPAC) held its first show of the new season. A funk band from Chicago took the stage. Admission was free, with entertainment paid by a sponsor.

This tends to be the way of the island as the busier season begins. Following long periods few activities, suddenly several events compete with one another. It's a sign that ferry traffic and business income will rise.

Monday, April 16 –

Today is Tax Day, the deadline for postmarking federal income tax returns because the 15th fell on a Sunday.

We had a beautiful morning with a light northerly breeze. There were many ducks on the harbor, and geese and swans, some of them flying north.

***

Our upstairs phone rang at 6:15 a.m. It was Rich informing me there was an opening on the second run due to an illness among that crew. Would I fill in?

I was ready to get up and going, anyway, and it was a pleasurable change in my routine to head to the dock and get the *Eyrarbakki* started. Erik Foss joined me a few minutes after I had started the generator. We removed snow shovels and de-icing chemicals from the ferry, wondering, had we seen the last of winter snow? We took a chance and removed them anyway, cleaning up the small space by the engine room entry.

Eight vehicles waited in line to leave the island, and after we loaded and were underway, a pair of swans flew toward us coming from Plum Island. They sailed overhead past the *Washington's* decks, headed for Detroit Harbor.

At Northport, a semi and a dozen cars awaited us. During our turn around time, I opened the outside spigot on the terminal building, heated the spigot with a flame, and filled two water sample bottles, one for nitrates, the other for a bacteria test. These two samples were later sent to the state hygiene lab to satisfy state regulations for safe public drinking water.

Even though recent days have been warm, the Northport breakwall stones are still capped with ice, especially the north wall. Heavy rains and much warmer temperatures are needed to melt the ice completely away.

***

I rode my motorcycle to work this afternoon, and it felt great to ride in warm air and glide over clear roads.

Tuesday, April 17 –

A new face joined our employee group today, Gay Hecker. Gay is Tully Ellefson's sister, and Rich Ellefson's aunt. Gay and Dick, her husband, have moved to the island recently when Dick, a physician's assistant, accepted a position at our island clinic. The Hecker's daughter, Grace, sold tickets for several summers as a college student. We now have quite a complete Ellefson family representation!

***

The *Robert Noble* reconstruction project is really shaping up. Joel cleaned in the engine room, picking up bits of wiring, metal pieces, and other refuse, and then he vacuumed the bilges. Topside, Tully worked on restoring insulation that had been removed when new piping was installed overhead for the cabin and heads on the passenger deck. Strips of fiberglass material slathered with paste adhesive hold the bats of canvas-faced insulation in place. Inside the cabins, Bill Crance and Rich Ellefson installed specially shaped steel mouldings to create a coved effect along the base of each wall. When covered with epoxy material they will help to keep moisture away from the wall sheeting.

There's more installation and a thorough cleaning yet to be accomplished in these spaces, but the hardest, dirtiest work is nearing an end. Tomorrow morning a Coast Guard Marine Safety officer will be here to inspect our work and note deficiencies. We're hoping for on-the-spot approval so that our work can continue toward completion. Throughout this process Rich and Hoyt have kept the Marine Safety Detachment in Sturgeon Bay appraised of work progress with correspondence and photos and phone conversations. We don't expect any surprises.

Thursday, April 19 –

The clear, calm morning was outstanding. I heard passengers remarking on the clarity of water and the fact the lake bottom can be seen all the way out the channel, and all the way to the Plum Island buoy, to depths of 35 feet and more!

I cleaned windows on the way to Northport with Eric Brodersen, a new employee of two weeks or so. Eric told me how much he appreciated and enjoyed working on the ferries and said, "I've found that it's good for my psyche." A most thoughtful comment expressed in a very personal way. I can relate to his sense of appreciation.

I rode the 7 a.m. ferry to Northport and met John Fitzgerald to discuss spreading topsoil over our new drain field and other areas torn up when new concrete tanks were installed. There is a sizeable disturbed area, and since topsoil isn't in large supply on this end of the county, John's trucks will haul soil from southern Door, reversing work done by glaciers in the last ice age, when rich soil was scraped by ice and moved by water erosion to points further south. John will level, seed, and cover the area with straw, and in thirty days we should see a cover of grass begin to grow.

***

By noon the temperature outside our island office approaches 60 degrees, a perfect day to accomplish outdoor work. Bill Jorgenson and Eric Brodersen are grinding and chipping rust and thick paint from the *Noble's* main deck, while Rich Ellefson, Bill Crance and Ken Berggren are final-fitting toilets and setting moulding trim strips in the cabin and pilot house. I began working in the men's head in the late morning, cleaning, sanding, and then, finally, applying a coat of white paint over the old, light yellow walls. A new poured epoxy flooring system will be installed in the heads when painting is done.

While we work, the boat crew makes the scheduled trips with the *Eyrarbakki*, carrying tankers, visitors, and service people back and forth. In the channel, the U.S. Coast Guard Aids to Navigation Team from Sturgeon Bay is working the Detroit Harbor buoys, setting #2A and repositioning other buoys that moved with ice during the winter. The Plum Island Middle Ground buoy #2, a red nun between Detroit and Plum Islands, was swept off position during the big ice shove in early March, and it hasn't been seen since. In over 30 years, I don't recall when that buoy budged from position.

***

I ended the afternoon with a motorcycle ride to Jackson Harbor and around the "block" on Swenson Road.

Friday, April 20 –

A few of the current demands for my time are: the Northport restaurant operation; time as occasional fill-in crew on the ferry; meeting with a landscaper and gardener for work at both terminals; review of our company's 401(k) plan; consideration of termination of the current, frozen, defined benefit plan; review of the employee handbook; and, when time is right, work outside the Ferry Line, such as at the Stavkirke on Saturday work days.

***

I am one of the crew this morning on the *Eyrarbakki*, and what a beautiful morning it is. There isn't one person I've met today who hasn't remarked on the exceptionally fine morning. A slight frost melted before I got up at 6 a.m. It was still cold enough, as Ken Berggren pointed out, to cause formation of a light skim ice in the middle of Door waters. If you looked closely in the low light, a slight patch of broken skim ice could be seen, only visible because the morning was dead calm. One passenger spoke about paddling a canoe across the passage some day soon. Just three weeks ago we needed a Coast Guard ice breaker's assistance to get across. A canoe in June, maybe, but not yet, is our advice.

On our return run to the island, our deck is filled with trucks and trailers. We have a fuel oil semi, three fishing rigs towed by pickups, and a small trailer on the back of Pastor Frank Maxwell's Jeep filled with pizza supplies for the youth group fundraiser. Saturday morning at Trinity Lutheran Church, Frank will supervise the youth group and assisting adults. Their goal is to produce 500 pizzas, most of them presold, made either fresh for baking, or freezing. Funds earned will support the youth on their trip to San Antonio, TX, in June. They will stay in a San Antonio church and assist in mission work such as cleaning, repairs, house remodeling...whatever is asked of them. The intent of their trip is to make it a working session helping others, and along with the work, an opportunity for personal and spiritual growth.

Saturday, April 21 –

Special to Washington Island are the everyday, natural experiences that happen with regularity. There is reassurance that cycles will occur: ice will form; ice will melt; water levels will eventually rise again, just as they've fallen. And, tourists will come, just as they departed in the fall.

The arrival of tourists in numbers also coincides with the swarms of tiny bugs that hatch from the water, because both follow warm weather north. Within a day of the arrival of the first bugs, swallows arrive to eat the bugs and to nest. Tourists seem to follow the bugs and the swallows.

***

Washington Island is an average community in many ways, the kind of average from years back, the kind many people can't take for granted any more in their home town. Here "average" is an absence of crime and vandalism, nights without threatening fear of darkness. Then, too, there is overwhelming calm and natural beauty, the ability to be alone and find one's self. Island experiences can seem spiritual. Yesterday morning, with perfectly calm waters, for the first time as a ferry captain, I witnessed a lady down on her knees in the bow of the ferry. This may be an unusual sight in the middle of Death's Door, praying openly on the steel deck of the ferry, but why not? Muslims by the hundreds pray several times per day, wherever they may be. If our spirit is moved, then neither time nor place should matter.

We've witnessed far more unusual happenings on the ferries over the years: fights between family members; displays of sexual habits of people who don't think (or don't care) they're being observed — and other ranges of human behavior.

Our local galaxy is Death's Door and the surrounding islands where spiritual contentment may be found.

Sunday, April 22 – Earth Day

Hoyt and Joel applied epoxy to the deck in the *Noble*'s heads. In order to properly bond the epoxy product to steel, cabin heaters were turned up high. It was above 80 degrees in the cabin, over 100 degrees near the ceiling as measured with a heat gun. The finished product when applied and cured shall be impervious to weather.

***

In a few days I intend to spend time in the woods hunting for turkeys. An advantage in turkey hunting is to be settled in a spot well before daylight, ready to listen to their calls as they wake up and the toms and their harems get organized for the day.

***

In Madison, according to the radio, the day's temperature reached 85 degrees. Here on Washington Island, the southerly lake breezes are in the 20-plus mph range, great kite flying weather, but a warm jacket or sweatshirt is required.

Earlier this morning we visited Arni with Kirsten and Aidan. He was in the shower when we arrived, and we waited as he dressed for the breakfast table. He was in good humor and apologized to us for oversleeping.

***

Saturday evening the Island Party was held at Karly's hall. This tradition began over fifty years ago when local leaders and key summer families raised money enough to purchase and refurbish the old general store in Jensenville. It became the island's community center. This was where Arni Richter had worked as a young man, delivering grocery orders and ice with horse and wagon for the owners, Lawrence and Ruth Gislason.

Gislason's Store community hall, located adjacent to the present Red Barn theater, preceeded the modern day Community Center, a steel structure on Main Road built in 1970. Today's Island Community Center houses the medical clinic, the dental office, an optometrist's office, the town office, a library, gymnasium, the Island Archives, a general meeting room, and a kitchen.

***

Approximately 31 years ago I drove to Milwaukee and wrote for my U.S. Coast Guard Captain's License. It was only a few days after our daughter, Evelyn, had been born. I had studied for the test for quite some time, building on knowledge of Rules of the Road and vessel navigation I had learned as a U.S. Navy quartermaster. Fortunately, I passed the test on my first attempt.

Mary Jo had passed a longer and much more grueling test with a nine-month preparation followed by birthing at Shirley Atkin's home on Townline Road. Shirley was Dr. Paul Rutledge's assistant at the time, and in her home was a bedroom prepared for expecting mothers.

I drove Mary Jo to Shirley's early in the morning when labor pains began, and Dr. Rutledge stopped by periodically through the day to check on Mary Jo's progress. At around 5 p.m., he sat down in Shirley's kitchen to a bowl of navy bean soup, a favorite made just for him. In the nearby bedroom, labor had quickly taken its course, and by the time Dr. Paul put down his spoon, Evelyn had begun to emerge. Dr. Paul had no time to put on gloves. Within minutes we had a breathing, crying, healthy baby girl. I went with Dr. Rutledge to ring the Trinity Lutheran Church bell, a tradition of his to signal a new baby had been born.

Evy's birth was among the last of baby deliveries at Shirley's. Before Shirley hosted deliveries, there was Pearl Haglund's home, and in fact, Pearl was present to assist Shirley for many years. After Dr. Paul Rutledge, no medical provider dared follow the practice of island delivery, it seemed, in the light of malpractice suits. We were fortunate two of our children were born on the island, both healthy babies. Thordur, our third child, was delivered in St. Vincent's Hospital, Green Bay, and because of complications including a breech birth, it proved to be a wise decision.

Today, expecting parents typically have prenatal checks with their mainland obstetrician, and when the due date is close, they are often advised to stay on the mainland. In a few instances, surprises of early labor have occurred, and we've been called out with the ferry to rush the mother on her way to the hospital. No births have occurred on board our ferries, but it's been close several times, with one birth occurring in the Door County ambulance alongside the highway in Ellison Bay shortly after transfer from the ferry.

Tuesday, April 24 –

Mid afternoon the *Eyrarbakki* slid up to the island dock with a fertilizer spreader hitched to our Allis Chalmers tractor on the foredeck. We carry a number of fertilizer spreaders in spring for island farmers, and waiting on the dock with his diesel tractor for this one was Tom Koyen. He recently plowed Coppersmith's (a farm adjacent to the golf course once owned by a man named Coppersmith) and will fertilize the sandy soil prior to planting wheat. A surprisingly good crop of wheat grew from that land last year, harvested in late September along with crops from other island wheat fields.

Brothers Tom and Kenny Koyen took on wheat planting and harvesting initially to provide the Washington Hotel with whole wheat for their wood-fired oven. The Hotel bakes fresh bread weekly, sells some loaves locally, and ships the rest to an associated restaurant in Madison. At one point, the wheat supply had a surplus, and it was at that point that hotel owner Brian Vandewalle approached Capital Brewery in Middleton, WI, to see if there was interest in using some of the wheat for brewing beer.

Capital Brewery, by coincidence, had earlier looked into producing a wheat beer, trying to figure an angle to enter that market. They already brewed many beers recognized with national and international competition awards. A recipe devised by Brewmeister Kirby Nelson for a wheat beer, and a marketing program under the Island Wheat label proved to be a very successful combination. The product sold briskly, and within the year Island Wheat had become the number one selling Capital product. This, in turn, gave the Koyen brothers even greater incentive to plant wheat, and they worked to obtain permission to plow island fields that hadn't been touched by a disk since the days of potato farming over forty years ago. More recently, using the same island grains, the Death's Door Vodka label began. The bottle and label are distinctive, with the clear alcohol content further marketing Washington Island.

Island farm fields in general have not been planted for several decades. A brief effort by Havegard Farm to grow and sell island sun-flower seeds for bird food lasted only a few years. Occasional corn or alfalfa has been planted, and the fields have been used as pasture for cattle or horses. For the most part, these fields have been fallow. But the absence of fertilizers and pesticides over recent decades has placed island crop fields in the category of organic land.

Due to lack of active agriculture, in most fields, choke cherry trees, juniper, cedar and other plants had taken over, growing beyond stone fences and borders. With the sudden impetus to groom fields, perhaps the largest cultivation effort since potato farming in the '50s and '60s, the island once again has an agricultural look to it. The island economy has been infused as a result. These farming efforts also slow the advance of homes in the center of 20- or 40-acre fields, quite commonplace in recent years as old farmsteads were split up and sold in small pieces.

A downside, if there is one, might be the reduction in grassland habitat for birds, given the fact hedges have been uprooted and fields tilled. Wheat crops may be beneficial to game and songbirds, but once the harvest is completed and the food source is gone, the open fields provide little cover.

Wednesday, April 25 –

Today is sunny, in the low 40s, with a predicted warming to the mid-50s.

I was up at 4:30 a.m., ahead of my alarm, just as light began to show over the wood line to the east beyond the golf course. It was the start of my five-day window for turkey hunting, and I was eager to get dressed and outdoors. I picked up Hoyt and we loaded a sack with tur-key decoys. One was a large plastic tom with a fan of real tail feathers in display, courtesy of Bill Crance. If realism translates to success, we'll have that part covered. We drove to Lobdell's Point, both dressed in camouflage, to set up before daylight emerged and the turkeys stirred.

We stopped along the Point Road near a sweeping curve Hoyt calls "Coastie Corner," the scene of many an accident by wayward Coast Guardsmen in the wee hours of morning. At Hoyt's request, I shut off the motor and we rolled down our windows: darkness in the woods and total silence. Even the treetops were still. No wind had yet come up. Hoyt called a few short crow caws with his mouthpiece to see if a tom turkey might respond. Turkeys don't care for crows, and a tom will often respond excitedly if a crow is in his territory. Once more, total silence.

We drove on, turning right onto Henning Road, a graveled track that cuts through the Lobdell Point woods. I turned off the truck lights and the motor and Hoyt called again. He got no response except the general emergence of noise from other birds who now were beginning to awaken and start their day. We walked into the woods single file, Hoyt with the bag of decoys, me with a 12-gauge shotgun under my arm.

Hoyt pointed to a large maple tree. "Sit over there." So I did, after first scraping away dried leaves and sticks, creating a quiet spot in which to sit, turn, and stretch if need be. Hoyt, meanwhile, planted the tom decoy in full display, and three hen decoys. He grouped them to look as though they were a small flock, about 15 yards from me, and then he took up a position behind another large tree, behind me.

As daylight began to glow in the east, more and more bird sounds were heard. Overhead, a pair of swans flew toward Figenschau Bay and the island's west side. A flight of ducks followed the swans minutes later. On and off, crows cawed noisily and songbirds interjected their sounds. No turkeys were heard.

When Hoyt set the decoys out, I saw only dark shapes, but as the sun rose I made out each decoy clearly. We sat on a ridge about 15 feet above the surrounding woods, and from that vantage point I could easily see several hundred yards into the hardwoods. Nearby, young, green leek shoots were popping through the matted leaves everywhere I looked, creating a pungent aroma where we had trod on them. Vibrant spring growth would continue to emerge over the next month and more, and by Memorial Day weekend these leeks would be joined by delicate Mayflowers and thousands of white-blossomed giant trillium.

Hoyt tried a gentle, soft, contented hen call, followed by an excited tom call. Still, no response. Only crows answered, irritated to hear a turkey in their midst. From high on a tree nearby, a pileated woodpecker drummed away looking for breakfast, sounding out to the world.

Every few minutes Hoyt called, but no turkeys responded. The southerly breeze of the day gradually sprang up. I had dressed warmly, but my fingers were cold, so I slipped on knit gloves and shifted myself around the base of the maple, and as I twisted, my boots dug into the soft earth. The dampness and decay gave off a pleasant, woodsy smell. In my comfortable new position I could easily have nodded off, if it hadn't been for the regularity of Hoyt's turkey calls.

It was full daylight by 6:30 a.m. By that hour, any turkeys within a mile would have been out of their tree roosts and dispersed, pecking and scratching their way to various parts of the woods. We gave up. It was strange not to have heard a few live calls returned, because just days before we knew there had been turkey activity in those same woods. The early morning air had been so still that a turkey within a mile radius of us would have heard Hoyt's call and answered, regardless of whether or not he wished to advance aggressively toward the sound source.

On Lobdell Point just a few hundred yards away, I heard traffic heading to the early ferry. We gathered our gear and headed back to the truck. With four more days left on my permit, we'll try again tomorrow.

Thursday, April 26 –

A drizzly morning didn't slow the ferry traffic. Joel said the outbound trip at 7 a.m. was nearly full owing to several large trucks and trailers, and the inbound trip from Northport had four fishing rigs onboard. Fishermen are here for the weekend to cast for northern pike, members of a club that has fished the island shoreline regularly for years, especially in late fall for smallmouth bass.

Washington Island has a variety of harbors with good bottom structure, weed beds, shallows and ledges, a favorable geography such that in nearly any wind these fishermen can find a lee or a decent spot in which to fish. Their success rate reveals they have the knowledge and skill to catch fish better than the average fishermen. Using catch and release methods, these fishermen have caught 6-pound bass, claiming this is one of the best spots for bass anywhere in the Midwest.

We appreciate their business, too, both on the ferry and on the island as a whole for the rented rooms, food, beverages and fuel purchased. Their economic support is often at the beginning or end of the regular tourism season, an otherwise slow period of activity.

MAY

Tuesday, May 1 –

I drove out to our east side property to see how the logging operation was going.

Yesterday afternoon, along with Hoyt, I observed a mature bald eagle in a hardwood tree perch, not but a couple hundred feet from the gravel road. He remained there for 45 minutes. Still there when we returned.

We came to observe the tree harvester at work on our property, which had been marked for selective cutting. Ryan Krause of the Algoma Lumber family, grandson of founder Reine Krause, sat behind the controls in the cab of the harvester, a large beech tree locked in the jaws of the machine. This type of timber processor is commonplace now days in logging operations. It's safe, efficient and especially effective in cutting repetitive lengths such as pulpwood for paper mills. The machine's claw encircled a tree, and a saw within the jaw cut it neatly at the stump. Then the entire tree was turned 90 degrees, sideways, and the branches lopped off by ramming the piece back and forth between knurled wheels. Finally, in seconds it cut eight-foot lengths for firewood, lengths preset by the operator.

The processor rolled about on its three axles, articulated in the center for snaking around trees and stumps and over hollows. The oversized tires, high and fat, allowed the machine to climb over downed trees and up and down the ledges in the rough terrain, even when carrying a rack filled with logs.

This was only day two for the logging operation, and already most of the machine harvesting had been done. A second machine, called the "forwarder," specialized in hauling the heaviest log payloads out of the woods, and with its own mounted boom and grapple, the operator quickly loaded the machine's bin. Later, he stacked these saw logs alongside the gravel road for access by semi trucks.

The second man of this two-man crew was busy with a traditional chain saw as we walked in. He stopped to analyze which way a large maple would fall. These were the prime maples whose logs would bring top dollar as veneer, but they were too large in diameter for the processor. Also hand felling would avoid splits on the bottom cut, the butt log, which could reduce the log's value. At the rate the cutting had progressed, our entire 20 acres might be completely harvested by Wednesday evening.

Smaller and less marketable trees, generally beech, birch or ironwood, were being thinned to improve future growth, and in some cases, to make a trail for access to the prime maple trees. Logs not intended for the mill, but firewood, were snipped into 8-foot lengths. They were generally less than 10 inches in diameter. The additional cost of truck and ferry transportation and the questionable value of some tree species didn't allow for transportation to the mill. Already, several island homeowners had contacted Jeff Krause, Ryan's dad, to obtain a semi load of the 8-foot sticks for firewood. Many island homeowners have recently installed free-standing, outdoor wood boilers with fireboxes that accept 4-foot lengths, which eliminates the work of re-sawing and splitting.

***

Reviewing the job done by the Algoma Lumber Company on our property, their use of modern equipment, payment by check in full prior to setting a foot or tire on site, brings admiration for their professionalism. From conversations I've had with the Algoma Lumber people, each time they return to log a piece of property the yield is higher than before, indicating that their methods employ good forestry practices through selectively marking, cutting and removing logs from the woods.

In addition to a landowner's gain from sale of timber, there are the other economic factors for the island that logging brings, such as lodging and meals for the cutting crews and the considerable income for ferrying the log trucks and equipment. These have a positive impact, and in my view it's a fortunate thing Algoma Lumber bothers to come to the island at all when there is abundant forestland on the mainland, closer to their mill.

***

The evening was pleasant and clear as I raked our lawn after supper next to the roadside. From across the road at the island ballpark I heard voices, a boom box, as island ball players worked on the grounds, readying the diamond for their home opener in a few weeks.

Wednesday, May 2 –

It's 46 degrees with NE winds early. Later the day was sunny, and temperatures reached the low 60s.

Bill Shepherd stopped at our home while we were finishing breakfast, about 7:15. I had mentioned to Bill that Mary Jo wanted to make a few landscaping changes in our front yard. Her guideline was this: whatever Bill plants, it must come up each year, be easy to maintain, and not be too expensive.

With that in mind, Bill had a few quick suggestions, like moving bushes from locations in our yard where they weren't doing well, placing them in visible, sunnier exposures. That would be quick and cheap! Bill consulted Mary Jo's tastes in flower colors, a smart move on Bill's part, and then Bill was off by ferry to Green Bay with his trailer to pick up plants. Bill also maintains our Northport and island Ferry Terminal grounds.

Bill Shepherd has a good eye for what plants work well, and he's tireless, often completing his first hour's work on flower beds as the rest of us arrive for work.

Friday, May 4 –

Sunny, blue skies, with light ENE winds.

***

Terrie Cooper from the Door County Land Trust is here today at our office for a visit. Part of her island routine includes a Land Trust meeting, of which Hoyt is a participating committee member. After looking at maps, Mary Jo, Terrie and I walked the Potato Dock area and the bayou near Arni's home as a way to start a discussion for how these properties might best benefit the island long term. Although the Potato Dock upland property has had soils disturbed and it isn't completely natural, it is undeveloped. Is there any use that might bring low environmental impact but still might add economic value to the island and to our business? Is it unrealistic to think a property such as this can be preserved when elsewhere in Door County half a million dollar condos are jammed along the waterfront? There must be other, useful, alternatives that can also bring income and pay the taxes.

Saturday, May 5 –

I worked with John Herschberger at the Stavkirke boardwalk project. John, as it turned out, had begun at 6 a.m. setting up his saws and laying down numerous 2 x 8s in the gravel as foundation for the boardwalk. Visiting with John when I arrived was Trygvie Jensen, camera around his neck, his two young children beside him. Tryg was on the island to help put his grandmother's home in shape for eventual sale.

Tryg is a son of Richard, one of three Jensen brothers who initially were island carpenters under the name Jensen Builders in the 1970s to the mid-1980s. Norbert became a plumber and moved to Sturgeon Bay; Emil worked as a state building inspector out of Green Bay until his recent retirement; and Richard had his own home construction business in Green Bay for many years.

Tryg is in the final steps of publication of a book he wrote about Door County's commercial fishermen. The project was immense, with several hundred pages and over one hundred photos and illustrations, many interviews, in addition to writing and editing. His enthusiasm for his project was dulled only slightly when he was forced to become his own publisher, too. The lost time pushed the date of publication back by at least a year. He anticipates having copies available for the public by July of this summer. It was Tryg's devoted interest in his subject matter that turned him into a writer, photographer and historian. His island perspective as a descendant of local commercial fishermen, the Bjarnarson family, gives his voice credence that a scholar may not easily emulate.

Monday, May 7 –

It's 50 degrees at 8:30 a.m. Somewhere, temperatures will reach the upper 60s, but we doubt it will be so on Washington Island.

Today is a day for introspection. In fact, that's all I can manage. Just thinking can be hard enough some days, when ideas that do present themselves are difficult to act upon. My head cold is in full bloom and the contents of my skull must be 90 percent phlegm. My eyes burn and my head throbs. My nose is red and sore from repeated wiping and blowing, yesterday and through the night. Such a miserable head cold fits the winter routine much better than spring.

This will be a morning with hot tea and Regis. Or, public radio to clear the head and the soul. But now, as befits my condition, my declaration is to write down a list of the worst and dirtiest words I can think of, expunge them from my system, so that I can once more think outside of "self."

***

Island life is recorded in various ways. Land sales and deeds are recorded at the County Registrar's Office, as are births, deaths, and marriages. Artist paintings, and photographs, and letters mailed and saved can be found in attics, trunks, and at the Island Archives. And, there are personal journals and community newspapers.

A local newspaper is an invaluable source of community information, in addition to becoming a valuable historical record. To this end, the *Island Observer* fills that niche with varied degrees of success. Editor and owner Gail Toerpe, when she was newly in the editor's chair, wore a brown porkpie hat with a "press card" stuck behind the hatband ribbon. At that time this presumptuous reporter covered many island events. But her reporting coverage grew less over time as more "filler" crept into the pages. There tends to be lots of "looking back" material — pieces reprinted from other papers, articles submitted by readers and writers of varied quality and of questionable interest to the community at large. The work of attending meetings and events and then distilling those events and reporting them in a fair and readable manner is a skill, and it takes resources and commitment.

Recently, a "Letter to the Editor" to Gail Toerpe was printed that summed up my thoughts:

"Is expecting real news of a community too much to ask for from a local newspaper?

I am a long time summer visitor and subscriber to the Observer. *I look forward to my issues all year round in the hope that I will get news of my Island family, friends, and community. Unfortunately most of what I get is too much news of the publisher/ editors' family and dogs and filler articles about cleaning, birds, trivia or ever more enormous ads. Honestly, I'm reduced to searching the classifiers(sic) to try to glean real news...I love the Island because of the wonderful people who live there and know that their lives are worth writing about."*

Actually, this writer's comments can be applied to other local and regional newspapers, too, like the *Door County Advocate* and the *Green Bay Press Gazette*, newspapers that have strayed from the original purpose of being a community newspaper. It takes extra effort to research and write good news stories, and the publisher has to want to provide the space to print them. Often, it seems, hard news stories are avoided because that might mean taking an unpopular stand.

With so many people using the internet as a news source, the gap in local news has opened up further with the few conglomerates like Gannett controlling their stable of papers more tightly than the old green-eye-shaded publisher ever did his own.

***

A bowl of soup, a long nap in bed under covers with all my clothes still on, and after I awakened, sunshine streamed through our living room windows, performing wonders to my head and body. My head no longer pounds, and now I can gaze upon the bright green grasses emerging in our yard and appreciate their struggle to fill in the thin, vacant spots of soil. Even the daffodils seem brighter after my nap, opened wide to the rays of the midday sun.

A gentle, all night rain would do nicely. I can see buds on the maple and oak trees, swelled in preparation for those first few genuine 70-degree days. But in upper Wisconsin and Michigan, the earth is now so dry that fire warnings have been issued. We need rain.

Across the road at the ballpark is an old island school bus, purchased by the team for away games. Makes sense when a few fans whoop it up with beer at the ball games, then drive home in a stewed state, putting our roads under threat of death and injury. Not too comfy, bus seating, but better than most ballpark bleachers. Let's hope the idea works out.

***

At 3 p.m. I went to the basement to carve. Two St. Andrew's crosses removed from the Stavkirke await decorative relief carving. I cut a pattern from an old political campaign placard of simple, intertwined lines. It was based on a design I was given by a shop instructor in Eyrarbakki, Iceland. He carved the design into wooden spoons and gave them as gifts for weddings and anniversaries. I modified his design by stretching it out over a 20-inch span. This design is as close as I can make to authentic Icelandic Viking, and it works well on the four arms of the brace. Fourteen crosses, 28 sides at approximately six hours per side of layout and carving time.

While I carved, my ears cleared and my head pressure neutralized, and I broke a sweat. A real sign of recovery.

Tuesday, May 8 –

The day is warm and the breeze is light. This is our warmest day yet, and temperatures will hit 60 degrees by noontime.

With heat and humidity comes fog. By 2 p.m., the breeze shifted to the SE, from the lake, and the fog rolled in. The ferries began using their air horns in addition to radar and GPS to navigate safely. The last ferry of the afternoon as the sun goes down on a foggy day is often the hardest, with virtually no visibility at all. That will be the case today.

Wednesday, May 9 –

A soft spring rain fell as I awoke this morning and dressed, preparing to drive out to the Ferry Dock.

This is a day for me, a benchwarmer, to get in the game, to be a deckhand. The reason is that two crew, Hoyt and Bill Crance, are out turkey hunting this morning, and Rich has the day off. It's my turn!

Some mornings, stepping outdoors into cold and rain can be a miserable experience, bracing for the inevitable. However, today's rain is soft and welcomed, and the tree buds have opened further overnight. The puddles on the pavement as I drive to the dock indicate it has been a rain of some significance.

Erik Foss and Eric Brodersen are out on the *Washington* getting the ferry ready when I arrive. I can see lights from the engine room companionway. By 6:30 a.m. the ticket booth is occupied, and Patty Cornell has her first customer at the window.

The Algoma Lumber Company "forwarder" and "processor" are in line, along with the loggers' pickup trucks and several other autos. I made a quick trip into the office to grab my cap and check the daily truck and trailer board before warming up the Gator, the small dock vehicle we use to pull freight carts. There will be no way around getting a wet seat from an open vehicle that was parked outdoors overnight.

Eric Brodersen worked the lines on deck while above, in the wheelhouse, Erik Foss warmed the navigational instruments, the radar, GPS, and radios. The main engines were idling but still cold, and a plume of whitish diesel smoke rose from each outboard corner of the transom. We unfastened the last mooring line and slid around the corner to the hydraulic ramp. The harbor was still. Several ducks took flight from beneath our bow. I couldn't see them, only heard the fuss they made flapping wings and slapping their webbed feet against the water, trying to get out of our way in the fog. The visibility is about half a mile and ought to stay that way as long as rain continues to fall.

There was no wind as we rounded Plum Island's northwest corner and a fog bank rolled in. Within seconds the visibility dropped to less than 100 yards, and we navigated solely by compass, radar and GPS. By the time the mass of Northport's break wall stones appeared, we were within 150 feet of the opening. Over the tree line the fog looms like a mountain range, but behind it some distance to the south is a patch of clear, blue sky.

Twenty minutes later, while loading the ferry for our return trip, the fog bank began to lift as quickly as it set in. Plum Island, across the Door from Northport, is shrouded in a thick, smoky fog that hangs in the treetops, but to the north, four miles away, I began to see Washington Island. The rain had nearly stopped and our passengers got out of their cars and mingled on deck to view the changing weather and to look over the side at a school of suckers. Drivers for Verizon, 7-Up, the Carpet Shop, and Van's Fire and Safety were represented.

The last item loaded onboard is a used hay binder for Lee Baxter. Rod Cochart hauled it to Northport on his trailer for Lee, and he'll use the same semi flatbed to haul the two large, off-road pieces of equipment for Algoma Lumber Company to their next logging site near Valmy. Before leaving, one of the loggers kindly used his pickup truck to back the hay bind on the ferry foredeck for us. Our scheduled semi for this return trip, Sysco, didn't show as planned. Our load is quite full, just the same.

Friday, May 11 –

It's sunny, and breezy from the NNW at 15-20 mph. Temperature is in the low 60s.

***

We held our Annual Ferry Line Shareholder Meeting at Sievers School in one of the classrooms used for weaving. The setting was comfortable, quiet, sunny, and private. Joining Hoyt and me were a number of shareholders, our accountant, legal counsel, and Board of Directors. The meeting began at 10:30 and lasted until 3:30, with a working lunch.

Arni Richter was not present. He had tendered his resignation at the April Board of Directors meeting, and so he was not nominated as director for another three-year term. This occasion marks an end of active participation with the Ferry Line for Arni, age 96, who has over 65 years in the ferry business. He is still a shareholder, but with hearing and mobility problems he's unable to sit at the table for long periods of time, or join discussions due to hearing loss. The reading of materials in preparation is also difficult because he has macular degeneration.

While we recognized this meeting as one step farther from the business he and Carl began, we also tipped our hats to his leadership and insight over the years.

Saturday, May 12 –

In the afternoon, Mary Jo and I gathered at Schoolhouse Beach Cemetery with about 30 others, friends and family members including Arne and Eric Orman, who came to pay respects to their brother, Carl Orman.

Carl was the son of Lloyd and Evelyn (Richter) Orman, and he was named for his grandfather, Carl Richter. He would have turned 53 in early May, and his untimely death was determined to be caused by a heart attack.

Carl had a wonderful sense of humor, as do his brothers, always quick with a line or a corny joke, with timing and persistence that made others laugh. He was a career veteran of the U. S. Coast Guard. He began his career in the Navy, then transferred to the Coast Guard where he rose to Chief Quartermaster, spending much of his time navigating on cutters.

The cemetery setting was sunny and pleasant as participants arrived. Just before the 2 p.m. scheduled start time, Pastor Frank Maxwell arrived on his green Vespa scooter. He then waited a few minutes more until everyone had assembled around the gravesite. There, with Tim Jessen's help, a small hole had been dug to receive ashes adjacent to Evelyn's grave. Flower arrangements were placed on the grass alongside the grave.

"Would everyone come in closer so that we can hear one another?" Pastor Frank asked. As the crowd drew closer, Hoyt, who happened to stand near Arni Richter, felt a tug on his pants leg. Arni, sitting on the memorial bench erected there in his wife Mary's memory, whispered to Hoyt, "Tell him I can't pull this bench any closer." The granite bench was anchored to a concrete slab, and it weighed in excess of 300 pounds.

Following prayers and scripture, Arne and Erik poured Carl's ashes from a plastic sack into the hole dug in the earth. Another prayer and the service closed. We visited and hugged before reassembling at Carol Lemon's home for food and refreshments.

There, more stories flowed. Jill (Jessen) Jorgenson and Arne Orman swapped stories of their childhood on the back deck as I listened. Karly Jessen and Lloyd Orman, their respective fathers, had been best of friends. Jill recalled the only time she ever saw Karly in a bathing suit, when they all went to Pedersen Bay to dig freshwater clams. Back home, the clams were placed on a rack in a washtub.

"With the oatmeal sprinkled on the bottom of the wash tub," Arne corrected.

"Yes. With the oatmeal," Jill said.

"What is the oatmeal for?" I asked.

"The clams eat the oatmeal, then they shit out the sand," Arne informed me. "Then Karly and Dad steamed the clams. Oh, were they ever good."

And so on until the sun went down.

Sunday, May 13 – Mother's Day

The day is sunny, in the low 40s early, then the temperature climbed to low 60s until a strong lake breeze sprang up. Inland, within 100 miles, temperatures are pushing 80 degrees.

Before the warmth of the day wanes, we take a Mother's Day tour of the island by motorcycle: to Jackson Harbor, the east side roads to South Point, to West Harbor, and home. Only occasionally do we exceed 45 mph. Much of the time our speed is under 35, because island roads are often winding, with blind drives and intersections hidden by foliage. Add to that the possibility of deer or 20-pound turkeys, and there is plenty of incentive to proceed with caution.

At one intersection near the Witness Tree — a tree stump with 1864 surveyor's mark blazed in the side — where Townline Road meets the beach at the easternmost end, there is a profusion of light blue forget-me-not flowers. Their heads seem to float 10 inches above the forest floor on thin stems amongst the cedars. It is one of the largest blankets of delicate blue anywhere on the island. And in wooded areas with better drainage, growing where the sun penetrates part of the day and where cool lake airs are not overbearing, the giant trillium flowers have opened. The white petals are profuse, and they will only be more noticeable in the weeks to come as the soil warms and plants spring to life.

Monday, May 14 –

Strong southerly winds and cool air greeted us this morning.

Bill Crance and I headed to Northport to complete several projects at the restaurant there, and at Gills Rock. While at Northport, the company producing a video on "Ghosts of Door County" arrived to board the ferry. There were 16 people in all including cameramen, soundmen, behind the scenes people, and a group of specialists who've made a business of identifying and verifying paranormal activity. These islands of Death's Door are a subject matter with potential for ghost presence, and they intend to produce a film of local, ghost-related stories.

Traffic is fairly brisk with trucks and cars in the morning, but it slacks off in the afternoon. Within the terminal building, Bill replaced a broken toilet seat in the men's restroom, wrestling with corroded bolts while standing on his head in a confined, twisted position. Meanwhile, I moved a display case from the basement and swept gravel from the pavement at Gills Rock where cement had recently been poured next to the steel sheeting. We caught the 3 p.m. ferry back to the island, where I spent the remainder of the afternoon with correspondence and phone messages.

Tuesday, May 15 –

Last night a major thunder and lightning storm passed through, dropping a fair amount of rain. The ground outside our home is soaked and there are puddles on the pavement.

The sky broke open occasionally with rays of sun, then reverted back to cloud cover. The *Eyrarbakki* returned at 9:30 a.m. with a full load including a logging truck from Algoma and a Coca Cola vending truck.

***

The "Ghost Busters" are on board the 10 a.m. ferry leaving the island, and I have been asked to go along and talk on-camera about Death's Door. In the confines of the rather tight pilothouse along with Jim Hansen, captain this trip, and Bill Jorgenson, there is a sound man and a camera man besides Dave, the host/narrator, and myself.

On nearby Pilot Island, according to Melanie Koyen and Sara Wood who used to stay there overnight in summer, unusual events occurred, like the slamming of doors and flushing of the toilet, signs that one or more spirits might inhabit the lighthouse. Around the turn of the century, a young assistant light keeper who was despondent cut his own throat on the island's rocky outcropping. His supervisor later found his body, and the death was reported as a suicide. Perhaps it is this young man's spirit that still inhabits the lighthouse?

The sky was heavily overcast, and a gray pall hung over Pilot Island as we passed by, helping to create mood for the film people. A Gills Rock gillnet tug sailed across our bow several hundred feet away, returning from setting nets on the lake, and their cameraman captured that, too.

Supporting evidence of ghost activity had been observed at

Nelsen's Hall on Main Road the evening before, too, the producer/ director told me. Their ghost meter needle — what kind of meter, I didn't find out — pegged on "high-likelihood-of-spirits", and that wasn't a reference to the booze bottles in the barroom below. I must see the finished DVD to find out the rest.

***

On our return trip into Detroit Harbor, Bill Jorgenson pointed out three pelicans with white feathers and black-tipped wings flying ahead of us. Then, after leading us up the channel into Detroit Harbor, the pelicans turned 180 degrees and joined another four pelicans that had been resting in the waters near the island ferry dock. Together, the seven pelicans cruised at low altitude, gliding above the water's surface past the Potato Dock and around Willow Point where they disappeared from view as they flew west.

More and more pelicans are seen each year in this area, although we still consider them unusual, not the type of bird we'd expect to find in northern Lake Michigan waters. But pelicans are no longer a rarity, and their nests have been documented on lower Green Bay islands for several years.

Thursday, May 16 –

Yesterday afternoon, while I pressure washed the deck of the *Robert Noble* in preparation for rolling deck paint, the wind shifted. This occurred around 4 p.m., and with the wind shift came a sharp drop in temperature. Perhaps the north wind will blow the bugs away.

These flying insects are the size of gnats, but they don't bite, and they don't seem willing to fly away, either. When brushed from an arm or cheek, they smear. Attracted to oil-based paints, these bugs present a challenge for painting, and so it's best there is a breeze blowing, enough to keep the bugs moving.

***

The first group tour bus of the year came in this morning with 48 passengers on board. Bev Hudson of Island Tour Guide Service is the step-on guide for the island tour today. She makes arrangements for lunch and coordinates island stops, including local museums not yet opened daily to the public.

Museum curators open up on request for her tour groups, since it's still too early for daily hours in facilities with no central heat and few potential walk-in customers. Group tours can bring in revenue to help fill gaps in ferry traffic, especially in the fall of the year. We have the equipment today, larger ferries and hydraulic shore ramps, that makes loading and transporting motor coaches relatively easy, and we've aggressively gone after the group market.

Not everyone is happy to see the large busses of senior citizens. Local critics of motor coach tours see busses roll past their place of business, unhappy that the tours don't stop. Their worth to the island is questioned. That complaint may seem true for a specific small business, but for the Ferry Line they represent a piece of business worth having. Motor coach tours book ferry passage well in advance. They usually pay cash before boarding the ferry. If their experience is positive, the tour broker or tour guide will often repeat a successful itinerary the following year. We know patrons from such tours who have later returned on their own, having been favorably introduced to Washington Island.

Ferrying these large vehicles requires special consideration. Motor coach suspension is notoriously soft, and a bus loaded with passengers can rock in seas, making passengers sick. In the most extreme, there is potential for the bus to rock so much, due to the high center of gravity, that the coach wheels could lift off the deck during a severe roll. To avoid chance of this happening, we generally cancel a motor coach when the winds are forecast above 25 kts. We've returned the coaches ahead of schedule by asking the guide to cut the tour short when winds have shifted to the northwest. The prospect of finding accommodations for 40 seniors overnight on the island, when they have their clothing and medicines on the mainland, is not a good situation.

We believe the group tour business is an economic benefit to the island as a whole, and that this segment of business helps enable our ferries to operate profitably. This, in turn, results in better service year around for the general public. With increased motor coach business years ago, we were pushed to improve loading ramps and docks, a benefit all of our customers now enjoy.

***

Atlas talks to, or through, the crystal Mary Jo gave him as a Christmas ornament. It is a clear, quartz crystal in a long, hexagonal shape, polished, with a hole for a neck string. Mary Jo hung it on our tree as an ornament, but it went largely unnoticed by Atlas who at the time had more exciting things to play with. Then in late April when he visited, Mary Jo placed the same crystal in a nightstand drawer by his bedside where he rediscovered it, this time as an unusual knick-knack. He took the crystal home with him in a small plastic tackle box Mary

Jo gave him, along with acorns, small fossils, shells and items he found on our walks. He brought it with him in the car, and on long drives with time on his hands he would open the box and look over the items. One day in their car, Evy noticed Atlas was whispering and holding the crystal. She turned and asked what he was doing. He had the crystal to his lips and whispered, "Ssshh. Quiet. I'm sending a message to Gramma."

"What are you saying?" Evy asked.

"I'm telling her, 'I love you, Gramma. I love you, Gramma.'"

Thursday, May 17 –

Sunny and not a cloud in the sky. North winds dropped down to 15 mph or so. By afternoon the direction shifted to the south, from the lake, but it remained clear and the day warmed up.

***

Today the Red Cross Blood Mobile visited the island. It is always this same time of the year when this truck and the Red Cross personnel arrive from Green Bay, bringing portable cots, tables and blood collection equipment. The day's production line for blood collection is set up in the Community Center gymnasium with the help of local volunteers. American Legion and American Legion Auxiliary volunteers unload and set up equipment for the Red Cross workers. They process island donors and man the "canteen" where donors are furnished beverages and a light snack afterward. By 2 p.m., with three to four dozen pints of blood collected, the trucks are repacked and headed for the return ferry.

Herb Gibson told me last night he began giving blood when he was 17. That was when the Red Cross Blood Drive set up in the Trinity Lutheran Church basement. Herb is now 62 and has one of the island's longest continuous records for giving blood.

***

Mid-afternoon as I worked at my office desk with the window open I heard the sound of motors, and I thought nothing of it until I spotted the research vessel *Sturgeon*, a government-owned vessel operated by the U.S. Geodetic Survey. The large, blue hull, nearly one hundred feet in length with a draft of 10 feet, moored at our Potato Dock. Their routine is often to rest during the day and obtain water samples and net samples for fish and other aquatic life at night. The *Sturgeon* was formerly an offshore fishing vessel, seized by ATF for its role in drug trafficking, then converted at an Escanaba ship repair facility as a research ship.

Hoyt and Rich sailed the *C.G. Richter* to Bay Ship this morning, experiencing excellent conditions. This trip to the shipyard is the first time this ferry has been underway since late last fall when it was moved from the service dock in front of my office windows to the Potato Dock. When the *C.G.* returns from Bay Ship in a week or so, we'll moor it nearby at the service dock once again to avoid roosting seagulls and the acidic mess they create. This seldom-used ferry is due for a 5-year hull inspection. Except for two round trips over the last four years, it hasn't seen active duty. We maintain the hull and the Coast Guard certificate, hoping we'll find a potential buyer soon.

Friday, May 18 –

Although ferry traffic in general has picked up, today the first ferry to the island appears to have only four cars on board. That's unusual given the typical semis, service vans and sport fishermen that we carry on early incoming trips. The pace picked up as the morning continued, however. With this being the Door County Lighthouse Tour weekend, we anticipate extra traffic from people interested in seeing the lighthouses of Death's Door, and the light on Rock Island's northern bluff.

While it's easy to understand the public interest and the development of romantic notions for the days of light keepers past, the movement to recreate history and make lighthouses more accessible has created icons out of old lights and abandoned or wrecked ships.

Lighthouses were often in very remote locations, a solitary form of work, but there were also men well suited for that sort of life. The work and pay was steady, and for some, living alone for long periods of time wasn't considered a hardship. The fact they were seldom bothered by supervisors and managed their own situation much of the year may have held appeal.

Unfortunately, making romantic icons of remote lighthouses doesn't substantially change the position of today's Coast Guard, a very practical organization whose mission it is to provide safe navigation, not restore relics. The deteriorating Pilot and Plum Island light and life saving facilities are prime examples of neglect due to a Coast Guard policy of not repairing what is no longer needed.

A recent transfer of land and lighthouses on Plum and Pilot Islands from the Coast Guard and Bureau of Land Management to the U.S. Fish and Wildlife Service is slated to happen soon. But in the meantime, no restoration work can be authorized. The roof on Pilot has a big hole in it, and nearby the machinery shed roof has already fallen. This is a shame, because the lighthouse was built prior to the Civil War in 1858. It was a critical aid to guiding ships through the Door Passage. The roof and bricks need immediate attention. The pier is mostly gone, former wood cribs torn apart decades ago by ice and seas. The more modern the steel and concrete jetty has also nearly washed away. Landing there in a small boat is next to impossible without anchoring and jumping into the water to wade ashore. While the government agencies prefer to keep people off Pilot Island, it's not really necessary to post a warning because the stench from the hundreds of seagulls and cormorants that nest there each summer is deterrent enough to drive even the most curious away.

So, this weekend, more than at any other time of year, lighthouse aficionados will have an opportunity to see the areas' many lighthouses from the water, shore, or hiking trail. Several lighthouses will be open for visitation with docents on site to answer questions. We'll run our regular ferry trips and sail a tad closer to Plum Island, if weather permits, for a closer view.

Saturday, May 19 –

Last night we were invited to a gathering of people active with the Island Players, the local theater group. Mary Jo recently passed along her set of books as the organization's treasurer after six years on the board. This gathering was a gracious way to express thanks to her, and also an occasion for visiting with the many dedicated, enthusiastic Island Player members. Their latest production was *The Diary of Anne Frank* which opened for several dates at Karly's dance hall this winter and was very well received. It will be replayed this summer at the Trueblood PAC.

***

Margie – In writing about the play, I am reminded of island resident Margie Franks who has appeared as an occasional Island Players cast member. I saw her an hour ago as I drove the mail van to the island post office, riding her bicycle in the rain.

Some call her "Margie Buckets" because Margie rides her bike everywhere she goes, often balancing two galvanized steel buckets from the handle bars, preferring buckets over a basket. In winter when ice or snow prevents bicycling, Margie walks, towing a sled. Probably one of the island's healthiest adults because of her regular exercise, she can often be seen pedaling along Main Road, coming from Mann's

Store, her two buckets loaded with grocery items.

Approximately 45 years of age, Margie grew up and attended school on the island, then lived for a number of years in Green Bay. She returned to the island to live with and assist her mother, Lois, who later passed away. Margie continues to live in the home in which she grew up. There, the yellow Ford Granada with flattened tires is a permanent fixture in the driveway. She has no phone, doesn't drive a car, and there may be doubt as to the state of plumbing in her home. She chooses to live and travel as she does. Part time in summer Margie has cleaned rooms for Holiday Inn. Occasionally, she contributes an article to the *Island Observer*, often an instructive piece on the topic of music composition and notation.

On the few, very rare occasions when Margie is seen walking, which is usually on the coldest days of winter when roads are icy, she refuses to accept a ride despite the bitter cold. Pedaling or walking remains her choice, and to those who see her on a daily basis, the sight of Margie and the buckets swinging from her bicycle handlebars is just part of the island landscape.

***

New little islanders – Three Ferry Line wives are expecting babies soon, within six weeks of one another. Mothers-to-be are Kirsten (Hoyt) Purinton, Kerstin (Rich) Ellefson, and Krista (Joel) Gunnlaugsson. These birthing events could result in quite an explosion in island school enrollment in a few years' time, as well as providing future employee material. Besides these announced Ferry Line family events, Courtney (Mann) DeJardin is also expecting. We can be quite certain there will be a class of four, at least, entering the island grade school six years from now.

***

Lunch at Island Pizza – Mary Jo and I walked from the Ferry Office to Island Pizza, next door, for lunch. We each ordered a sub sandwich, our first of the season. Dan Mathy and his pizza understudy, nephew Ethan, worked behind the counter. They prepare two or three pizzas ahead of time, anticipating customer demand, and if the slices don't sell, which is not often, Dan moves them at a special price, just to keep the product fresh.

We were joined for lunch by a zillion of the tiny bugs that hatch this time of year, and although they tended to be worse near the cedar trees out on the deck, they were also thick under the covered porch. While we ate lunch a large straight truck was loaded on the departing ferry, leaving a smaller one on the pier, a 30-footer, for lack of deck space. The truck driver approached Dan's window and spoke with a Russian accent. He wished to buy a slice of pizza and showed his credit card.

"Sorry, we don't take credit cards," Dan said. "Just cash or a personal check."

Unfortunately, those weren't options for the customer, so Dan asked, "How often do you come up here? Look, I'll write it down, and you can pay me next time you're here."

Dan is a trusting person who would rather furnish lunch to a customer on credit than lose a pizza sale. The truck driver lived in Green Bay and he agreed to mail Dan a check when he reached home. While a $3.50 slice of pizza and a Coke isn't huge, Dan's gesture is, and it's greatly appreciated by his customers. Dan claims he hasn't yet been hung out for his generosity.

Sunday, May 20 –

We experienced two consecutive days of overcast with rain showers and cold winds, first from the south, then the northeast. Finally, today, we're blessed with a clear sky common with a high pressure system.

***

News of J.J. Ehlenfeldt's death appeared recently in the *Island Observer*.

JJ was known also as the "Collinsville Locksmith," the calling card lettered on the side of his truck. He was also known on the island for being an active Lions Club member, a member of the American Legion Post, organizer of the MS Benefit Bicycle Ride each June, a participant and winner of medals at the Midwest Senior Olympics, and the guy you call when you need lock work done...or locked your keys in your car.

JJ's beard was a pointed, graying goatee. His speech pattern included what I would call a "juicy S," and when he pronounced the lock manufacturer, Schlag, it came out sounding like an edible fruit.

When it came to installation or the repair of locks, re-keying of doors, or opening autos to retrieve keys that ferry customers locked inside, he was always JJ-on-the-spot. When he installed locks for us, he often returned several times to make minor adjustments. Over a 15-year period, JJ reworked every ferry pilothouse door lock.

The memory of JJ that stands out for me was when JJ's teeth went missing. In the early 1990s, Dr. Tom Wilson had JJ as his dental patient, and when the new set of dentures arrived at his Sister Bay office address, Tom drove them to the Gills Rock dock and passed the small box off to the ferry crew. They, in turn, were supposed to deliver the box to the island ferry office where the patient, JJ, would call for it. The box never arrived on the island and no teeth ever washed up on the Gills Rock shore afterward, or were discovered later that summer by fishermen in the mouth of a hooked salmon. They were never found. Of value to no one but the owner, it was hard to imagine anyone taking a box with a set of another's teeth as contents. The *C.G.* crew recalled receiving a package from Tom, but the memory trail went cold at Gills Rock. In fact, it wasn't until JJ called at the ferry dock later that day to pick up his set of teeth that anyone at the Ferry Line office realized that a package had gone missing.

Many customers would be anxious, angry, and frustrated to learn their package had disappeared, with out-of-pocket expense and inconvenience. JJ, however, rather than placing blame, told Arni he would apply for a new set of dentures under his health insurance, sparing the cost of the loss to the Ferry Line. It was a most gracious gesture.

Over the years, we came to know JJ better as he and his wife, Jackie, spent more and more time on the island each summer. We called on him regularly to solve our Ferry Dock lock problems. I hope over time our work orders repaid JJ, at least in part.

To date, JJ's missing dentures remain shrouded in mystery, perhaps awaiting discovery by a future underwater archeologist who may claim them as state historical shipwreck property.

Wednesday, May 23 –

A cloudy morning brought a threat of rain with temperature in the low 50s.

In the Bay Ship conference room we were joined by Todd Thayse, General Manager, machinists Steve Krauel and Wayne Kasten, Rich Ellefson, Naval Architect Mark Pudlo, and Hoyt, who had just returned from his trip to Cincinnati late that prior evening.

We reviewed the *Arni J. Richter's* starboard shaft history and the symptoms of vibration, spoke about probable causes, and tossed out a few ideas for solutions.

No definite answers or direction resulted from our discussions, partly because we hadn't agreed on the problem. Were the vibrations experienced a symptom or cause? In order to further set out a plan we agreed to meet afterward in the dry dock to look first-hand at the section of underbody where the skeg, shaft, propeller and rudder are located.

At 11 a.m. the machine shop crew loaded the props on my trailer. I cinched the nylon tie-down straps tight, added chains with load binders, and headed for Two Rivers and the Kahlenberg shop.

Thursday, May 24 –

It was a sunny and bright day with a southerly flow of air that increased in velocity as the day progressed. I pulled *Moby Dick*, my 33- x 13-ft., 1970 pontoon boat on its trailer with hazard lights flashing, down Main Road and out to the steel building at the ferry dock. A launch will soon follow.

At the ferry office, a woman driving a red jeep called for a package. I had noticed her earlier at the post office where I stopped during the noon hour, and although her face looked familiar I couldn't remember her name. When she came to the customer window to pick up two UPS packages, I had to ask. She was Joanne Nelson, and I remembered one of her sons, Peter, from about 15 years ago when he frequently fished near the ferry dock.

Joanne told me of a day when young Peter, who was fishing near the Ferry Dock, met Mary Richter. Mary had been working in the flowerbeds near the office. She went home, made a sandwich, returned and give it to Peter. He never forgot her kindness.

My conversation with Mrs. Nelson reminded me of a story Arni told, a singular story, one that Arni enjoyed retelling whenever the timing was right and he had an appreciative audience. I first heard him tell it when I rode with him to Madison, nearing the sweeping highway curve outside of Beaver Dam. Arni had run out of gas on that same curve with his wife, Mary, as passenger. Arni got out of his car to flag down help, and the first car to come along stopped. The couple asked if they could be of assistance. Arni got in and they drove to a nearby filling station.

Small talk enroute to the filling station revealed this couple was returning to their Madison home from a vacation in Door County. Arni said he and Mary were from Door County. Then, the lady recounted her experience of the previous day when they had visited Washington Island. She had forgotten her purse at Holiday Inn on Washington Island where they had had lunch, and she didn't discover her purse was missing until they were aboard the ferry and nearing the Gills Rock dock. Once ashore, she called Holiday Inn and confirmed that her purse was there. Owner Martha Stelter said she would phone the ferry dock. Answering the call, Arni then picked up the woman's purse from

Holiday, and he saw to it the ferry crew would deliver it to the Gills Rock dock on the next ferry.

Finishing the story as they neared the Beaver Dam gas station, the lady turned to Arni and said, "I couldn't believe how nice everyone was. It was so good to get my purse back."

"Mam," Arni replied, "you won't believe it, but I'm the guy who picked up your purse and sent it over on the ferry." At this point, as he always did when he told this story, Arni savored the stroke of providence that connected the people and events in this story, and he exhibited obvious pride in his home, the island, his ferry service, and chance opportunity to be of service.

Friday, May 25 –

Down in the bottom of the dry dock beneath the *C.G. Richter's* hull, I met the two Coast Guard inspectors, Travis and Dale, who brought with them an ultrasound instrument used for obtaining hull readings to determine thickness of the shell plating. We tested eight separate points near the aft portion of the hull, a broad sampling of plating aft to determine if "wasting," heavily rusted or thin plating, was isolated, or if there was reason to examine the entire hull. A pinhole through the plating on the port side, aft of the generator, had been found by Bay Ship personnel who were sandblasting. The cause appeared to be a pocket where frames intersected and water collected, corroded from inside the hull outward.

They were satisfied the shipyard had already addressed our isolated problem by proposing to cut out an 18- x 18-inch piece, with radius corners, and to weld in a new piece of steel. Only one such patch would be required, not a major job. Considering the hull is 57 years old, it is still in very good condition. Metal loss is not unexpected, and according to the readings, we are still well within accepted standards for loss of plate thickness, according to tables cited in Coast Guard regulations. These tables actually pertain to larger hulls, according to the inspectors, where loss of metal at mid ships can create stress, flexing, and possible fracture or collapse of major sections. But that's not the situation with the *C.G. Richter*.

***

On my drive through town past Sturgeon Bay's new City Hall on Michigan Street, I happened to observe the setting of the ornamental eagle and globe on the top of the new Door County Veteran's Memorial.

Around the memorial's base, workers swept up construction debris and laid sod in preparation for a special dedication ceremony next Monday afternoon.

✳✳✳

Our ferries continued to bring full loads of vehicles to the island throughout the day. This is what our ferry crews do so well: shuttle back and forth to stay even with or ahead of incoming weekend traffic. As soon as one ferry is ready to depart with cars and people, the next ferry is ready to load. We hope to see cars continually rounding the corner of the highway at Northport so that our ferries will be busy through the evening.

For the first time since October, all island restaurants will be open, as will motels and gift shops. The long hibernation will be officially over. This weekend's splash of income is sorely needed by all business owners, and to make the weekend economically successful, several good weather days are needed to make a difference and to create a happier crowd of visitors.

Saturday, May 26 –

A sunny, bright morning. The late traffic last night was steady, but not gang-busters. Each ferry carried nearly a full load and we ran two extra, non-scheduled ferries. The morning's first ferry arrived at Northport to find a full load already waiting in line, and each subsequent ferry since has also filled with traffic. This is typical holiday routine, expected and welcomed. With sunshine and blue skies we ought to see the walk-on and day traffic pick up by late morning.

The 10:30 a.m. ferry from Northport arrived with the presence of multiple human forms silhouetted on the upper deck, enjoying the view and fresh air and open skies. These are day trippers. As a ferry-boat captain, such trips are a pleasure and the reason so much energy is spent on maintenance for six months. Operating the ferry through the Door, swinging it about for a perfect landing without fanfare, loading, navigating and then unloading once again with safety and efficiency is a pleasure, and it's also pleasurable to note the positive reactions of passengers moving across the water, headed toward an unknown destination, surprised and satisfied by their experience.

✳✳✳

On our island dock, Ed Livingston awaits the discharge of passengers with tickets for his Cherry Train Tour, an island tour extremely popular as an alternative to bringing a car to the island. Ed incorporates several short stops on his tour designed to give variety and offer further island information. One stop is at the Ostrich Farm, owned by Wayne and Kristi Oscor. Another is the Stavkirke. The most popular stop, especially in warm weather, is Schoolhouse Beach with its smooth stones and clear waters.

But many day visitors bring their own conveyances such as cars, bicycles or motorcycles to help them see more of the island by touring roads and harbors. And, our roadsides now are quite beautiful. Blue forget-me-nots line the ditches and borders of swamps, cool and damp, and the flowers are more profuse than ever, it seems. People comment on the blue haze floating low in the woods, for low-lying smoke is what the soft blue carpet appears to be from a distance. Giant trilliums are out in bloom now, too, making a showy statement of their own. It's hard not to be excited about living on Washington Island on such a day as this.

***

With our boat crews set and our shore staff working at full measure, my self-appointed afternoon task was to begin sealing our parking lot behind the freight garage. I worked for several hours rolling the black goop. I had made a good start when raindrops interrupted my progress. There's much more asphalt to cover, and it won't be completed in one day.

Our first official day of the Memorial Day weekend ends with steady incoming traffic right up to the last ferry of the afternoon. Our day traffic has been solid, too, with nearly a full load leaving the island on the *Washington* at 5 p.m., our last scheduled island departure.

Sunday, May 27 –

The big news this morning was brought to us by Hoyt who came knocking on our door with little Aidan around 7 a.m. He had been on a special emergency ferry last night at 2 a.m. He and Rich transported two ambulances: a father in one, a son in the other. A major 'slashing' injury was administered by one on the other, returned in kind it appeared. The jugular of the young man was partially severed, and the ambulance crew took turns applying pressure to the spurting neck wound. The two men were separated for their own safety and placed into two separate island ambulances. The father had a deep laceration to his scalp, from a hatchet, it was guessed. The young man's blood pressure was very low, and although he might have expired along the way, instead he survived under good care of the ambulance crew. The night was thick with fog that followed a light rain through the early evening hours, and it presented Rich and Hoyt with a challenge navigating the narrow Detroit Harbor channel. Fog at night with a rising wind is very difficult in close quarters. At one point, they spotted in their searchlight the Washington Island Coast Guard boat alongside one of the channel buoys. Later, they learned the Coast Guard had been underway, intending to bring back-up support from the mainland for the island's lone law officer, but they experienced radar unit difficulties and weren't able to safely leave the channel. As a result, the Door County Sheriff's Department investigator came to the island on the return emergency ferry from Northport, after patients had been transferred to County ambulances. (Through a rather strange arrangement, Door County does not operate the emergency medical services on the island, although they pay a partial support fee.)

More details concerning this incident will come out, no doubt, in days to come. Was it drugs? Booze? Plain old bad blood between family members? Or, a combination of these things?

Such incidents are totally out of keeping with the island's pastoral reputation. It was thought these same family members were tent camping on a piece of property they own off Swenson Road.

Monday, May 28 – Memorial Day

There is no breeze this morning. The flags on the poles along the ferry dock water front are limp. There is a beautiful, blue, sky overhead.

There will be hundreds of Memorial Day ceremonies across the nation today, but none will compare to the setting on Washington Island. First, an indoor program is held at Bethel Church, and the church is usually packed with veterans and their families, young and old, from all walks of life, islanders and visitors. Afterwards, the Legion Color Guard marches, with many participants following on foot, a few driving, to the nearby cemetery at Schoolhouse Beach. There, a wreath is gently placed at the flagpole base, and names of buried island veterans are read, from the Civil War to present. A rifle salute and taps, and then the march resumes downhill to the edge of the beach. From the loose, white stones of Schoolhouse Beach a second wreath of island cedar fronds and flowers is floated upon the waters. A short prayer is offered, and taps again follows the second rifle salute.

Our march to the cemetery this day was accompanied by three bagpipers, and two drummers, a snare and a bass drum. This is one more bagpiper and two drummers more than any time in the past that I can recall, and it added greatly to both the march and to the rendition of "Amazing Grace" that followed taps. Newest musicians to join in the ceremonies are Emmett Woods, bagpiper, Tom Noonan, bass drum, and Jens Hansen, snare drum. Their drums provided cadence throughout the march to the cemetery, and later, to the beach.

Bob Gillespie and his son, Michael, an Island high school senior, have played bagpipes on Memorial Day for many years. They are self-taught, practicing with the determination to participate in such events. Bob's inspiration took hold shortly after the death of Michael's grandfather, Thorsten, an ex-marine, who died tragically 10 years ago in April. Michael's uncle, Rick, was an island soldier killed in action in Viet Nam. Mae Williamson, grandmother to Michael, wife of Thorsten, mother of Rick, would join our group later that day to travel to Sturgeon Bay for the dedication of the new County War Memorial there.

Today's blue sky reflected from the equally blue waters of Washington Harbor. There was little wind, and with temperatures just so, light waves were refracted in the clear atmosphere. I spotted Burnt Bluff and the Stonington Peninsula, small blips on the horizon separated by Big Bay de Noc, at least 25 miles away.

That is the Island's Memorial Day program outline as it has been for years. From the beach, community members take their time as they wind their way through the cemetery, pausing at family member graves, then up the gentle hill over the old beach trail through the woods. Here there is often a profusion of May flowers, and the opening of leaf buds on the trees. In all, the hike is about one-third mile, a pleasant time to visit with reflection along the way.

Family grave plots are planted with fresh flowers. Over the gravesites of buried veterans fly small American flags, each thin staff stuck in a holder by Legion member Herb Gibson prior to the Memorial Day Weekend.

These moments on Memorial Day, shared among the nearly 200 people present, are among the best memories we have of the island as a community.

Tuesday, May 29 –

The morning is sunny, but dark clouds hang over the lake to the south. Bryan Stefancin has returned for the summer, and he jumped right into shore maintenance work, joining Matt Kalscheuer and Tully Ellefson. They made excellent progress on scrubbing the topsides of the *Noble* and were ready to begin painting when an overload of vehicles appeared on the island dock just before 11 a.m.

With Rich and Hoyt unavailable, away to the shipyard to oversee activities, I started up the ferry engines and took Tully with me as crew. We loaded seven cars and an empty oil tanker truck while the regular 11 a.m. crew filled the *Washington* with other cars. Most of our customers leaving the island represented the last of the Memorial Weekend traffic, people who enjoyed an extra day of great weather before returning home. Painting was suspended as we got the *Noble* underway.

Although our trip to Northport was clear and sunny, by noon on our return trip, I couldn't see Pilot or Detroit Islands. A fog bank had quickly rolled in from the lake. I made out the *Washington* as it ran ahead of us, and also the tripod entrance marker to Detroit Harbor, but I was concerned if the fog bank continued to roll in, then the island's channel would be thick. It was. By the time we were a mile from Washington Island, where visibility had dropped to less than 200 feet.

I slowed the ferry as we swung northward and proceeded up the West Channel, alternately watching compass, radar, GPS, and depth sounder, in addition to eyes-out-the-window. Soon we were alongside the entrance buoy, our course set 010 to pass each buoy with a margin for error from the channel's edge. I signaled with the ship's air horn, one prolonged blast every several minutes, to warn any other vessels of our approach. Down on deck were two young ladies with bicycles, wearing shorts, appearing shocked by the cold, damp lake air. As they departed the ferry a few minutes later, I assured them it would be different, probably clear and warm, inland from the ferry dock.

Fog continued to hang in the channel until about 3 p.m. Then it cleared slightly, with a thick haze that remained until dark. There was a feeling of impending thundershowers, heavy air and southerly breezes pumping moisture northward over the lake. Typical of spring weather.

Wednesday, May 30 –

The evening was still, and so is our morning. Blue skies and sunny, with a light breeze on the water. To our west several hundred miles in Minneapolis and beyond are thunderstorms and heavy rains.

***

I began selecting old photos of Ferry Line employees from the various photo albums I keep. Saturday, June 16th, our company will host a Ferry Line alumni picnic at Karly's, and my intention is to show these photos as a rotating slide show. Harmann Studio of Sturgeon Bay has offered to scan the selected photos and put them on DVD.

***

Our first-ever Island Birding Festival now has over 50 names entered, and we're quite pleased. Details are coming together, and we'll meet with all of the volunteers and supporters tomorrow afternoon to finalize plans.

Thursday, May 31 –

Sunny and warm, light SE breeze. A bit hazy. Threat of rain later in the day, which is the same threat we've abusively taken the last couple of days. But this time, it looks as though the weatherman may be right. More abuse.

***

On this last day of May, my observation is that traffic tanked after the Memorial Day Weekend exodus. This is not unusual, but it is disappointing there aren't more visitors in the Door Peninsula to fill the void. Since nearly all families are back home, to school and work, it is the retirees we're depending on to travel and spend money. There are almost no Cherry Trainers today and very few bicyclists. Our ferry loads consist of mostly commercial vehicles, service trucks and the like.

***

We ended May on opposite ends of a sine curve. The upper curve peaked when Eric Brodersen brought in the oil painting of the *C.G. Richter* crossing the Door in winter. Approximately 4 x 3.5 feet, this terrific winter scene quite accurately depicts ice in the Door with Plum Island in the distance, a cold winter scene. No passengers are visible on deck, but there are a few gulls in the scene. While there are certainly times in winter when there is practically no human or animal presence, the stark seascape with ice cakes and cold water predominates. I liked Eric's painting as soon as I saw it, and so have others. For several years before this, it hung on the rear wall of the Middle Bar tavern.

Eric is a self-taught artist now working with us at the ferry dock. His painting hangs prominently behind our customer service desk. In order to make room for Eric's oil painting, we moved the portrait of Arni Richter done by John Davies into our lobby. Both paintings show great talent by island artists.

The low sweep of the sine curve came at 11 a.m. Matt and Bryan had finished painting the *Noble's* stern, backed in toward the dock. Ready to move on to their next task of chipping paint in the steering room, they suggested moving the ferry back to its port-side-to position alongside the pier.

I went below to the engine room to start the engines, and as I moved past the generator I grabbed the handrail and my palm landed in wet, black paint. My verbal reaction consisted of four letters in sequence, four times. I wiped my palm with a rag as best I could and, distracted by the wet paint, I started first one diesel, then the other. Satisfied we had propulsion power, I climbed the engine room steps to the main deck. The generator was left cold, since we were just twisting mooring position 90 degrees from stern-to-side.

At the wheelhouse controls, I spun the ferry. My crew retied the mooring lines and reconnected shore power. This entire evolution took, maybe, all of five minutes, and I went below decks again to the engine room to shut off the motors. It was then I saw lube oil running down the interior shell plating, seeping through limber holes of frames, beneath the floorplates toward the bilge.

I headed up to the office and marshaled available forces, plenty of oil rags, oil mats, and oil absorption floats, and we began the process of wiping up. More than the oily mess, I had concern for the engine running dry with low sump oil. We could only guess as to how much oil had been pumped out until we measured what was left in the engine. We would refill the motor sump after Bill Crance finished installing a new (and missing!) oil line on the port engine filter assembly.

That amount turned out to be six gallons out of a possible 9.5 gallons of oil total, meaning, maybe 2.5 gallons ran into the bilge. The motor sounded OK when I shut it off, and it sounded OK after we refilled and restarted it. My maneuvering had been for short duration and at low rpm's, so we had good certainty there had been no harm to bearings and parts. As it turned out, during our three-hour drill, we were able to wipe up much of the pockets of oil plus soak the skim of oil that had flowed into the bilge.

Lessons learned and learned best are often learned the hard way. Greater damage or pollution had been avoided. We found out how well bilge oil absorption socks work, because they very readily soaked up the oil. They are said to absorb four or five times their own weight in oil, while not absorbing any water.

We could ill afford to have had a recent major reconstruction of this motor only to blow it through miscommunication, a missing $10 hose, lack of tags, and my haste. The human factor, the Coast Guard has found through accident investigation statistics, is responsible for the vast majority of vessel groundings, pollution incidents, and loss of life. Our near-miss incident was also due to human error.

That's the month of May. Soon traffic will jump upward again in volume with more consistent mid-week tourism. Our company books still show a long way to go before we are out of the red and into the black for the year.

JUNE

Friday, June 1 –

Fifty-five degrees for an overnight low. At 7 a.m. the air is still, and there's little to no wind. We had no rain last night, and none for the past several weeks. Just 100 miles to our south, parts of Green Bay received 2.5 inches.

***

Fog was predicted and fog we got. Driving to work down Main Road to the ferry dock, I found visibility was, maybe, 100 yards, and at the dock visibility was 200 feet at most. Looking toward the water, I could see less than 100 feet.

I completed a few office tasks before getting in my truck to catch the 9 a.m. ferry. It was one minute before 9, and I hurried because I couldn't see if the ferry *Washington* was still at the pier with the crew ready to raise the ramp, or if it had already departed. It was an eerie sensation, driving toward the water without knowing what lay ahead. As it turned out, the ramp wasn't yet raised, and I drove aboard the *Washington* and parked my truck.

Underway I stood in the port bow in a lookout position. Al Stelter was in the opposite, starboard corner, and we watched for buoys, landmarks, and other vessels. Our course was true and we passed all channel buoys with good clearance.

The Detroit Harbor West Channel was dredged by the Army Corps of Engineers to minus 14 feet in 1939 according to nautical charts, and it hasn't been dredged since. Charted channel width is 150 feet, and there is slight filling in here and there, mainly in the area opposite the ferry docks. The channel edges slope upward quickly to less than 8 feet of water. Because each of our ferries draw at least 9 feet when loaded, and the *Arni J.* draws over 11 feet loaded, there's little room for straying from the channel in fog. For that reason, our captains place a security call over the VHF Marine Channel 16, letting other vessels know when we're proceeding out the channel and across Death's Door shipping lanes.

Passing ferries are often our only radar targets, but bulk freighters also navigate the Door passage, and we encounter occasional salmon fishermen who often loop their trolling course without warning.

Commercial gillnet tugs head to or from the lake at unknown times, and Charlie Voight's *Island Clipper* runs a regular daily schedule May into October, to Detroit Harbor from Gills Rock. The U.S. Coast Guard patrol boat from Washington Island Station also gets underway at unspecified times. The result is that you never know who might be out there, or who is paying attention, so a visual watch is necessary and required. Besides visuals, we also use time, compass, radar, GPS, and a depth sounder. It's enough to keep two and even three people busy, on edge with increased tension. Small craft such as kayaks or low aluminum fishing boats may not show well at all, visually or on radar, until you are right on top of them.

On this day, we had a visual on the tripod entrance buoy as Captain Jim Hanson swung the bow west and steadied his next leg parallel with the west shore of Plum Island. Fred Hankwitz, also a licensed captain, placed a security call to alert other vessels of our location. All eyes were on the water and the grayness that lay ahead.

After approximately nine minutes on our final leg, our radar showed less than one-eighth mile to the breakwall entrance at Northport and Jim slowed the ferry. I stepped out of the wheelhouse for a better look, because the pilothouse windows were damp with condensation. I was rewarded with fogged eyeglasses. Within 150 feet of the north wall, bright, white stones stood out in the fog, thanks to white seagull shit splattered over the boulders, and we entered the Northport Harbor. Crazy though it seems, it often happens that once we're close to shore and secured at our landing, the sun pokes through the overhead. Now, just several hundred feet up Highway 42, blue sky appeared and I could see it was sunny to the west.

Alternating conditions were repeated as I drove my truck south along 57 to Sturgeon Bay: heavy fog near the lake, bright and sunny inland. I was on my way to check work progress on our two ferries at Bay Shipbuilding. At the shipyard I would meet our marine insurance broker, Peter Robinson, who flew in from Vermont for his annual policy renewal visit. As the morning melted into afternoon, the temperatures in Sturgeon Bay reached the high 70s.

***

The Door islands are shrouded in fog a good share of the time in May and June until, finally, lake waters warm up. The ebb and flow of fog, sunshine, moisture, and warmth, especially heavy hanging fog that condensed in tree branches, is a good thing for certain tree species. Plum Island has several excellent examples of hemlock trees that approach 10 feet in circumference.

Because landforms like Washington Island or Plum Island often aren't seen from Northport through fog, I marvel that first time visitors still buy ferry tickets, on faith that something lies beyond.

Saturday, June 2 –

I drove to the Community Center where Karen Huff was in the process of setting up coffee and donuts for early morning birders. As of late last evening, Carol Meyer had registered over 60 people for the Island Birding Festival, a number that exceeded our goal for this first-time effort. While the weekend forecast calls for rain, on and off, the only threat to a clear morning were wisps of fog over the harbor. This weather won't stop birders, but it will slow down ferry operations if the fog closes in.

***

Mary Jo and I were official greeters for the birders that Saturday evening at the Washington Hotel, where participants gathered to share notes on their day. Leah Caplan and her staff prepared a variety of cheeses and other appetizers and served wine and beer. The conversation noise level increased in the dining room threefold as the dinner hour approached.

Everyone's day in the field seemed productive in terms of seeing new places, meeting new people, and in bird identification. Ninety-five different species had been identified. The birders had split into three main groups, each led by a knowledgeable birder who also served as local guide.

When the reception ended, we left the Washington Hotel and joined the others at Karly's Hall where Lois Jessen had prepared a chicken dinner buffet. This was not "free range" chicken as someone had questioned. Dinner once again proved great for friendly conversation at the various tables. Chick Richards, host this event, welcomed everyone and raffled door prizes such as birding books, bird feeders and bird food, hiking packs, and bird houses. Sandy Petersen offered a short program on her field experiences in northern Sweden where she surveyed the buzzard (hawk) population over a period of several years. Her program was accompanied by slides and drew great approval from the audience.

Tuesday, June 5 –

Rich, Hoyt, Bryan, Tully and I walked through steps required for anchoring a ferry, and we also did man overboard drills on the *Washington*. Our Coast Guard inspection is tomorrow for renewal of the three-year certificate. It is primarily a walk-through inspection of the vessel, but attention will also be paid to crew responses during emergency drills.

A tossed life ring served as our "victim," and as soon as there was a victim sighted in the water, the drill to pick up the survivor began. Two crewmen on deck put on life jackets, one with a safety line, in preparation for positioning a ladder on the inclined bow ramp. By backing down the ladder toward the water's edge, it is possible to grab and retrieve a victim. Usually we do this in less than three minutes from first sighting to when the victim is brought aboard. We recognize the difficulty that would accompany such an evolution in rough seas or low visibility, or when the ferry has a full deck of cars. Also, an actual victim might be limp and water soaked, possibly several hundred pounds of weight. It would be problematic, too, if the victim were unconscious or hypothermic, unable to help himself. Or, too, a victim might be just the opposite — drunk, aggressive, or resisting help.

A young child overboard, we all seemed to agree, might warrant jumping into the water for rescue. The question remains: at what point do you place additional risk on yourself and, by extension, the vessel? Since we're not trained safety swimmers with dry suits, it would compound problems to have one more person floundering in the water, leaving a shortage of trained crew on board the ferry.

Wednesday, June 6 –

Mike Kahr, Death's Door Marine Construction, called me this morning. Mike's crew had been welding on barge sections for two winters, and now his plan is to transport the sections 10 miles down the highway on wheeled dollies to the Northport beach and assemble them there, then launch the barge.

This process of building a vessel on the beach, close to where it can be easily launched, is traditional shipbuilding practice. What makes this effort different is the attention our ferry company typically draws from neighbors who like to blow a whistle for intervention of some sort.

Thursday, June 7 –

Calls came in throughout the day asking about the weather, and "Would we continue to run if the storm got worse?" Impending severe weather, forecast in living color on all local TV channels since Wednesday, seemed to overshadow all other news, and has put the man on the street on edge.

One lady asked ferry captain Ken Berggren, "What will you do if it gets too bad to run the ferry?"

Ken's answer: "I know what I'd do. We wouldn't run!"

Friday, June 8 –

Hail as large as four inches, tornadoes, high winds and rain swept through Wisconsin yesterday.

While we were under the threat of severe weather, the storm cells moved in a NNE direction up the bay of Green Bay, and passed just north of Washington Island. As a result, we saw dark clouds, heard thunder roll in the distance, and felt the humid air of an impending storm. We even smelled ozone, but the most moisture we experienced were splashes of large rain drops, and not enough to wet the pavement.

Our Thursday conditions for ferry captains and crew consisted of a steady 25-plus knots of wind and even higher at times. After each series of dark clouds, a momentary sunny stretch appeared before the next cell moved near.

This morning's sun and balmy westerly breeze are perhaps the most pleasant of island conditions. There is no lake breeze. The sky has an immaculately clear atmosphere, like a window just given a sparkling cleaning.

There are no imperfections to this day, other than the ones we create within ourselves.

***

Following the storms on Thursday, ticket seller Jason Carr and I put up the flags on the poles in front of the ferry office. There are six of them: American, Icelandic, Norwegian, Danish, Swedish, and Finnish. They were taken down prior to the high winds and rain to avoid taking a beating. Several were already in poor, weathered condition. This row of flags along the ferry dock waterfront has been there for at least 25 years, an inspiration of Arni's to display Washington Island's Scandinavian heritage. They also happen to add a great degree of color.

When the Island Recreation Center was built in 1987, the job supervisor for contractor C.R. Meyer of Oshkosh was a Finn named Bill Knutti (with a hard 'K'). Bill was an avid cross country skier and had assisted in training the U.S. Olympic cross country team. For several months he had asked, "Why no Finnish flag at the ferry dock?" "No Finns," we answered. "Well, I'm one!" he said. In spring Bill presented us with a Finnish flag, and in time a sixth pole was erected to complete the major Scandinavian countries. Actually, we must note that Tom Hokkanen, Island Schools Art and Phy Ed instructor, is also of Finnish descent.

The true story of the Island's settlement is not found in the flag-poles at the ferry dock, though. Irish and Yankees were first among fishermen-farmers, along with Germans, who became early island pioneer families. The Norwegians and Danes, with perhaps a few Swedes thrown in the mix, came next. Icelanders made their first appearance in 1870. As if making up for lost time, over the next three decades Icelanders arrived in significant numbers due to difficult economic times in Iceland. A handful of Icelandic settlers drew even more of their countrymen, attracted by blood relations, common language and customs.

Arni Richter is named for his grandfather, Arni Gudmundsen, among the first Icelanders to settle here. Arni and Mary Richter had enhanced the island's cultural image by naming the new ferry *Eyrarbakki* in 1970 after a major port of embarkation for Icelanders. Well water, hand-pumped from the schoolyard in Eyrarbakki, was flown by Icelandic Air to North America for the one-hundredth year celebration, and Gertie Andersen, first Icelandic offspring born on Washington Island, christened the vessel.

From the late 1960s until just four years ago, Arni made it a point to visit Iceland every few years. He told of the first visit he and Mary made to Reykjavik, Iceland's capital. He knew the name of a distant cousin with whom he had corresponded but never met. He and Mary waited in their hotel lobby for an arranged first meeting, not knowing who they were looking for. But instantly, Arni said, he recognized his cousin, so strong was the family likeness. Arni and Mary returned to visit his cousin and her family many times, often accompanied by other Washington Islanders with Icelandic ties.

In 1987, Mary Jo and I had the opportunity to join approximately 75 others with Washington Island/Iceland connections — a visit arranged as a "home-coming" trip. Lots of work went into planning the group tour by Ted Jessen and his Icelandic counterpart, Kolbein, who arranged for historical and scenic stops, and visits with unfamiliar relatives.

The highlight of the tour fell on an Easter Sunday afternoon when dozens of native Icelanders and their visiting U.S. relatives met one another for the first time in the banquet hall at the Loftleidir Hotel. It was amazing to see the similarities in facial shapes, the sparkle in the eyes, the shapes of noses and ears, carried forward by family genes on opposite sides of the globe through several generations.

Most recently, we've read about a strengthening Icelandic economy as they welcome the establishment of tech businesses on their shores. Geothermal energy and human genetics are two specialty areas in which Iceland has excelled, along with the traditional commercial cod fishing. Like another small island nation, Ireland, Iceland is now a leading nation in the European Economic Union in terms of growth. The GDP and standard of living have brought stability and new jobs to a nation formerly plagued by high inflation, easing dependence on a flagging fishing economy.

Sunday, June 10 –

Another beautiful morning, possibly finer than Saturday, and a perfect day for a motorcycle ride down the county. Larry Young, riding his '66 Harley, and I took the 8 a.m. ferry.

We purposely take as many back roads as we possibly can for the scenery, the rural homes and farms and landscapes we've not seen before. We get lost occasionally, happily so, because eventually we arrive at a familiar crossroads or landmark. Our route wound around the backside of the Village of Ephraim, past a dense cedar swamp on the southeast side of the village where we climbed the hillside and emerged among farms and fields. Mixed among older farms are new homes, some rather pretentious. We slowed to peer through trees at a fenced in area with a pair of camels.

It wasn't until we were on County F between Fish Creek and Baileys Harbor that we began to see sizeable working dairy farms and field crops. The change is subtle but constant from one section of the peninsula to another. Visual appeal is great as the land opens up and closes in again, depending upon terrain and tillable land. Closer to Egg Harbor and Institute, dairy farms as large as any found in the better known dairy sections of our state can be seen.

Our pleasure ride continued with smells from blossoming trees and fresh cut hay, and from the herds of farm animals, as we rode slowly, never exceeding 45 mph. The only early Sunday people we encountered were bicyclists or morning walkers. The peninsula's interior roads were very quiet this Sunday morning.

At Sturgeon Bay we were joined by Cal Holvenstot, a Sturgeon Bay resident and father-in-law of Hoyt. We continued to ride, this time south of Sturgeon Bay as Cal led us along the Lake Michigan shoreline toward Algoma. Like myself, Cal is a relative newcomer to motorcycling. He bought his first bike at age 70, just a year and a half ago. This association with two friends on motorcycles added to the day's enjoyment.

Monday, June 11 –

Skies are sunny and clear blue, with a southerly breeze. Hoyt and I left the island on the early ferry for Bay Shipbuilding. We discussed what we hoped to achieve at the yard prior to bringing the *AJR* back home. Hoyt noted the starboard shaft still had vibration Friday when it came out of dry dock, even after all of the various things that had been tried to correct the problem. We, and the yard, are running out of alternatives and new ideas, and time has run short before we need to put the *AJR* back into rotation for the busy season.

Joel Gunnlaugsson is in his final student day of the Door County Leadership course. Our company helped sponsor Joel through enrollment fees, and we adjusted Joel's work schedule so that he could attend classes over the previous 12 months. Joel said he learned about county government, the major organizations and businesses within the county, and he established contacts with people who influence County economics and government.

Tuesday evening is Joel's graduation ceremony and reception. Hoyt will join Joel, representing Washington Island Ferry Line as a sponsor.

✳✳✳

The evening was warm and still. Mary Jo and I worked outdoors around home until dark, taking advantage of the long daylight. Anyone vacationing here now, in particular someone camping, should appreciate such a beautiful evening. Insects also appreciate warm, still evenings, and mosquitoes are out in full force.

Tuesday, June 12 –

Several weeks ago, Capt. Ed Brown dropped by our office and I gave him several old photos for printing and framing. Three were of Northport in winter, perhaps the late '40s. Another was an old color photo, unusual in that it is square in shape, and it showed off the brand new Kahlenberg diesel in the *Griffin's* engine room, taken when the *Griffin* was new in 1946. The engine room bulkheads were white and sparkled, and the big diesel's brass gleamed, but the photo colors had faded. For many years this hung on the wall in the old ferry office, but when we moved to our new building in 1995, someone hung it just above the commode in the crew "engine room."

I had been looking for good artwork to put on the walls at the Northport restaurant, and the idea of framing historical photos seemed like a good connection. Ed Brown happens to have both the technique and the right equipment to make it work.

Photo work was now done, and each digitized photo was superior to the original. Ed printed them on archive-quality paper and framed them in black. Even the old color photo of the engine room is much improved, and local fishing families who enter the restaurant will recognize this engine manufacturer of many decades, the Kahlenberg engine company.

Capt. Ed's invoice has a line at the bottom worth noting: *"I'd like to die in my sleep like my Grandfather, not yelling and screaming like the passengers in his car."*

***

Our shore crew is painting on the *Eyrarbakki*, but because our incoming traffic level has increased, by 9:30 a.m. we need to get this ferry underway for Northport. Painting will have to wait. It's another super-fine day. Warm temperatures and ferry traffic will follow.

Wednesday, June 13 –

The harbor is glassy calm, not a ripple on the water this morning. A snapping turtle swam past the island ramp, and Capt. Bill Jorgenson said later he had to throw the engines in neutral to avoid scrambling the turtle in prop wash as he backed the *Washington* toward the tire fenders. The turtle later swam off, only to be seen 10 minutes later sunning and taking in air near the surface in front of our office.

At 9:30 a.m., as the ferry from Northport approached, the harbor was completely still and there were no clouds in the sky. We sent an extra ferry to Northport at 8 a.m., knowing there were several large trucks waiting to come to the island, plus the expected increase in auto traffic. When the *Robert Noble* landed at the end of the island pier, a large moving van held center position on deck, and several dozen people could be seen along the main deck rail, near the pilot-house, positive sign for a busy day.

Friday, June 15 –

A great traffic day is in store. The weekend build-up has begun, with people and vehicles coming in steadily through the day, requiring an extra ferry to keep up with the incoming cars.

The *Arni J.* was getting cleaned and touched up with black paint when Mark Edmonds, Sherwin-Williams paint rep, arrived on the island to discuss our painting needs, accompanied by his wife for a weekend getaway. We're seeking advice on paint products. For the new, two-part epoxies, application and mixing is much different than for the traditional oil-based paint we've used for years.

***

At midday I hauled my latest sculpture home with the Ferry Line tractor, carrying it suspended from the tractor bucket with a nylon sling, cushioned by a packing blanket. I dug the foundation hole the night before and believed it was ready to accept the base of my sculpture. As I turned into our driveway with the tractor and sculpture, Chad, Evy and Atlas surprised me by arriving minutes later. Perfect timing! I enlisted their help to square the 8-foot piece in the hole. That task took about 15 minutes, not bad considering the size hole needed was a guess. Eight sacks of cement awaited mixing, to anchor the base in the ground.

I collect scraps from the metal pile at the Town Landfill and also interesting cast-offs from the Ferry Dock. It's a matter of waiting patiently for the right parts to appear and being lucky, collecting enough scraps for variety and choice.

A few items such as the old farm discs, became a basis for one piece. I had already used one of the disk sets in a sculpture two years ago. Then in January, when least expecting it, two more sections appeared on the metal pile. I tossed them in the back of my truck, too, convinced they would make a good beginning for a new sculpture. Although several of the discs were chipped, I set them aside under a tree at the ferry dock and these same sections are now assembled as a sculpture, firmly fixed in our yard not too far from the old farm where they had been put to work for so many years.

I assembled the discs with pipe, pieces of axle and a flywheel, a combination that suggests a flowering plant. I painted it in bright colors after thoroughly priming the surfaces. Painting though time consuming, is the easy part, and it brings life to the welded form.

***

Grandson Atlas, after a big day outdoors, had gone to bed at 7 p.m. His parents, Chad and Evy, relaxed on the porch of the Kalmbach House not far from Arni Richter's home. They were happy to be on the island for a few days. After working at our home to nearly dark, Mary Jo and I joined them as the evening cooled ever so slightly.

The Bayou is an estuary near Arni's home in Detroit Harbor, and it's filled with songbirds, waterfowl and frogs, each making distinctive sounds as the sun set. Even after the sun had set we heard a blue heron call, disturbed from its roost. A prehistoric *aawwk aawwk* floated across the stillness of the evening. Aside from the occasional slapping of mosquitoes, there was complete serenity in this summer evening visit.

In the distance, the Friday night ferry diesels reverberated as the ferry approached the island landing, its sounds muffled by several miles of woods and water. The boarding ramp clanged against the steel shore ramp, cars were discharged, and soon a string of autos wound along the Point Road as new arrivals headed inland to summer homes or lodgings.

The process of filling up the island builds slowly, gradually, toward the Fourth of July. The heart of summer is around the corner.

Saturday, June 16 –

J.J. Ehlenfeldt was laid to rest in the early afternoon at the island cemetery. Pine boughs overhead were motionless in the nearly 80-degree afternoon sunshine as the American Legion color guard and rifle squad lined up in formation for a final salute. Bagpiper Emmett Wood, dressed in a wool Scottish kilt, long wool stockings and jacket, played bagpipes.

***

Approximately 140 people came to the first Washington Island Ferry Line Alumni Picnic at Karly's, and from all appearances, everyone had a good time. It was rewarding to see old friends and co-workers, each of whom shared as a common thread, past or present, employment either onboard or ashore in support of ferry transportation across the Door.

Everett Gunnlaugsson, connected with tubes to an oxygen bottle, was toasted by the crowd. In fragile health, he had been released from the hospital just a day or two before. Everett's response to anyone who asked: "If I die on the Island, so be it. It's as good as any place." Everett worked for the Ferry Line in the early 1950s, joined along the way by his younger brother, Nathan, a ferry captain who then continued to work until the mid-1990s, putting in 40 years of service. I had the good fortune of working alongside Nathan, particularly during my first years with the company. He was a great teacher and a professional mariner in every way.

Vic Cornell who worked in the latter 1950s stood and recalled a trip when an ice cake jammed the *Griffin's* propeller. A passenger with a camera captured Vic standing on an ice cake with a long pike pole in hand, working to free the ice from the ferry propeller. "Of course, that made it much easier to get going and make it ashore," Vic said modestly.

There were many others who followed these figures in later years, as deckhands and captains, as ticket sellers, and as office personnel. We played a shortened version of "Ferry Line Trivia", obscure questions with peculiar answers. Example: "What was the greatest number of fish boxes loaded on a ferry?" Nathan quickly responded: "801 boxes, in Jackson Harbor." That was during the herring run of the early 1950s, when herring were abundant in the lake and one of the idled ferries was put to work hauling boxes of fish to Marinette. Herring are all but absent today from Lake Michigan waters, and besides, a ferry today would run aground soon after entering Jackson Harbor for the shallow water there.

I read from a prepared list of Ferry Line employees who had family connections. Over two dozen closely related family members had worked at various times for the company: grandsons and granddaughters, nieces and nephews, sons and daughters, brothers and sisters.

A commonly expressed thought heard from many party goers was this: of all the jobs they held, they enjoyed this one the most. It was the work, the co-workers, the opportunity to learn from older captains, and the chance to be given responsibility for people, machinery and the ferry itself at an early age. We may never have another such gathering, for we're all getting older, but it was wonderful to have the time together with everyone, and it put people in an extraordinarily good mood.

The story of the evening, I think, was told by Al Stelter, our quiet deckhand who took the microphone. "When I was young, in grade school, my Uncle Elmer Mosak was a ferry captain, and he said if I helped get the boat ready I could ride with him for free, and I liked that. I'd wake up and go out to the dock with Elmer for the early boat, sweep the cabin to help get ready, and we'd leave the dock at 6:15 a.m. for Gills Rock. We'd get back to the island in time for me to get to school. But that wasn't all. Besides sweeping the cabin, he said I'd have to clean toilets and sinks, too. And I did it, too, because I enjoyed riding the ferry with them."

"Well, after high school I moved from the island, raised a family, retired and then came back to the island, and I got a job with the Ferry Line. And, wouldn't you know it, I'm back cleaning toilets and sweeping the cabin and riding the ferry, except now I get paid for it!"

Wednesday, June 20 –

We have a bus group scheduled this morning, and we anticipate a greater number of day travelers given the nice weather. An extra ferry is underway to Northport for the traffic.

I rode my motorcycle to work this morning, enjoying the ride past Martin Andersen's pastures with the cows and their newborn calves. Yesterday they were all pinched into one corner, headed in the same direction toward the intersection of barbed wire like filings under influence of a magnet. Today they are scattered, browsing on the sweet June grass.

The Point Road curve past Dr. Bass's home leads into a block of woods where it slopes downwards. At that point, the coolness of the woods is always noticeable. The difference in air temperature is dramatic as is the density of the cool air. It causes my motorcycle to shudder just briefly, like disturbed air from a passing semi out on a highway.

On my ride to work, I met only one car the entire trip, not unusual, and I didn't know the driver, which is also not unusual for summer. I have concerns for the odd deer darting across the road, more than for meeting motorists on the curves of Lobdell Point Road.

Sunshine today is in abundance, a perfect morning to work outdoors, and that is where Hoyt has the shore crew, out on the sun deck of the *Arni J. Richter*, painting to protect the steel and to spruce it up, making it look presentable for customers.

***

The day seemed to sail along too smoothly, good traffic, good weather, ample crew on shore engaged in meaningful maintenance, when the call came in from Capt. Bill Jorgenson on the *Robert Noble*.

Bill had just left Northport dock with a full load of cars and bicycles and quite a few passengers, when deckhand Ron Kleckner reported smelling something unusual in the engine room. Ron was in the process of reporting his observations to Bill in the wheelhouse when both main engines died.

Bill notified the Ferry Line office, and Rich Ellefson, Ken Berggren, Joel Gunnlaugsson and others prepared the *Eyrarbakki* to get underway. They took with them a long nylon line in case a tow would be required, and they disconnected and loaded aboard two, large 8-D batteries from the *Arni J. Richter's* generator battery bank. Bill reported that a terminal on one of the main batteries on the *Noble* had melted...and Rich suggested that Bill hold the battery wire lug by hand tightly against the melted terminal stub, after first screwing in the engine fuel solenoid.

Bill did as Rich suggested and the port engine fired to life, and that one engine proved enough to get the ferry underway and headed toward the island dock. Erik Foss on the *Washington*, meanwhile, stood by the *Noble* in case assistance would be required.

In the Ferry Office, Bill Schutz and I monitored the radio traffic. Rich requested we start the *Arni J.* and move it from the main ramp slip, making room for the *Robert Noble's* one-engine landing. By the time I finished checking and starting the *Arni J.'s* engines, Hoyt and Bryan had arrived, enough hands to back the *Arni J.* from the slip.

Bill made a beautiful, one-engine landing. He rounded the turn to the slip with just the right amount of speed and rudder, landing softly broadside against the tire-lined Standard Oil dock. After a slight rebound, he edged the ferry forward to the customary mooring position where the bow ramp could be lowered and cars and passengers discharged. Because Bill handled the boat so well and had kept his passengers informed, they applauded him. Many passengers also expressed thanks as they left the ferry.

An investigation of the burned wiring indicated the fault seemed to lie with either the starter solenoid or the starter switch. In the "on" position, a high draw of current continued to flow, we surmised, first melting the rubber from the grounding wire, the source of the odd smell, and then melting one of the lead posts on the main battery terminals. It all happened within a few seconds.

Hoyt placed a call to the Coast Guard Marine Safety Detachment in Sturgeon Bay, to inform them of our incident, reporting his version based on initial examination of equipment as to cause and remedy.

We had a spare starter, and given the extent of damage, all things considered, damage appeared minimal. A new switch, new starter, and a new grounding wire were needed, most of which we had on hand, with a few smaller parts ordered from Sturgeon Bay. As I left the island by motorcycle to pick up a new switch from Car Quest, we figured it would be late afternoon or early evening at the latest before the ferry *Robert Noble* would be put back in running order.

As the afternoon came to a close and the *Washington* loaded for the last trip of the day, dark rain clouds moved in, and the winds picked up sharply from the south. The rain came down hard from 5 p.m. to 5:30 p.m., then the sun came back out once again. As I rode home from the ferry dock on the wet pavement on my motorcycle, steam rose from the warm blacktop. Alongside the road I noticed small hailstone pellets, one-fourth to three-eighths inch in diameter.

***

That same evening, we had scheduled a crew meeting for 7 p.m., and the day's incident over loss of propulsion and melted wiring proved to be the main topic of discussion.

Some of the crew had started their day at 6:30 a.m., so we ran through the agenda of items as quickly as possible with primary discussion centering around that starter problem and the loss of power underway. Several suggestions were made for electrical system improvements: battery backup, new and better wiring, etc. We all agreed changes were needed to prevent a repeat of the morning's events. Our objective was to make solid repairs that would bring us through this high season, allowing for major changes after winter lay-up.

Saturday, June 23 –

Our weather meter is stuck on "beautiful".

Mid-60s at the start of the day, but it's now in the low 70s, great weather for being on the water. Saturday traffic is heavy with people coming in for the weekend, the cottage and room turnover day, but this day is so perfect, I think we'll see a good amount of day traffic, too.

The Jackson Harbor Fishing Museum whitefish dinner was held last evening outdoors at the museum, and approximately 200 people were served grilled whitefish, potatoes, cole slaw, bread and dessert. This annual museum fundraiser, operating as a non-profit under the Town of Washington, has been quite popular. The fish is delicious, but it's also an opportunity to visit. An exodus of cars came from the Jackson Harbor dock area as we arrived on motorcycle. It dawned on me later, this evening the Trueblood Performing Arts Center, or TPAC, featured a chamber orchestra presenting a Mid-summer concert, a special event to celebrate this longest day of the year. An evening ferry had been arranged to return the musicians and mainland audience members to Northport at 9:45 p.m.

***

Caitlin Stults, Kim's granddaughter, and Atlas, our grandson, will be dressing up as pirates for a photo session. These two were featured in Ferry Line ads last year, and we used their photo on the cover of last year's schedule brochure. Now several years older, they know each other and that should make it easier for them to sit still and have fun at the same time.

Sunday, June 24 –

Sunny, bright, and warm — another in a string of beautiful days. The lake breeze is welcomed for its slight cooling effect.

Main Road

Family cars with carriers on top, Jeeps with tops removed, motor-cycles and bicycles and mopeds, even the odd 4-wheeler. Main Road is the primary connector with all things Island: taverns and churches, post office and ferry dock, Jackson Harbor and West Harbor, School House Beach and realtors' offices, beauty shop and restaurant, marina and gas station, lumber yard and farm. We sit on our front porch warm summer evenings and watch as roller-bladers are passed by a tractor carrying a round bale in its front forks, Martin Andersen on his way to feed cattle. No cheers rise today from the island ball park because to-day the game is away. But the ball park premises are still in use. Sev-eral times this afternoon, Ivan and Micki Johnson pulled in behind the bleachers to drop a load of liquid waste into the town septic system from their pumper truck.

Yard Appreciation

Often we sit in our yard at home just watching and listening, happy to pay our property taxes for such an uninterrupted experience. Birds sing in the trees — my ears aren't trained to tell me what they are. There is June green everywhere, profusely bright greens of vary-ing shades depending on which tree type. A few spots of orange dot the yard: a poppy nearing its last days of bloom, large petals opened fully to the sun, and a monarch butterfly flitting over grass and bush.

My sculptures of welded metal fill in where nature has been tamed by mown grass, a garden centerpiece, a spot of form and color against the natural palette. Surprising how such a tiny bit of color will catch an eye, connect an idea with emotion, link sight with smell, love with being. Form, color, purpose, pleasure, plant perfume, love of living. It's all here, and available from this yard bench.

Monday, June 25 –

Two island men passed away last night: Bob Walsh and Bill Mason. Both men had retired to the island after serving in the military, raising a family, and retiring from careers elsewhere. Bill sang in the Trinity choir and Island Music Festival Choir, and he was Legion Adjutant. Bob was a faithful Lions Club member, and a musician, accomplished on the sax and keyboard.

Well-liked and friendly, Bob drove almost daily to meet the ferry and to pick up automotive supplies for Jim Van Ramshorst's auto repair business. At one time Bob drove tour train for Charlie Voight, but in the past several years he battled a serious leg infection, traveling across the Door every few days for treatment at a VA hospital. Bob's medical travels were nearly over and his leg had finally healed.

May Bob and Bill rest in peace.

Gibson's West Harbor Anniversary

In front of the white, wood framed main lodge the green of the rushes in the water fold into manicured lawn, Herb Gibson's pride. Further up from the water's edge is a low, stone fence. Then, there is a broad expanse of lawn abutting a high cedar hedge.

It was on this grand, sloping lawn in late afternoon that Gibson's West Harbor Resort held its 60th anniversary celebration. Joining in the celebration were dozens of people of all ages: relatives, former guests, neighbors, and friends of the six Gibson children. When an island box holder is sent out to invite everyone on the island to a party, as Herb and Marianna did, nearly everyone shows up!

We arrived at 5:45 p.m. and found people seated at tables or just walking the property, boys playing Frisbee and girls on their way to the beach. A long line of people started on the driveway and snaked up the front steps to the porch where the beer and lemonade were dispensed, through the screened doorway and into the front hall. Finally, there in the old dining room, tables held hot beef sandwiches, beans, salads and desserts. The line was maybe 100 people long when we arrived, and when we left it was just as long.

The old hotel housed workers of the Freyberg Mill from approximately 1870-1890, when white pine was logged from the west side of the island. Once the pines were logged, there was little undergrowth to take their place. According to Jack Hagen, whose family farm was on the hill one-half mile above the harbor, his grandmother said she could see all of the way from her kitchen window to where Flath's Cottages are now, well north of West Harbor and over three-fourths mile away.

That Jack Hagen made the party at all is a testimony to his stamina, and also to the close relationship he's had with fellow islanders over the years. He is a strong figure of a man in his early 80s with a thick shock of hair, perhaps even thicker since his recent chemotherapy treatment. For the past several years Jack has battled cancer, and the radiation and chemotherapy treatment nearly did him in.

Many people visited Jack's table. He wore leather gloves to protect hands that had open sores, skin peeled from treatments. But he was back on the island, and Jack had a sparkle in his eye. His daughter, Leila, expressed her appreciation. "Every day is one more treasure." He gains strength, it appears, from friends, family, and the familiar island surroundings.

"See that porch?" he asked me, pointing to the long porch attached to the front of the resort. "When I was four years old, I ran away from home and hid under that porch. My father came to get me, took me by the hair right behind my ear, and towed me home."

This resort holds memories for many. Some party guests worked at the resort while others had stayed there as guests, later finding and purchasing their own piece of Washington Island. For these former guests, there was always a love and fascination for Gibson's West Harbor and the hospitable treatment received there.

It's a credit to the Gibson family that rather than raze an old wood framed building and build new, and raise the rates accordingly, Gibsons chose to maintain what they had and keep rates low, among the most reasonable in all of Door County. The old buildings are cared for, and though obviously old and without modern-day amenities, guests seem to like the non-franchise look of things. There is the pool table next to the dining room, it's "Pirate's Den" refrigerator stocked with cold beverages. The comfortable living room has its fireplace, and the Gibsons have bonfires on the beach at sunset, water skiing, boats for rent, volleyball, a horseshoe pit (Herb is a champion and proud of his string of wins) and so on.

West Harbor Resort reeks so with nostalgia that even sticking toilet flush handles or rattling pipes don't dissuade guests from wanting to be put on the list for the following year. Marianna boasts that even when other innkeepers are begging for business, her units are always full. That's a formula that works, based on good service and known product, not on greed!

Tuesday, June 26 –

Morning air is warm and thick, a humidity not experienced often this summer and certainly not in the past several weeks. It is sunny early in the morning, but by 10 a.m. the humidity turned to fog as cool lake breezes edged inland. By 11 a.m. the channel was thick, and ferries used radar and fog signals from air horns as they entered or departed the harbor.

***

I checked on Mike Kahr's construction of his work barge. The bow plates are tacked in place. The welders are now finishing installing three bulkheads, with two top plates and a missing transom piece yet to be fitted. This may be a 4th of July event, the way it is shaping up.

Wednesday, June 27 –

On the way to work this morning, along the roadside and across from Dave's Garage, a young woman painter set her easel at the edge of the field we call Coppersmith's. Last year for the first time in over twenty years, this field was disked and tilled and seeded, and despite very sandy soils, it grew a great-looking crop of wheat for Capital Brewery. In fact, in midsummer a sign posted in the wheat field stated, "Wheat for Island Wheat Beer." We often saw visitors photographing each other next to the sign, identifying with the product.

The morning sun today pushed its rays through a humid haze, but the soft light made this field glow, and I gathered this effect might be what the artist was trying to capture in her painting. I remember quite vividly a similar scene years before, near midnight in early July with a moon so full and bright that shadows were cast on the ground. A painter had stopped along the roadside in nearly this same location, and taken by the beauty of the evening, was painting the scene by moonlight. I had just finished the Friday night ferry trips and was headed home when I came upon the painter, mood disturbed by the many pairs of headlights headed north on Main Road, on their way to cottages or up the road for a late night beer. Artistry in the dark. I would love to have seen the final product, to know what the moment produced on paper or canvas.

Thursday, June 28 –

Since launch of the *Arni J. Richter* in 2003, we've only done touch-up painting, and the main deck looks patch-work with various shades of gray paint. Because of the very aggressive non-skid, nearly one-fourth inch stipple in places, it wasn't easy to paint over. But several hours and about four gallons of paint later, we had covered all of the port side and most of the foredeck. Then we ran out of paint. The section of deck we painted set up well, baking in the midday sun. Twelve hours to cure, 24 for best service. It's a chemical reaction brought on by the hardener mixed with solids, but warmer, dryer days are the best to ensure good results.

The warmer the deck, generally the better the paint flows. We "stretched" the four gallons we used, because it was mainly color coating and protection for the paint underneath. In order to fill the small pits and crevices, repeated arm motion was required to coat even the smallest imperfections with paint. On cooler days when we roll paint from sunny deck to shade, there is a noticeable drag on the paint roller from the temperature difference. As an aside, a deck painter should wear old shoes and pants, because the splattering paint and grit sticks to everything nearby, including the painter.

When we roll the car deck of a ferry, we often use 15-20 gallons of paint, sprinkling in clean grit to make a non-skid surface. A second rolling after sanding helps to lock in the grit. The *Arni J.*'s deck, however, was the first to have a non-skid "system" whereby the grit is entrained in an epoxy paint. I had observed the shipyard painters apply the thick goo, rolling it on with a piece of pvc pipe, a makeshift applicator. The paint smeared on like a soft, sticky peanut butter.

"Coatings," as they are referred to by professionals, are intended to cover the surface being applied to block exposure to air or to chemicals, to water or to other materials. So special are the formulas that a specific coating is required for each job application, and the conditions of application must be adhered to, or else the product won't be guaranteed. When Bay Shipbuilding paints a thousand-foot ore carrier, or the interior of a 600-foot chemical barge, the conditions of humidity and temperature are critical. The manufacturer's paint rep is on hand to verify those conditions.

Friday, June 29 –

It is Friday, a beautiful but cool morning. Forty-one degrees on our ticket booth thermometer at an early hour. Fifty degrees at 8 a.m. Threat of frost last night in the Upper Peninsula. The water is calm, the air still, with perhaps a light northerly zephyr now and then. I'm headed to Northport, then down the county for a variety of stops and an appointment to find out what's wrong with my knee.

The *Washington* is the scheduled 9 a.m. ferry, and I assisted in getting the tractor and honey wagon assembled and ready for the pump-out during the next turn-around window. Fred Hankwitz, captain, notes that it has been far better, far easier, to pump out on a regular basis as we've done now on Mondays and Fridays, than to be caught midday with a surprise, a full holding tank of nasty liquid. The pump-out takes only five minutes when everything is ready and coordinated. Then, with nary a drop of offensive liquid spilled on deck — you can do this maneuver without gloves while you eat a sandwich if you do it right — the waiting line of traffic is loaded and the scheduled time of departure is kept intact.

***

Despite an afternoon appointment with a specialist who examined my knee and said a joint replacement would be the only answer to my problem, when I could no longer tolerate the pains and aches of my knee. I had an excellent day. At least I learned what my options are, and for the time being a shot of cortisone helped to mask the joint irregularity.

A Visit with Mom: Frieda Kalms Purinton

I love my Mom. She's 90 and lives alone at 1422 Memorial Drive in Sturgeon Bay, WI. Her home is the same home we four kids grew up in and came back to as college students, where I returned after graduation and then went off to the U.S. Navy as a Petty Officer. From that home, I married and began a new life with an island address and became a father.

Today I pulled in her driveway amid an overgrown lawn and limbs from a soft maple tree hanging low to the ground. Both grass and tree needed trimming. That maple, and the concrete driveway next to it, were projects I helped with one summer when I was about to enter sixth grade. I used a small wagon to haul dirt dug by hand, an excavation for the concrete drive. On one of the return trips from the backyard, my wagon carried a six-foot soft maple tree, and Dad and I planted it in our front yard. For years it remained a slender sapling, but now its trunk is several feet in diameter and its roots are beginning to raise the concrete at the edge of the driveway. Its limbs are numerous and hang low, and it dominates the front yard.

Often when I come to visit, I knock on the door and find it locked. By checking to see if the car is in the garage, I know Mom's home.

Then I peer through the front door window, and see her walker at the kitchen table, or at the end of the hallway near her bedroom. Mom is very hard of hearing, especially when she doesn't turn on her hearing aid, or, the more likely, doesn't wear it at all. I don't blame her, because from a distance I can hear the high frequency, whistling tones it emits.

One day I peered in and saw her walker, but despite my loud knocking she didn't respond. WDOR Party Line, a radio swap-and-sell program with intermittent chatter played at top level from her kitchen radio. I retrieved my cell phone from my truck visor and dialed. In a few seconds I heard Mom's phone ring, and so did she.

But today went a little differently. She didn't answer the door, but the door was unlocked, and so I walked in, calling her name so as not to surprise her. I continued down the hall to her bedroom, and found her sleeping with her reading light still on. The book she had been reading, a Reader's Digest volume, was overturned on her chest, rising and falling slowly as she breathed. She wore a white visor as an eyeshade to shield her eyes from the incandescent bulb above her head. She slept soundly, and I hated to interrupt her sleep.

I began to backpedal from the bedroom. I've found her asleep on visits before, and I left rather than bother her.

Today, I thought, I really should wake her. How many more times will we see each other? Ten, 20, maybe 50 times? As it is, I may see her only a dozen different occasions each year. This could be the one of 12. So, I shook her shoulder gently and called her name. She awakened, startled to see me, but mostly embarrassed to be caught napping at 3 o'clock in the afternoon.

"Mom," I said. "How are you? Do you want to sleep some more?"

"No," she said, reaching for eyeglasses on the shelf behind her. She glanced at her watch. "I think it's time to get up anyway."

"It's really nice outside," I said. My truck thermometer had read 69 F and there was no humidity.

"Outside?" she asked. "No, I haven't been out yet today." Then she remembered the lawn and the length of the grass, and perhaps wanted me to know she had it all in hand. "Someone's coming tomorrow to cut the grass."

"Yes," I agreed, "It does look a little long."

"It's been so dry," she added. "We had hail a few weeks ago, twice."

Hail isn't unusual, but it's unusual enough for even the casual observer to take note, and in this case the hail in Sturgeon Bay caused damage. Ken Chaudoir's strawberry patch had been destroyed, all of it, and when I drove by earlier on my way from the clinic, I saw his field tilled under.

"I'll get up. I've slept enough," Mom repeated. I led her toward the kitchen. She wore a long sleeve, golden jersey with three buttons at the neck. I recognized it as one of my father's shirts. He died in 1989. Mom continues to wear his shirts, not out of nostalgia, but out of thrift. She's a saver of all things, from oatmeal containers to newspaper clippings. I've inherited her traits, I'm afraid. When Dad passed away I took it upon myself the morning after his funeral to clear a path through the jammed utility room between the garage and kitchen. It was filled with paper grocery sacks.

But, other than her need to save, a treasure trove that sometimes produces amazing "blasts from the past," Mom is totally with it. She still drives herself to church, to the store and the bank, getting out of the house several times each week. She is a doer and a goer.

My older sister, Helen, kindly consents to driving her around, especially for evening activities, and they do lots of things together.

"Last weekend," Mom told me, "Helen and I went to Carl's graduation party, and then later that afternoon to the Gibralter High School reunion, held at the Reef." She has more plans for the upcoming weekend. I know there are times when Helen feels like she'd rather rest.

Mom and I visited at the kitchen table. She insisted I take with me a jar of preserves, always something to take back home. My visits are often short, limited by what we can say and hear, but I know she enjoys them just the same.

I'd better stop when I can, while I can, while we can visit.

Saturday, June 30 –

Lots of motorcycles and cars and pickups came in by ferry today, all day long. Never a long line, just steady traffic. Our summer ferry schedule has begun, and each ferry is now on the 15-minute turn around time with departures every 30 minutes. Today's traffic was mostly incoming, folks who will stay through the 4th of July or longer.

We've had one of the finest days anyone could ask for, as Islanders, as residents of this county and state. The day couldn't have been better...except for the last hours near sunset, when wiring from the starting switches on the *Robert Noble* overheated. Rich Ellefson went to the engine room to start diesels for the evening ferry leaving the island and watched incredibly as the wiring smoked and the plastic insulation melted. He quickly disconnected the power source by throwing a battery switch, but now we await help from an engine manufacturer to get it back in working order.

Our real summer season has just begun on a sour note.

JULY

Monday, July 2 –

Light drizzle during the night, then cool and overcast during the day. Skies cleared around midday, then turned cloudy again with high humidity at dusk and the feel of rain in the air. Traffic was good.

***

Passengers often point toward Pilot Island, then ask, "What's happened on that island? Forest fire?"

The sticks of cedars, once green and beautiful, give Pilot Island the appearance from a distance as though a fire swept through, but it was chemical heat rather than open flames that killed these trees. The cormorant, a bird that swiftly built its numbers into flocks of hundreds and then thousands, claimed Pilot Island as a private nesting island. Many of those first nests were built in the cedar trees. Branches and twigs were pulled for nest building, and from those nests this strange water bird with webbed feet, shaped somewhat like a loon, crapped and spilled their waste, killing trees and ground vegetation.

What cormorants didn't mess up, the seagulls did. On my last foray onto Pilot in June of 1994, I wore a raincoat. I balanced over the uneven rocks with a stick, and held my nose against powerful bird odors on this overpopulated island. Youngest son, Thor, and I walked as far as the old lighthouse as small, fluffy gull babies scurried underfoot among the weeds and dead brush.

Cormorants took to the air when we approached their roosts, but the more stubborn birds hung in their nests until we got quite close. There were dozens of birds that day sitting on nests. It's no wonder Pilot Island's waters on a still day have floating feathers everywhere. Also, it's no wonder that Door County's beaches have been fouled, given the population of cormorants, gulls and geese.

A recent news item in the *Peninsula Pulse* by a Park Naturalist described an oiling operation on several small islands (I presumed near Fish Creek). The operation required a trio: one person to apply oil, one to tally nests and eggs, and a third to mark the oiled nests with water soluble paint.

The recent expedition on one island alone counted 2,973 nests that contained 7,929 eggs. Between two islands, a total of 25 gallons of corn oil was sprayed onto 14,833 eggs. That is an obscene reproduction rate, and it has been allowed to persist for too many years, unchecked. This bird isn't just a threat to water quality and vegetation on these small islands, they're also very efficient fishers, either singly, or more commonly as a flock, herding game fish toward the shallows where they are easily caught and eaten. I observed a cormorant work near the Northport dock in 1992 as it chased a smallmouth bass round and round until it caught the bass in its beak. It swam like a snake, fast, with fluid movements and corners tighter than the smallmouth could possibly make.

A statistic I read indicated each adult cormorant eats a pound or more of fish per day, a pound that could be made up from perch, small mouth bass, or nongame fish.

There can't be resolution soon enough for the cormorant situation.

***

Jeff Rowsam, FABCO/CAT Technician from Green Bay, responded to Rich's request to examine the *Robert Noble's* engine wiring and advise us if a new, complete wiring harness with new gauges to match, is a realistic, achievable goal in a week's time.

Jeff has done CAT field work for many years. He supervised our engine and gear installation on the *Arni J. Richter* and now oversees new projects, as well as selling engines for FABCO/CAT of Green Bay.

The mechanics of engine motors are quite similar from land to sea, from heavy construction to marine applications, but the installations are considerably different. For one thing, the engines operating in a closed space such as a vessel engine room, a steel box with limited ventilation, must be adequately cooled with fans. Piping raw seawater through the block and through oil coolers is often the best, and easiest, way to remove internal engine heat. The marine atmosphere, as compared with trucking or construction, is clean, with little dust in the air. Regular oil changes and maintenance will extend the working life of the components beyond that of landside applications.

Another advantage of marine power systems is that the motors often run at a fairly constant rate, with rpms seldom varying for long periods of time. This constancy also helps to extend the engine's life, and it is possible to find an optimum rpm range that gets the ship to its destination on time, yet balances speed through the water with fuel consumption.

Operating engines that run freely, don't labor, and that will burn fuel efficiently for a given speed from dock to dock is an important part of what we do, and we've discovered that 1200-1400 rpm is a good operating range. Our interval between overhauls seems to be above average for engine hours, and that, in turn, may ultimately extend the working life of an engine pair. The *Robert Noble's* engines were given a top-to-bottom overhaul after some 60,000 hours, in 2004. They were installed as original equipment in 1979 when Peterson Builders, Inc., built the ferry in Sturgeon Bay. We're hoping these motors give us a few more years' service. But the engine wiring installed by the shipbuilder consisted of separate gauges and switches, each wired separately.

It is this wiring that now appears to have met outer limits of usefulness. The deteriorating plastic coating from the start switch wiring of the starboard engine appears to have been the culprit of Sunday night's meltdown, and we're not going to chance a repeat performance.

Tuesday, July 3 –

In order to get a head start on the *Robert Noble* repair, I pulled duty as captain on the *Washington* in place of Ken Berggren. Ken then worked with Bill Crance and Rich to configure a new mounting bracket for the steering pump. Repositioning that pump will make way for an alternator on the port engine, and, in turn, that becomes the first step in creating an independent battery bank for both port and starboard main engines. In the future, with totally independent starting systems, including wiring and batteries, if one engine goes down, it should not affect the other.

The change in my routine is a good one. I headed down the sidewalk to the dock to involve myself in the loading and unloading routine. Ron Kleckner and Matt Kahlscheuer are my crew, and we work well together. The fifteen-minute turn around requires us to keep moving, with little time for delay on either end of the run.

We filled up the vehicle deck on the several incoming trips. On our 12:30 p.m. trip leaving the island we had just left the pier when a call came in from the Island Rescue Squad. I turned the ferry around in the channel. The *Washington*, like each one of our ferries, is capable of turning in its own length within the narrow channel (rather than motor beyond the entrance marker, turn around, and then retrace the route.) By the time we moored at the ramp we had just departed from, perhaps five minutes had elapsed, and the ambulance plus three more customer cars were ready to board.

By the time we left again, we were 15 minutes behind schedule, but I was confident we could make that time up on the next run, or over the next two runs, with quick turn around times at Northport.

When we arrived at Northport 25 minutes later, the Door County Emergency Services ambulance awaited.

Ron, a U.S. Postal worker of many years who retired as Postmaster of Itasca, IL, is full of fun and comments, and my day goes quickly as a result. Today, Ron elected to address sloppy dock lines left by the crew running just ahead of us in the three-ferry rotation. The ideal is to leave the mooring lines neatly coiled and in an easy-to-reach position so a boat hook isn't required to retrieve them. He got on the radio to let the crew ahead of us know there was no place for amateur line handlers. Joel Gunnlaugsson responded with, "You're always whining!"

***

At Northport, I noted that Mike Kahr's barge project had approached final stages, and that the deck, stern and bow plates were now tacked in place. I observed activities between runs as his crew of men constructed launchways from H-beams, creating a steel grid over which the barge would slide. We're as anxious for Mike to launch his construction barge from our beach as he is to have it floating and working. The number of sidewalk superintendents has increased. So far, onlookers have respectfully stayed clear of the equipment and work. According to one source, Mike's barge is supposed to be the launch platform for the Sister Bay fireworks for the Fourth of July. By the day's last ferry departure, launch ways had been set with cross members between the H-beams. Welding sparks showered down from above as other workers welded deck plates.

The barge appeared nearly ready to push in the water.

***

As we put the *Washington* away for the evening at the service dock, the skies had become cloudy with winds still light from the south, but in the west sunlight continued to poke through the scattered clouds on the horizon. Rain is needed badly.

Wednesday, July 4 – Fourth of July

The morning began with overcast skies and high humidity, requiring our captains to use their air horns to blow low visibility signals. But by 11 a.m., the fog had burned off nicely, the skies had turned blue, and day traffic began to pick up.

Today is the first day of our official "Pirate Day" campaign. Although not all crew have joined in by wearing pirate gear...pirate scarves, hats, beads, tattoos, eye patches and plastic swords...most do, and they seem to enjoy playing the part for our visitors. A selection I made was a Kerr canning ring as an earpiece, hung by a loop of string over my ear.

I went to Northport at noon to see Mrs. Eller, and upon arrival there I noted the barge had been moved at least 20 feet toward the water's edge. While I stood with other onlookers and watched, Mike and his crew had scooted the barge another 15 or more feet, close to the fulcrum point where it might tip the launch ways and begin the downward slide to the water. By stacking timbers to create a fulcrum, he used a stout length of H-beam as a lever, and then by twisting and pushing this lever with his excavator bucket the barge moved, sometimes an inch, other times a foot or more. It was slow progress toward the water's edge.

Watching from the pier were many people, some who were there simply because their car was in line for the next ferry to the island. Other onlookers were locals whose interest in the construction show intensified as launch day approached. Among the onlookers was Captain Paul, Paul Voight, of Gills Rock, dean of local charter fishing captains.

I spoke with Paul about his early years on a farm at the top of the Gills Rock hill in order to learn more about Chester Thordarson, owner of Rock Island, and the Chicago prohibition characters who used to visit Thordarson's island estate. Paul spoke of Mayor Thompson and his followers, body guards who parked their automobiles in his dad's five-car garage (a machine shed with multiple doors). The Voight family farm was situated near where the Shoreline Restaurant is now, overlooking the fishing docks and the old ferry dock. The Chicago mayor and his friends were assumed to be connected with the mob underworld, and because no weapons were allowed on Thordarson's estate (only sporting guns) they placed their machine guns in Edna Voight's closet. The autos and machine guns remained there while the men were transported by ferry, or private boat, to Rock Island 15 miles to the north.

Paul also spoke of his great-grandfather, Gottlieb Voight, who became the first Postmaster of Gills Rock, an event that established this fishing community by creating an official post office there. Gottlieb was responsible, according to Paul, for naming Gills Rock after John Gill, an old pioneer, because the accepted common name, Hedgehog Harbor, contained too many letters to fit on a cancellation stamp.

***

Joel Gunnlaugsson, who is also a volunteer island fireman, told me there are plenty of fireworks in store for the evening at the Island Ballpark, the location where everyone gathers for the annual event. First, there's a children's parade from the Legion Hall to the ballpark, aimed for kids with bicycles and scooters, buggies, and so on, decorated with streamers and balloons. There are usually a few dogs in costume, plus horses with riders, and other family pets. All follow the Legion color guard down Main Road. Most children wave small flags given to them by Legion members.

The children's parade ends at the ballpark with sufficient time before darkness to allow for socializing and settling in before the fireworks begin. Legionnaires Ted Hansen and Kirby Gunnlaugsson pass out dollar bills to each of the participating children as they lined up along the first base line. Last year Kirby and Ted gave out $130 in singles to the parade children. Immediately afterward, these same children form a long line at Time Out Concessions, the snack wagon owned by Karen Baxter. The trailer is towed from its home base on the Jackson Harbor dock to the ballpark for this one evening. Popcorn, cotton candy, hot dogs and cold drink sales are "through the roof."

The Island Volunteer Fire Department shoots the fireworks and takes responsibility for a safe program. It is a simple, yet traditional, up-close Fourth celebration.

Mary Jo and I found ourselves alone as the Fourth of July sun set behind the ballpark trees. I had marched earlier with the American Legion color guard as flag bearer in the children's Fourth of July Parade, and I came home warm from the exertion, overly dressed in polyester uniform. We sat in our backyard and watched the fireworks launch from the ballpark across the road, while plumes of color and smoke crested far above our maple trees. This fireworks show was the best we've seen so far, with short gaps between rounds.

***

Earlier that afternoon, I had come home from work early and took Grandson Atlas to the Art and Nature Center (ANC) to see their nature exhibits. Atlas brought his Pirate's Treasure Map so he could checkmark the list of special island places before he could return to the dock and open Kim's treasure chest of trinkets for kids. The map and directions is a part of our Pirate theme to encourage children and families to seek fun in various parts of the island.

The ANC has been going strong for over 35 years, ever since the old Washington Harbor schoolhouse was emptied. A group of attentive citizens saw value in starting an interpretive center that would double as a small art gallery. So the old schoolhouse is a combination of the two elements: artist's work displayed in the east classroom, and exhibits in the second classroom depicting the island's natural history. Original wooden floors with outlines and screw holes from desks arranged in rows are still seen there.

The nature room is for all ages, but children, especially, enjoy an aquarium of native lake fish species, terrariums with toads, snakes and island plants, microscopes and mystery boxes, and perhaps most fascinating, the bee hive with a chute leading outdoors.

Atlas checked the beehive off his Pirate List and we departed for the Mountain Tower. This lookout is some 180 steps up the side of the cliff to the tower's top. Atlas ran ahead of me, and I met him descending while I was still on my first trip up the tower. He decided to make another complete round trip to the top and back while I waited on the lower stairway for him. His muscular legs and wiry torso are built for speed, and in no time, we had checked off another Pirate List item and were back in my truck for the ride home.

Thursday, July 5 –

Mike Kahr and three of his men stood on his floating barge as we entered Northport harbor this morning. The barge was officially launched about 5:30 p.m. on the Fourth of July. It draws only 18 inches, so that once the forward portion was afloat, the aft end needed less persuasion to push it down the ways. The last few feet of steel-on-steel screeched and smoked, despite bananas used for lubrication, until the entire barge was afloat.

As a follow-up to the launch, today the work crew stacked timber blocking and picked up steel scrap and equipment. Launch way beams were torched apart and piled on a low-boy trailer. Mike's perseverance and hard work paid off in an economically built barge of a size and design that best suits his construction operations. We hope he'll have a busy work schedule to help pay for his barge.

While his crew cleaned up the beach, Mike transferred spuds with excavator from old barge to new. These tall steel stakes can be planted to stop, spin, or anchor the barge in position.

***

A day following a holiday is often busy, and that was the case today, July 5th. A long line of vehicles and people, plus bicycles and motorcycles, waited to board ferries for the island. We also received more than the usual amount of freight. UPS delivered 97 packages to our Northport freight garage, and each label was scanned as the parcels were off-loaded from the UPS truck to our cart for the trip down the dock to the waiting ferry.

I am not normally the "dock jock," as the crew sometimes refers to that position, but I was the Official Dock Attendant this day. I joked with Thor, our youngest son who arrived at mid-morning to get in line, that I had taken his old high school summer job. Actually, most of our current captains began their Ferry Line association as dock boys before they reached 16, the age where they graduated to the decks of the ferries. While at Northport, I installed a parking signpost, hosed off the front patio, swept portions of the roadway and the building, trimmed weeds and spread Weed-B-Gone, and hustled freight. After a rather active six hours of freight and projects, I was quite ready to head back to the ferry office.

Friday, July 6 –

The morning was beautiful as most have been of late, but the humidity was high. Atlas had slept at our house last night and joined us in bed at 5:30 a.m. to watch "Noggin," a children's TV channel. The sun had begun to cast a glow on the maple leaves in front of our home, and the birds were singing. It had rained, perking up grass and flowers noticeably overnight with our first genuine shower in several weeks.

I boarded the 8:00 a.m. ferry with Thor as my companion to attend a meeting in Egg Harbor. Shortly after we departed the island pier, a few hundred yards down the channel, Capt. Jim Hanson blew five short blasts on the air horn, twice, an emergency signal to get the attention of a bass fisherman who lazily trolled down the center of the channel ahead of us. We passed several salmon fishing boats trailing lines over the stern, trolling the depths of the Door near Plum Island for salmon. A light NW breeze blew at their backs as they headed on a southerly course, parallel to our own.

The meeting I planned to attend was a briefing for Door County businesses regarding an upcoming Travel Writer's tour. Thirty writers from around the nation will be hosted, and they will spend the better part of four days traveling from one Door County activity or business to another.

Where does Washington Island Ferry Line fit in? I'd like to think we are, first of all, reliable transportation, but we're also an attraction that thousands of people find fun, just for the ferry ride. We hope each of our customers chooses to do far more than ride the ferry once they're on the island, but we like to make an equally strong impression for both the ferry ride and the island destination. We hope to obtain positive comments and referrals through upcoming articles written by the various Travel Writer participants.

Saturday, July 7 –

There is nothing wrong with this day unless it is the attitude of the beholder. Sunny once again, with a light SW breeze. I awoke shortly after 5 a.m. Unable to sleep, I went downstairs, read, and enjoyed a cup of coffee as the sun rose, intense bursts between the cedars, golden shafts across the grass that lengthen and turn to yellow as the sun rises in the sky.

***

With portable marine radio and binoculars, I headed down to the Bayou docks at Arni's property, where I spun the *Moby Dick* around by hand and started its motor.

This is our family "yacht," a 33- x 13-foot platform with benches extending over two ex-houseboat pontoons. These pontoons are painted white, making it a natural candidate for Moby Dick: "It's the white whale." I lettered the name near the stern to resemble the logo of a leading Frisco band of the late '60s, Moby Grape.

This morning at 11 a.m. is the Blessing of the Fleet, a program organized by Tim Lyons and the Washington Island Yacht Club each year. My craft can stand divine help. The outboard motor has no neutral or reverse, only forward. It's an early model 1970 Mercury, a stacked-cylinder Black Max, a popular motor design for many years with parts now near-impossible to find. I'm fortunate to have two old motors to scrounge parts from. Both Bill Crance and Marine Diesel mechanic Butch Jess have worked on this motor, however, after we launched we still could not get the propeller to reverse. Butch showed impatience at having to work on such a hopelessly designed model.

Bill Crance on the other hand, patient as the day is long, thinks it is simply a matter of adjusting the control linkages. I hope he's right. But for now, there is no reverse, the second such summer in this state of operation. But I'm not particularly concerned. My biggest problem is in getting the boat turned around in close quarters and before squaring away, so I can start the motor and surge ahead.

At my mooring slip in the Bayou at Arni's, the two pontoon bows cleared the sheet piling as I swung toward the channel and open water. Once I had turned the key and the boat began moving ahead, in my opinion, the motor never sounded better. The *Moby Dick* was soon on a near-plane. "Like a giant carpet," Hoyt once described it, a huge aluminum rectangle gliding gracefully and effortlessly across the harbor, skimming the surface at perhaps 12 knots. Within minutes after casting off from Arni's dock at the Bayou, I was at the Ferry Dock. I approached with caution, anchor at the ready, turned the key and cut the motor as I coasted alongside the dock wall, as graceful as if I had two engines and a bow thruster at my command. Moored at 8:30 a.m., *Moby Dick* was the first "yacht" to appear for the Blessing.

***

The Island Yacht Club is a largely social organization, but this morning's program is meaningful thanks to Tim Lyons' insistence that elements pertinent to a blessing are included in the program. For one thing, deceased and retired island sailors are recognized, and the names of commercial fishermen are mentioned, as are members of the U.S. Coast Guard, and also those who lost their lives by falling through the ice or by falling overboard, or having their ship sink out from under them, or having been struck by lightning on the water...these are among the myriad of chance events that take a waterman home to his maker.

Jens Hansen had warmed up the Blessing crowd with a few folk ballads accompanied by his own acoustic guitar and an electric bass. As he played the crowd assembled on the grass between our office and the water's edge and sat in the semi-circle of folding chairs.

Retired fisherman Jake Ellefson entertained and informed the audience with history of fishing on Washington and Rock Islands. He held up examples of early birch bark and carved cedar net floats, working his way toward the most modern floats of plastic. Major island fishing families and notable commercial fishermen were acknowledged for their contributions. Then Jake gave several examples of legendary fish caught in local waters, including a 70-pound trout and a sturgeon seven feet long. "No fish story," said Jake.

Jake's ringing baritone sounded loud and clear, as it does each Memorial Day at the cemetery when he reads over 250 names of deceased veterans buried there. His historical, authoritative overview on commercial fishing was appreciated by everyone.

Tragedies of the past are as real as are the surviving friends and relatives, and the Blessing program serves to recognize these maritime relationships, past and present. With the past in mind, Jacob Ellefson, now one of the few living retired island commercial fishermen, recounted the days gone by. Jake and brothers Steve and Klemmet Ellefson, and their father before them, fished for a living from Jackson

Harbor. During his lifetime, Jake noted the many changes in fish stock numbers. Perhaps at no time, he said, have threats to commercial fishing been so great as right now.

So, we may be looking at an historical moment, Jake told us, actually a gradual moment, in which the whitefish population nearly disappears. Always in the past it was cyclical, but who can be certain? Are we past the tipping point?

***

Aside from asking for guidance from above on this very critical natural balance upon which many island families historically have depended, there is a general belief that blessing an inanimate object like a vessel will bring good things to the craft, its occupants, and to those who rely upon it. If those are honorable enough reasons, then we at the Ferry Line can unashamedly ask for an extra dose of blessing for our ferries upon which the entire island depends, especially the currently laid up *Robert Noble*.

The Blessing event on Washington Island, I think, has especially strong elements of the genuine and sincere. The message this morning was delivered by the Rev. Elizabeth Ward, wearing her Episcopalian vestments, who spoke of humility in the face of an overwhelming natural world, and the fact that the Holy Spirit, God, Our Creator, watches over us in many ways, including through the love of neighbors and friends. Rev. Ward likened the Island to a ship out on the lake, surrounded by water, subject to the elements, but with a sturdy and caring crew.

Her message was witnessed by perhaps 150 persons who listened intently in the 80 degree sunshine. Several found shade from a lone spruce tree along the waterfront, but no one moved.

When the program ended, the island's surviving commercial fishermen, most now in their 80s, and family members of commercial fishermen, posed for a photo. Perhaps because he wasn't aware of the group photo being taken, Arni instead chose to pose separately with Hannes Andersen against the ferry building. The two men had taken trips together to Iceland in prior years, both very proud of their Icelandic heritage. Hannes, as he has every year since the Blessing of the Fleet has been held here, was snappily attired in his Naval Captain's uniform. He is a WWII naval veteran who spent nearly 30 additional years in naval reserve duty.

***

I liked the tone of this morning's event, the honoring of the island's commercial fishing families.

A small bonus to the morning: *Moby Dick* was voted "Best Look-ing" pontoon boat. Actually it was the only pontoon boat there, but nevertheless it was recognized for sleekness and a uniquely utilitarian appearance.

One disappointing note: Thor, Mary Jo and I cast off for a lunch cruise around the harbor. Upon pulling back in to pick up Hoyt, sans reverse, I rammed the steel ferry dock at a fair clip. It wasn't pretty. In fact, the starboard pontoon bow took a major hit. About an hour and half later, when I returned again to drop Hoyt and Mary Jo at the same place along the same ferry dock, the same exact thing happened, and I slammed the pier again with teeth-jamming force. Upon closer scru-tiny, I discovered that not only was neutral missing, but by reversing I had actually increased rpms in forward! My adjusted solution will be to shut the motor off before I approach the pier, coasting to an easy landing. My family passengers seemed embarrassed that a ferry cap-tain and company president wouldn't operate a craft in full working order. Well, sailboats don't sail in reverse, either, was my reply. A skip-per must think ahead, something I will try to improve upon.

Monday, July 9 –

Our refrigerator at home holds fresh smoked salmon, thanks to Hoyt, Rich Ellefson and Bill Crance. The smoked fish are from Rich, who has been learning the art of smoking fish in his grampa's smoker from Uncle Tully. Hoyt, Rich and Bill had a successful fishing trip in Bill's boat, the *Carol Ann*, several days ago. The smoked salmon are delicious, and we turned some of it into a fish paste.

Like loaves of fresh bread or sacks of ripe tomatoes passed be-tween neighbors, we're really fortunate to have frequent gifts of fish. We used to handle dozens of boxes of whitefish on the ferry, unloading them from the fishermen's trucks to the ferry deck, and from the ferry deck to Harvey Olson's truck. With Harvey, the Ellison Bay fish whole-saler, directing us how to stack them, we placed 35 – 100# boxes on his one-ton Ford pickup. Actually, each box weighed over 100# with ice, and Harvey's truck groaned as he gingerly crept in low gear up the Gills Rock hill and back to his cooler shed in Ellison Bay. There, some-how, he managed to unload them alone. Harvey wholesaled local whitefish to dealers in Chicago and New York. Throughout this fish transport process, every so often island fishermen were kind enough to bring us a bucket of whitefish livers, or whitefish fillets, ready for the pan. Most often, such gifts occurred in springtime when fishing was good and the water was cold.

A study of the elderly on Washington Island done sometime in the early 1970s found many healthy, elderly islanders, a surprising number in their 80s and 90s. One conclusion was that low stress played a factor. Another contributing factor was thought to be a diet heavy in fish.

***

Nothing is as disconcerting to a ferry captain as the customer who locks keys in his car on the deck of the ferry. Unless it is a corner car, this makes loading and unloading nearly impossible. We call a nearby locksmith who considers opening car doors a part time job. If we alert him early enough in the trip, he'll meet us at the dock. If not, we're stuck with a car that won't move. We've made round trips with a locked car on board, buying time until the locksmith arrives. We also have a set of window jimmies, long blades that can trip internal locking mechanisms.

The other morning, when we pulled in to Northport on the *Washington*, we had a passenger whose key would not work in the ignition of her small Ford car. The key was slightly bent and so well worn that it wouldn't catch on the tumbler pins. So, in order to get the car off the ferry with the steering wheel in the locked position, wheels straight ahead, we attached a chain to the car and to our little 4-wheel-drive John Deere Gator. We were going to "bounce" the front end over as the car moved forward, and in so doing, clear the bow opening. The metal to which the chain was attached was extremely light and rusted. On the second pull, the metal crosspiece ripped from its fastenings and the small radiator core dropped down to the deck. Damage done, we reconnected to an axle and pulled again, skidding the car over smooth steel and rough concrete to the Northport ticket booth. After exchanging information with the owner, I called a tow service, and several hours later, assistance arrived from Sturgeon Bay.

Following an increase in temperatures, the black flies came out at Northport. With an offshore breeze they are quite thick near the ticket booth, where they are a major problem for the captive ticket sellers, biting ankles and any place there is bare skin. Our ticket sellers are heroes for putting up with them in the booth all day long, but we've not found a foolproof way to keep them at bay.

Late Saturday afternoon, Northport ticket seller Jason was "getting eaten alive," and I was told he was in great distress. I went to Mann's Mercantile with the mission of picking up supplies that might help his black fly situation. I bought two bracelets advertised to keep the wearer fly-free, and a fly swatter, the last swatter on the shelf. I also bought a pack of flypaper rolls and a small fan to create an artificial breeze within the booth. I also bought a can of Outdoorsman fly spray, recommended by Eric DeJardin to be the *only* fly spray that seemed to really work. I also picked up a jug of car wash as I walked by the automotive section, recalling that we were completely out at the ferry dock.

Then, I hurried back to the ferry dock with my purchases, just in time to catch the *Washington* as it finished loading. I placed the plastic sack of supplies in a storage area for the crew to give to Jason.

This morning, Jason worked the island ticket booth. I remembered the fly applications I purchased and asked Jason, "How did those things I sent over work? How about that fly spray?"

"They worked great," he replied. "I put the bracelets over my socks, and I don't think I had one fly after that. Then I used the spray, and that seemed to work, too. I rubbed some of the car wash on, and that wasn't bad either."

Tuesday, July 10 –

Warm and sticky weather. You don't need a weatherman this day to tell you there will be significant changes. We monitored thunderstorm and tornado warnings on the marine weather channel, and when we shifted to the NOAA and Fox 11 weather radar links we discovered a line of intense thunderstorms with high winds about 30 miles to our west.

If the storm line continues, the larger and heavier cells will split north and south of us with a less intense section passing over Washington Island. We'll miss the rain if that happens, but we won't mind missing the heavy winds. Carol Stayton, ticket seller on the island, removed flags from the poles in front of our office to spare them a wind whipping. The band of storms is not deep, perhaps less than 10 miles, and within 15 minutes it should pass over us with colder and clearer air behind the line.

***

Our ferry crews waited approximately 20 minutes, and the sky cleared to the west. High, dark clouds with lightning passed to our north. Winds slackened as the skies became clear and blue again.

Wednesday, July 11 –

The frontal boundary between warm, humid air and the cooler Canadian high pressure brought brisk northwest winds.

Wind velocities in the early evening might have reached the 30-40 mph range. It blew through the screens of our upper story bedroom windows, billowing the curtains. About the time I turned out my bedside reading light at 10:30 p.m., our power went out. I fumbled my way downstairs to the utility room and groped for a flashlight.

Island power outages are fairly frequent, disconcerting if you are connected up on computer, or have something baking in the oven, or own a business where there is no getting around lighting and electricity to serve customers. But we also have a distinct island advantage. Because an electrical cable underwater from Northport feeds most of our power needs from Wisconsin Public Service, as it has since 1981, we're still self-reliant if connections from that cable fail us. Standby generators at our electric co-op can be started within minutes.

Thursday, July 12 –

Clear, blue skies, low 60s, and fresh westerly winds this morning. It's another outstanding day on the island.

I spent my morning writing a letter in response to the Federal Register Notice regarding the transfer of BLM properties, namely Plum and Pilot Islands, to U.S. Fish & Wildlife Service. This transfer has been years in the making, with at least part of the delay coming from a cleanup process to remove soil contamination. Other delays can be pinned on the slowness of the system, from bureaucratic government that always has "bigger fish to fry." A prime example was the soil clean up contract completed in 2005 on Plum Island at a taxpayer cost of $860,000. Then, there was the wait of more than a year and a half following that work for Coast Guard to post signs stating there was "Danger of lead contamination in the soils" (just in case you were thinking of ingesting soil).

The shuffle of paper work seemed unending, the reviews of documents, signing off between various bureaus and desks, so that in the end we feel so fortunate there was progress at all, given the complexity commonplace with such transfers.

Finally, to allow for objections, there is the required Federal Register Notice that gives the opportunity to request a public hearing (but with no guarantee such a hearing would be granted), and to receive public comments on the transfer.

I thought it was worth my time to comment, if for nothing else than to vent my frustration about the lack of apparent leadership in this decade-old transfer under purview of several federal agencies, none of which really seemed to take a heart-and-soul approach to what

ening with buildings on Plum or Pilot Islands. The waiting
i   i, U.S. Fish and Wildlife Service, stated years ago it has no
interest with the island buildings. Their mission is to provide nesting
and migrating habitat for birds.

This quest to protect the birds has been so dominant in the past
that Pilot Island has been allowed to become a sorry mess of seagull
feathers and cormorant poop, caustic waste from fish-eating birds who
consume a pound or two each of fish daily, then sit in the trees and on
rocks and defecate.

The USFWS is now the Federal organization we need to befriend if
we expect to restore any of the buildings, but it remains to be seen
how willing they will be in this partnership to promote historical restoration and visitation. So far, Pilot Island has not gained USFWS
support for restoration work.

Saturday, July 14 –

The NW winds were sharp today and temperatures were in the
upper 60s. When clouds scudded overhead around 11 a.m., winds
piped to 30 mph or better and stayed at that level much of the day.
Charlie Voight shut down the *Island Clipper* after the first trip. He has
a tight docking situation in Gills Rock, and with WNW winds the seas
pound against the rocky shoreline. We carried a number of Charlie's
passengers back to the mainland via Northport on our ferries.

Lines of traffic were brisk on both sides of the Door, with day visitors and families starting or ending island vacations. It's what we refer
to as "Saturday turnover." There is an island wedding for an island girl,
Andrea Small, at Trinity Lutheran Church this afternoon. The Island
Lion's Club's huge tent is set up in the field adjacent to the church for
the reception to follow. This evening at the TPAC, a totally separate
event, Corky Siegel and his blues band will play.

This evening the sky has cleared, perfectly, and winds have
dropped, setting the stage for a beautiful sunset in a few hours' time.
The jackass over at Wayne Oscor's ostrich farm is braying a loud and
obnoxious sound, begging for attention. It may be his feeding time.
The sound of the donkey carries on the light northwest breezes. Along
Main Road the traffic of the day has calmed.

Monday, July 16 –

Rich drove to Green Bay to determine progress on a new wiring
harness for the *Robert Noble*. Rather than locating and replacing one

bad wire at a time, for only the one engine, we've decided to redo all wiring, gauges, switches for both engines, and to add new gauge panels in the engine room and pilothouse. Anything less, it seems, would invite future problems with aged wire. A photo sent earlier by the company Rich is working with showed the new gauge panels designed for retrofit in the pilothouse, with minimal alteration to the binnacle. The new panels are ready to be picked up.

***

Numerous bass fishermen are in the harbor. Their fishing boats run the gamut from simple, open wooden or aluminum boats with a 10 hp motor to fancy bass rigs with twin 200 hp motors and swivel seating and electric trolling motors in the bow. The more knowledgeable fishermen can catch fish no matter what the boat looks like, although it's handy to be able to motor to different locations with ease. For the most part, an 18-ft. Lund with a 10-20 hp motor will push you along nicely and take you to most any part of the island shoreline you wish, and the lighter rigs are easy to beach or pull up on a trailer. The simplicity of this type of boat has made it a favorite with fishermen here since the wooden boats went out of favor in the 1960s.

Tuesday, July 17 –

I'm up and ready to get to the Ferry Dock by 6 a.m. for the early ferry. It's impossible to be earlier than Bill Crance (Grampa Willie) or Tully Ellefson, my deckhands. I don't get many chances to run the *Arni J. Richter* as captain, but today I will.

The morning is beautiful, with no breeze and a clear, blue sky. While this broken record of a weather pattern plays over and over, each day does seem better than the one before it.

Margie O'Connor is selling tickets in the island booth, and Jim Rose, veteran of some 28 years of ticket selling, is in the Northport booth. Our first several trips were light on traffic, half-full or less, with a few commercial trucks. We had Paul Novak in his semi truck onboard our first run. His open-top trailer is used for hauling scrap metal from the Town Recycling Center. He cleaned up the scrap metal pile in early spring, a heap at least 100 feet across and 12 feet high, but already the new pile has grown through the accumulation of old tanks, grills, washing machines, refrigerators, lawn mowers, and so forth. By the time Paul lined up to leave the island in the early afternoon, his load was heaped above the sides of his trailer. We watched closely to ensure the few highest metal pieces didn't snag the *Arni J.'s* overhead.

On an earlier outbound trip from the island, we carried a trailer of wet garbage and a second bin of recyclables hooked up to the Veolia truck. Al Hiller, driver, is a regular on our ferry, almost one trip per week even in winter. On this day Al joined me in the wheelhouse. I also invited Pastor Phil Green of Bethel Church who said he'd never ridden in the pilothouse. Our conversation ranged from jokes about garbage ("It's still picking up," Al laughed), to the cormorants on Pilot Island, to the status of ferry traffic as we passed the *Washington* headed to the island with a full load of people and cars. Phil and his son each had roles in the recent Island Players production of *The Diary of Anne Frank*. Last week Phil led the audience in song with voice and trumpet at the evening Hymn Sing for the Forum conference.

Part way across, Phil noticed he was missing his typed notes, and trucker Al spotted them flapping in the breeze on a deck bench outside the pilothouse, about to blow away. "Sermon rescued?" we asked Phil. "No," he replied and tapped his temple with his forefinger. "That's still cooking up here."

Our work day, from 6 a.m. to 6:20 p.m. when we tied up passed by quickly. We had hauled a great number of cars and bikes and people safely, had fun, and the day was such a beautiful one that I don't think there was a displeased passenger. From a captain's point of view, the *Arni J. Richter* is a pleasure to operate, with an excellent wheelhouse, good instrumentation and engine controls, unobstructed view of the surrounding waters, and easy passenger access to all decks. It's also the easiest of our ferries to load and unload.

Wednesday, July 18 –

Humidity is high and there are patches of thick fog moving in and out. At no time does the sun burn through near the ferry dock in the forenoon. Each captain is guided by radar and GPS and places security calls on the marine radio channel 16, informing other traffic of his whereabouts and intended course.

Saturday, July 21 –

Another beautiful day. Who can complain when the temperatures are low 60s at night, and mid-70s by day?

I awoke early and then spent the next hour or more turning over a newly-completed metal sculpture in my mind. Where to place it in our yard? Was it finished, or did it need additional welding, more pieces? Should it be painted or left natural? Completion of a creative project once it's begun becomes an obsession. After thinking it over for several months, I spent seven hours in one stretch assembling and welding thirty feet of chain, three old wagon wheel hoops, a stout buggy axle, and a light engine flywheel. When I welded a second pass over chain link joints, the top part of the sculpture collapsed on me. My welding hadn't penetrated enough to hold up the springy, cantilevered, several-hundred pounds. Disappointed, I hooked the fallen section to the tractor bucket and hoisted the piece back to its former position and welded it up once again. For good measure, I added a heavy truck spring coil for support, giving it added stiffness, yet movement.

This sculpture was intended be free-standing. Now I needed to find the spot in our yard where light would strike the shapes and I could enjoy it from the windows of our home. My mid-morning mission was to trailer it home, set it in the yard, and free myself to work on other projects. By 10:30 a.m., with only one minor adjustment, I had completed the job, lifting it to a resting place on the lawn with the tractor bucket.

***

This is the day of the W.I. Lion's Club's annual Fly-In Fish Boil, an event that attracts small plane pilots and flying enthusiasts from around the Midwest. The Lion members begin boiling water in the kettles in mid-morning, start serving at 11 a.m., and by 1:30 p.m. three to four hundred pounds of fish has disappeared, feeding six to seven hundred.

Ferry traffic is brisk today, both directions, and with the *Robert Noble* now back in the running as the fourth ferry, we are just managing to keep up. It's one day short of three weeks since the *Noble* was last underway.

Sunday, July 22 –

Today was an excellent day to get away for a motorcycle ride down the Peninsula, and it's also a good sensation to return safely home, a home with many great memories.

Our house was built circa 1915 by J.W. and Clara Cornell, parents of nine children, Mary Jo's maternal grandparents. Little has changed physically with our home except for the trees in the yard having grown larger. A photo in our front hall shows Mary Richter as a very young girl standing in the lane with her lunch pail and books. A horse harnessed to a grader and a pile of gravel is behind her, perhaps the spreading of gravel for the initial driveway. The sugar maple trees in that photo are small, only 6 to 8 inches in diameter, and now some are two feet and more in diameter. A black band can be seen around each tree in the photo, taken when the bark was young and smooth. If I look closely today from a distance, I can just make out those same bands, now about five feet above the ground. These bands were painted in tar, supposedly as prevention to ward off an infestation of worms that would otherwise crawl up the trunks and eat the leaves.

It is a privilege to live in such a home. In the living room where I'm sitting now as I write this entry, Tim Jessen was born. His Aunt June (Gunnlaugsson) was midwife to Tim's mother, Evelyn. In the next room, where we now have a sofa and TV, Julia Thordarson lived out her last days as a ward of Jake and June Gunnlaugsson, dying in 1958. The Gunnlaugssons bought the house, barn, garage and 40 acres from J.W. Cornell and operated the upstairs as a rooming house called Maple Grove. Room decal numbers are still on the doors. Later, the Gunnlaugssons sold it to Ethel Anderson, another daughter of J.W. Cornell, which brought it back into the family. Ethel sold her home to us in 1976.

How did Mrs. Thordarson, wife of the famous inventor and industrialist, C.H. Thordarson, come to live in this house on Main Road? Tom Guinan was June's father, and he had also been caretaker on Rock Island for many years and knew the Thordarsons well. Some Guinan family members would link Tom with Julia romantically. It's entirely possible. Her husband, Chester, was absent for long periods when away on business, and when he was present, he appeared to others to be totally absorbed in his own work and thoughts. The old lath-and-plaster walls tell no tales. My sources are descendents of Karly Jessen, and an interview with June and Jake Gunnlaugsson in the early 1990s.

Monday, July 23 –

A friend who helped me when I assembled *Over & Back – A Picture History of Transportation to Washington Island* came to the island for a visit today.

Jim LeGault is a man with many interests who has friends and acquaintances all over the country. He's been a serious amateur photographer and at one time published an environmental book about Lake Michigan back in the early '70s called *Reflections in a Tarnished Mirror*. He sailed on Great Lakes freighters. He sold automotive replacement parts to shops from Door County to the Upper Peninsula. He built a small sharpie, a double-ended ketch of Herreshoff design, and sailed as far as Drummond Island on the St. Mary's River. Then, when the opportunity arose, he bought the steel-hulled, junk-rigged *Friendly*, and began sail charter tours. Besides having his Coast Guard captain's license for chartering, Jim works on yacht deliveries and as crew maintaining yachts for owners.

Somewhere between his sailing and interest in travel, he bought a home in Mexico, in the Yucatan Peninsula, about 100 miles inland. "People ask me, do you get bored? What a stupid question! I've been doing basically nothing for many years, why would moving to Mexico make me bored?" Jim's laugh that follows is a snuffle, an intake of air that might make me think he is deprived of oxygen. It is as much a joke to himself, about himself, and doesn't matter if no one else appreciates it. His smile is slightly off-center, hidden by his thick moustache, a Yosemite Sam model. His Spanish is improving all the time, he said, and when he masters that, there is always ancient Mayan to learn, the language still favored by the indigenous people of the Yucatan.

He showed me an album of digital photos he's taken, stunning photos of ancient Mayan ruins just miles from his home, of flamingos so bright they are beyond pink, and of tropical bird life found in abundance among the low, mangrove lands of the sea coast. It is an area maintained as a wildlife sanctuary.

There were also photos of native residents: a pretty young girl with dark hair and Mayan features; a female bull fighter in action; fans watching the bullfight from stadium bleachers made of poles, three and four rows high, their sandaled feet dangling just above the bull ring; and young people at a formal dance, dressed in formal costume.

"Busy?" Jim asks. "With a new language to learn, people to meet, I am at a loss to understand the question." Jim divides his time now between yacht deliveries, splitting his time between Florida and his new home in Merida, with frequent trips elsewhere as work and interests lead him. He still has family in Marinette, WI, and recently took the new ferry from Marinette to Sturgeon Bay with his dad. "There were only about eight of us on board," he said.

***

We got an early start scrubbing on the *Arni J. Richter* this morning. Cleaning the surfaces on all decks takes quite a bit of time, even when several people are involved with the project. I sprayed for spiders first to chase them from the smallest corners, then followed up with the pressure washer and a soapy sponge. The mess, the dirt, is mostly from insects, although there is still plenty of human dirt, too.

I am always surprised at the amount of hair found wound around and through screening and wiring. It takes a good five hours for a quick pass over the main surfaces. Meanwhile, another crew member cleaned the cabins and heads.

By 10 a.m., the boat is presentable, and just in time. We learn that there are two tour groups, numbering nearly 100 passengers, and the *Arni J.* will be called into action to pick them up along with some auto traffic. I stepped from ferry to pier with soaking shoes and sweatshirt to put away the equipment and change into dry clothing. We will repeat the process next morning on the *Washington*.

Tuesday, July 24 –

It was 72 degrees at 6 a.m. with a slight breeze from the south.

The scrubbing detail shifted this morning to the *Washington*. This ferry's not had a good cleaning since early spring, on the daily run because other ferries were either in dry dock or down for maintenance.

The adage "many hands make light work" applies to cleaning such a daunting spread of surface area. We confiscated a few "third man" deckhands where they could be spared to assist us with the job. Some four hours later we put away our equipment, pumped the waste tank and fired up the engines for running the remainder of the day.

I drove home, showered, and changed to clean, dry clothes. Then I crossed by ferry to the peninsula and headed to Sturgeon Bay for a meeting with Todd Thayse of Bay Shipbuilding to discuss our most recent yard period and the invoices that resulted from the work on our ferries. We were disappointed with the fact that we couldn't resolve the vibration problem on the starboard shaft of the *Arni J. Richter*, and I sensed the same frustration on Todd's part. We may go at it again in November when there is more time, hoping to finally resolve the problem. Currently, the packing around the shaft must be loosened before start up so that water can freely lubricate (and cool) the stuffing box, the gland where packing keeps exterior water from entering the hull. It's a finicky setting. When too tight, it gets hot and must be immediately backed off and allowed to cool down while the shaft is still spinning.

Our crew has pumped the sump under the stuffing box just about once per round trip due to influx of water, snugging up the nuts at night when the shaft is no longer turning to prevent excessive leaking.

Wednesday, July 25 –

We have an injured reserve list going. Two men are currently out with ailments that potentially could shorten their ability to work over the next month or so. Tully Ellefson hurt his leg jumping from the tractor over two weeks ago, then worked with a knee brace and a limp. He will find out tomorrow if the ligaments are torn or if there is a better prognosis for recovery. Bryan Stefancin ran into another bicyclist on his carbon fiber road model, destroying the bike and putting his shoulder down hard. He has possible tendon tears in his shoulder and may require surgery.

***

Because of the shortage of crew in several slots, today I found myself the third man on the *Robert Noble* with Joel Gunnlaugsson and Al Stelter. Joel is an experienced captain. Al is experienced at many things, including heating and air conditioning, is retired and now works part time for us as a deckhand. Al's mother and dad, Martha and Al, were island stalwarts and business owners for decades.

Al Stelter Sr. barbered in Milwaukee for years and also ran a shop on the island. Good memories are stopping at Al's for a cut on a Friday afternoon or a Saturday morning. Rarely would there be a wait. A few times on late Friday afternoons, though, I happened to come during cocktail hour. Hannes Hannesson brought a bottle of brandy which he and Al would share between cuts. Martha, an artist and hairdresser, and who happened to love martinis, had her beauty shop in the next room. She managed Holiday Inn successfully for many years. Martha brought her martini glass and sat down to join the conversation with the men. If a haircut was underway, the customer just waited until Al and Hannes had a drink or two, then cutting would resume in no particular hurry for the end result, which was sometimes imperfect.

Son Al told us a few stories while in the pilothouse this morning about Martha and Al. "Classics," as he referred to them. We had been talking about campers and motor homes and the fact that we had seen more of them onboard the ferries this summer than before. I asked Al if he still had the old motor home that belonged to his parents.

Al said he sold it. Martha, who was always the driver, had backed over a stump and opened up the exhaust manifold in the process. Later, when Al went to start it up, the hot exhaust hit the dry lawn and started a grass fire. He decided to peddle it while he could.

Had he remembered the accident Martha and Al were in with their motor home?

"Yaas," Al said. "They drove all the way back from their trip, thousands of miles, returning just a few weeks before Thanksgiving. They hit a slick spot on County S partway between Sturgeon Bay and Algoma, went into the ditch and rolled the camper completely over. Martha and Al had to crawl out through cold swamp water to get to the road. They both wound up in the hospital where I visited them. Martha wasn't thinking much about their situation. She worried about the frozen turkey she bought for Thanksgiving. The frozen turkey flew out of the camper and into the swamp when they rolled over. We were coming up from Illinois to spend Thanksgiving on the island, so I went out and bought her another turkey. That made her happy."

"Once Martha and Al were driving at night on the Pennsylvania Turnpike. Something went wrong with the camper and Martha pulled off to the side of the highway. Martha always had her paint box with her, and her artist's brushes, so she made up a sign that said, 'Just knock on the door. We're sleeping.' Here they were on this big Turnpike and she and Al crawled in the sack and slept on the side of the road, never thinking about who might stop or what they might do. Fortunately, it was a state trooper who first saw the sign in the back window of the camper, and he knocked on the door and woke them up."

A short pause, then, "Here's another classic," Al continued. "One time they drove up in the mountains, out east, in the Smokies. They towed Dad's VW beetle behind the camper, and when they stopped at a truck stop they decided to unhitch the beetle and look around to see the sights. So they left the camper behind and drove off. Later that day when it came time to relocate their camper, they forgot where they had left it. They drove into North Carolina, South Carolina, and finally, on the third day, guessing correctly they had crossed over the mountains, they found their camper again at the truck stop." We all laughed at the thought of Martha and Al spending days on the road looking for the mother ship.

With that final story, we entered the break wall at Northport and had to "get to work." On earlier trips that day we had compared gardens. Al always has great produce from a large garden, and he does lots of canning with his wife, Helene. He fills his lunch pail with good things to eat from his garden each day in summer. Joel and I are the amateurs. We're proud just to get seeds to sprout, and we hope they will result in something worth picking later. Every trip, Al is into his lunch pail. A cucumber here. A sandwich there. Some fruit. A cup of potato salad. This routine lasts the entire day. My routine, on the other hand, is to eat it all when it's there, and as a result I usually have an empty lunch bucket by 11 a.m. We also got into a discussion of who prepares lunches. Does your wife fix your lunch, or do you? If he wouldn't pack his own lunch, Al says, he wouldn't have any lunch, or as much.

The morning passed quickly with such banter, and in between we had guests in the pilothouse, "little pirates" as well as adults who are curious about the ferries and how the ferries are powered. Today is a "pirate gear day" for our crew, and Joel encouraged Al to put on a pirate headscarf and neck chains. I wore a Kerr jar ring for an earring on my right ear, drawing comments from passengers when they boarded. We've managed to get some of our customers to laugh, not a bad thing. I was asked to pose with one lady for a photo, and I suggested her husband might not approve. "He's golfing," she replied. Well, OK then.

We especially enjoy it when families of young children use our pirate's treasure map to find suggested island stops. Today, with pleasant temperatures, Schoolhouse Beach is a place where parents — anyone for that matter — will be happy to cool off in clear water.

***

Our ferry leaves the island at 1 p.m., and it will be less than half full, not an unusual occurrence this time of day. I'm the 'third man' on board, and as such I'm not essential this trip, so I shifted to shore mode for a while, to help with freight and do paperwork.

At 2:15 the *Noble* returned, carrying the UPS cart, generally a load that sometimes spills over to a second cart, and that is the case today. While helping Bill Schutz unload and sort packages on our shelves, our crews switched ferries during the 15-minute interval between trips. Joel moored the *Robert Noble* so that Jeff Rowsam, CAT technician who helped us get started on our engine rewiring, can inspect the job on the *Noble*. Jeff arrived the day after Rich called him, and he gave us advice and direction, connecting us with a known supplier of wiring harnesses. This shortened our search for a vendor and got us immediate results. Jeff has been considerate enough to follow up with a visit.

Friday, July 27 –

The air is heavy and oppressive once again, but the forecast is for clearing skies and a high pressure with NW winds.

That is exactly what happened, and on the *Eyrarbakki* with Ken Berggren and Jack Nehlsen, we have a steady lake breeze to keep us cool, and by noon the drop in humidity is noticeable.

***

Two young girls with their dad were guests in the wheelhouse on our first trip to the island. Most visitors consider it a significant part of their experience to be allowed to join the captain and to steer the ferry.

The *Eyrarbakki* is a bit harder to steer than the other ferries only because the wheel is connected to the rudders by cable rather than hydraulic cylinders, and it takes more muscle power to turn and to hold the wheel against water pressure. On the straight away, cable steering isn't difficult. In tight turns, or backing away from a pier, power steering has advantages.

Steering may be the most visible part of our job as ferry captain, but it's just one of many tasks. There is the check of engines and bilge prior to start up, and again each time we leave the dock (a deckhand's duty). There is the need to keep on schedule, and to deliver the safety message to the public, to load or unload vehicles, bicycles and people quickly and safely, to keep a weather eye out for wind speed and direction, to observe current, and to keep a watch on other vessels.

Then, there is also the matter of controlling the motion of the ferry, and the course. Skills of knowing when to speed up, slow down, fall into neutral, or to reverse the propellers will mean a soft landing with correct positioning, so that the ramp can go down as soon as lines are made fast. It's a fluid movement within fluid lake waters, sliding around a turn — twisting and sliding at the same time — around the ninety-degree bend into the slip. Rare is it that the ferry ever goes straight ahead. It is always sliding slightly to one side or another, influenced by wind, current, and the energy of the ferry propellers.

So when we invite little pirates, big pirates, and other guests into the pilothouse, it's with the appearance that all is well and that our job of steering, the most visible job, is a piece of cake. Most of the time, it is.

Tuesday, July 31 –

I awoke at 5:30 a.m. The air was still and it was 68 F.

I went downstairs to read, joined by grandson Atlas 45 minutes later. We read, played games, and then I fixed breakfast, Mann's Store breakfast sausage and toast. Atlas is a light eater, but he liked what I fixed him, especially when there is a story with the food. In this case, it was the honey container and discussion about the beehive we saw at the Art and Nature Center.

Tully and I started early on the blacktop sealing, hoping to finish by midday. Before I got out on the pavement I received a call from Tim Kroeft of the WDNR research boat *Gaylord Nelson*. They had moored at the Potato Dock overnight, and he called to say Walt Jorgenson's truck had its front wheels drop into a sinkhole in the pier. Tim said they had helped Walt get out of the truck, with great difficulty, from the uphill passenger side.

When I got there, I expected to see one front tire stuck in a small hole, but actually the entire front end was in the hole, and the rear bumper was in the air, about level with my waist. Tully, following with our tractor, put downward pressure on a nylon sling attached to the truck frame, while I pulled on the rear hitch with a chain on my pickup truck. With the help of the DNR crew who straightened the front wheels, we pulled the truck backwards out of the hole. The sinkhole measured 12 feet in diameter and was approximately three feet deep.

We then returned to our seal coating chores, completing the outer dock area by approximately 1:30 p.m. with temperatures pushing 90 degrees. Our ferry traffic seemed fair, considering the heat. Many day visitors had Schoolhouse Beach on their mind, I'm sure.

***

A comment heard much later in the day by someone at the Customer Desk in our office:

"How come the beaches are so rocky? Doesn't the stone break down with wave action into sand?" A fair question.

If this stone were other than limestone, that would probably happen, but a sand beach on the island is rare. I think most of the abraided material dissolves into the lake water. A small amount becomes sand, no doubt, but it's within the harbor depths, not along shore. So we enjoy a rare, smooth, stone beach, stones polished by the grinding in the waves. The real advantage to Schoolhouse Beach is having water deep enough to swim in very close to shore.

AUGUST

Wednesday, August 1 –

My afternoon was spent on several tasks: I delivered a load of garbage and recyclables to the Town Landfill, the Island Recycling Center; I wrote a letter to attorneys about our permit for Northport Pier. I commented by letter to the federal docket. The topic was the EPA's interest in assigning overboard discharge permits to all vessels, large and small. The purpose of the proposed regulation will be to eliminate all sources of pollution, the incidental as well as the intentional.

Intentional pollution is already covered, so what is meant by incidental? Washing off decks, circulating sea water through engines or refrigeration systems, pumping ballast water, and so on. What our company opposes is another government agency to issue permits and regulate this industry segment.

My suggestion to EPA is to first seek out real and extensive pollutant sources such as tons of farmland fertilizers (phosphates and other chemicals that run off farmland into streams and lakes), or the City of Milwaukee's sewage treatment system that regularly overflows millions of gallons of untreated sewage into Lake Michigan, or island bird sanctuaries such as Pilot Island (with protected bird populations that produce nitrogen-rich guano that washes into the lake). Pursuing those sources would net major improvements in water pollution and bring easily measured results in a short time.

Thursday, August 2 –

A great breeze off the lake late yesterday cooled things down in the closing hours of the afternoon, but as evening came on the wind died, and night became rather oppressive. Humidity was up again this morning. The temperature at dawn was 74 degrees.

Yesterday's early ferry from Northport carried only one car and a semi truck. This morning it was three vehicles incoming. That poor payload may be a sign of warm mornings and people sleeping in. By noon the pace seemed to have picked up.

Office Manager Bill Schutz totaled July's traffic and we were about even in vehicles, but up 11percent in people over last year. That's encouraging because each of the three prior years numbers trailed off instead of rising.

Friday, August 3 –

An almost imperceptible front moved through yesterday afternoon. The visual clues were dark clouds that marched across
Michigan's Upper Peninsula to our north. Then, the atmosphere
cleared and the wind shifted to the NW. Overnight the temperature
cooled and the humidity dropped. It was a beautiful morning with not
even slight dew on the grass.

This is "yard sale" day. Mary Jo's partners and friends arrived before 7 a.m. to begin setting up their tables and wares for the "Uniques
& Antiques" sale in our backyard. The day's cooler air and sunshine
will help attract customers, and a small band playing live, contempo-
rary music will keep them in a buying mood. I'm confident they'll have
a good crowd and sales. For me, this is a good day to be at work.

***

Ron Kleckner worked feverishly for at least three months on his
days off, evenings and weekends, rebuilding a boat he bought from
Jack Hagen. The hull was in great shape, but the wooden decks, hard-
top canopy and trim were rotten. The engines, a pair of gasoline
Chryslers, were frozen and needed a fair amount of work. Ron kept at
it, putting in long hours on his days off, and now it's finally launched.
The engines turned over and fired up, a relief after the considerable
attention given them, but a few plugs were found missing from the exhaust manifold and the water pump impellers were torn up, brittle
from sitting so many years.

Jack Hagen had chartered this boat, the *Jule II*, for salmon fishing.
While Jack wasn't a fastidious yacht-keeper, he was an excellent charter captain, successful in terms of catching fish. But most importantly,
he satisfied his customers with local knowledge, stories of the island,
and his enthusiasm. I recalled going out with Jack years ago with Hoyt
and Thor, and we caught three salmon. I remembered the sounds of
his gas engines (he shut off one motor for trolling), and the crude stick
propped against the glass edge to hold the sliding side window closed.
Wooden trim around the windows was green with moss and there were
missing screws everywhere on fixtures, but Captain Jack was about as
pleased and at home as anyone could be, sitting in his cushioned chair
in the breeze, shirt unbuttoned, his trademark thick, bristly hair
trained back high over his head. Jack maneuvered his boat about with
ease and confidence, swinging the bow this way and that, occasionally

marking fish on the depth flasher, knowing it was just a matter of time before a salmon hit a downrigger lure. During long lulls waiting for the rods to trip, he freely expounded on stories of the island and local history, and it was his manner of telling them that made them special. He exuded a great deal of intelligence without polish and frippery.

Ron worked hard to convince Jack to sell him the rough-looking *Jule II*, a boat with lots of miles under its keel that had sat on blocks for so many years at Kap's Marina. One of the motors was seized tight with piston rings rusted to cylinder walls, sitting for years in a bilge partly filled with rainwater and melted snow. He needed a project, Ron said.

The very day Ron prepared to launch the restored *Jule II*, Jack told marina owner and friend, Will Krueger, that he wanted to launch, too, a newer model that had also sat on blocks in the boatyard. Sick with cancer, Jack might have believed this would be his last opportunity to be on the water, driven by the notion that he still owned a boat and how much fun it would be to fish once again.

For any one who loves being on the water, emotions are stirred by memories of cruising past the high limestone bluffs and islands, and of picnics with friends or family members.

Boats are catalysts for dreaming.

***

Nearly everyone's disposition is improved today, and that's directly related to cooler and more pleasant air. The sale at 1040 Main Road was a success. Dozens of shoppers were ready and waiting for the gates to open at the stroke of 10 a.m. So many things were sold in the first few hours that stock was greatly depleted. There was no warehouse from which to draw more goods, a disappointment for shoppers who waited until the second day to shop. Everyone who has ever visited a yard sale knows being there early is the key. The large and more unusual pieces done by Mary Jo have left the premises.

***

This evening is also the annual Kaffe Fest — Scandinavian desserts and coffee — at Trinity Lutheran Church. More than 20 years ago, an annual Smorgasbord was hosted by ladies of Trinity Lutheran Church with such Norsk treats as smoked fish, Swedish meatballs, lefse, fruit soup, rosettes and other delicious and time-consuming delicacies. Many of those hard-working ladies have passed on, and the tradition as well as the workload became too much for those who took their place. Instead, the coffee and Scandinavian dessert event Kaffe Fest arose in

1995, with the Stavkirke across the road providing a good historical point of interest for visitors. Young girls in costume provide escort to tour the Stavkirke, and costumed ladies (and perhaps some men) serve as hosts in the Fellowship Hall of the church.

Fest Dancing is another highlight on Saturday evening, with approximately 100 costumed dancers of all ages. During Sunday morning worship at Trinity different Scandinavian countries are featured. This year a pastor from Ishpeming, MI, Finn country, will preach in English but recite liturgy in Finnish.

All Island Festival events are intended to extend tradition and honor heritage. While the tourism income for the community is greatly appreciated, I believe this Scandinavian Festival would continue in one form or another, even if no one came from off the island to see it.

Saturday, August 4 –

No rain now for several weeks. The other side of the coin is that our temperatures have moderated and last evening was pleasantly cool.

***

According to Mike McCauley, Dance Festival Master of Ceremonies, this year's Fest Dance had 133 dancers, a record number. This also is Mike's 30th year of participation. Mike is also a former Ferry Line deckhand of years back.

Atlas and other dancers in Scandinavian costume, young and old, gathered behind the screen of cedars and Scandinavian flags at the outdoor stage adjacent to the Community Center when we arrived. He was with Morgan Roberts, his dance partner for the youngest group of dancers. Mary Jo and I found open seats in the last row on the upper slope of the hill, but we chose to stand in order to see the dancers. Atlas met us with eye contact even though we were at the back of the audience. He and other 4- and 5-year-olds performed in front of the crowd of several hundred people, accompanied by a piano. After his dance, Atlas sat in Mary Jo's lap while the next age group came on stage, and he began to fall asleep. Along with his mom and dad, we walked out the back gate and headed home, telling him how proud we were.

Monday, August 6 –

A fledgling organization, Friends of Plum and Pilot Islands, is meeting this Saturday to work on formalization of their organization. Several email communications I received have taken up the topic of the old Coast Guard 40-footer sitting at the Rock Island State Park dock in Jackson Harbor. This retired patrol boat was used for a time by Kirby Foss and other Rock Island personnel to get back and forth to the state park. Now, after more than a decade of sitting untarped on a trailer, out in the open, with rainwater still in its bilges and paint peeling everywhere, it is being auctioned by the WDNR on WisconsinSurplus.com

Several of the Friends group members have this craft in their sights, thinking of the natural connection the old 40-footer might have sitting on the ways in the boat house. I agree, it would be a natural fit if you could restore it through volunteer labor. Bidding online closes Thursday, and we're told bids become more aggressive in the late minutes before closing. It's possible this boat could be snagged for a few thousand or less, in which case it might be worthwhile.

***

Rich Ellefson and I made a trip with the *Eyrarbakki* in late afternoon as the line of cars leaving the island began to build. As we loaded passengers and autos through the stern ramp, an elderly woman of 75 years of age tripped and fell as she came aboard. The rough nonskid surface of the vehicle deck scraped up her right knee, her right elbow, and her left palm as she hit the deck. Her right pinky also appeared dislocated. Her upper right arm also hurt her. I helped her to her feet and then up the stairs to the pilothouse with the intent of giving her first aid. We called the Northern Door First Responders as we left the island, and when we got to Northport the ambulance was waiting on the pier, lights flashing, to treat her abrasions and check her arm. Later, she complained of her upper arm hurting, too.

In the course of conversation I learned she had also fallen on a cruise ship about a month prior to this incident, and she still had bruises on her leg to show for it. She also told me, as we had climbed the stairs, that she had difficulty seeing out of one eye. She had been embarrassed by her fall and was briefly in tears from the trauma. By the time we arrived at Northport, she had relaxed and was able to smile.

Opportunities for such accidents are many, and yet, this was the first such trip I've been captain where someone fell and required medical care.

Tuesday, August 7 –

Quite warm today and humid. The sun was out in full force for several hours, then it clouded over, only to become suddenly clear once again. These rain clouds are only a tease. The sky looks like rain, feels like rain, but there is no rain.

I assigned myself once again to the task of rolling more asphalt sealer on the pavement near the island ticket booth. Because I was near the line of waiting traffic I fielded a number of comments from people who know me, and from those who are just visiting the island. Typical comments were these:

"I see they have everyone working."

"How goes the manual labor?"

"Look at what the boss is doing."

"Aren't you supposed to be supervising?"

"I just did my driveway. That's a lot of work!"

"Something about this picture doesn't look right."

"Hmmm. You're using a roller. I should try that."

"Good help must be hard to find."

...and so on.

What each of these sidewalk observers doesn't know is that I might appear to be bound to the roller and bucket, but it's my decision and not someone else's. It'd be different if I was on the clock and under direct orders to finish a certain section by sundown. That would be work. Instead, I can think about whatever I wish, do as much as I care to do, quit whenever I want to quit, and visit with people while I work if I choose.

For that reason, this work frees me, and I choose to continue to roll sealer on the pavement until the last ferry leaves the island. Rich Ellefson helped me with rolling for an hour in early afternoon, and ticket seller Carol Stayton swept the pavement ahead of me and brought me more buckets of sealer. I kept young Ben Gordon busy fetching cold bottles of water. In this manner, the day passed very quickly, and at day's end we had put on 10 buckets of sealer over a very rough surface.

Like any fourteen year old, Ben needs close supervision. Ben would like nothing more than to get his mitts on a roller and have the coating all over his shoes and shorts, the badge of a workman, like he did last week. I am thinking of his mother's reaction.

Looking for conversation and banter, I ask Ben this question: "Now, Ben, what is it you learn by watching me?"

"Well, I learn to ask questions. I learn how to be careful. I learn what it is to work hard and be diligent."

"Ben, you've got it!" I replied. "I was thinking of the word "patience," but you've come up with even better answers. Some people think it's the rolling on of product. It's really about personal choice. You put your mind behind the task, one small section at a time, rather than looking at the entire job as an impossibility with unhappiness as the result," I said. "Just think. On this island, maybe in this whole state, no one else is doing the same thing as we are. We're unique!"

Given time, Ben will be a great worker and helper. For the time being, with sweat soaking through my shirt, pants and underwear, I ask him to fetch me a bottle of cold water.

The wind, light and variable all day, switched dramatically to the NW.

Mary Jo and I sat on our garden bench watching billowing cumulus clouds to the south reflect the setting sun. They were full of motion, expanding as they rolled and tumbled across the sky, followed by a generous gap of blue that held the first star of the evening, likely a planet. The blue darkened, and the bats came out and began circling over my garden, catching insects, sometimes sailing close over our heads. A low cloud scudded directly overhead, crossed our property, and the winds picked up in a sort of mini-squall.

This summer when the fronts have passed through, there were seldom dark clouds, and no moisture, maybe a little wind, and very little temperature change. This evening, after the first line of low clouds passed, the sunset peeked through the trees to the west once more above the ball park across the road, and after half an hour the temperature seems as warm as ever, and the bats continued to make their circles over the garden and close over our heads.

Wednesday, August 8 –

Late in the morning Hoyt and I joined a conference call with our two legal counsels to determine if there might be alternative courses of action for the permit application to improve the south ramp at Northport Pier. WDNR, through the state legislature, creates an impossible set of rules, only vaguely addressing commercial ferry structures. We have little choice but to operate within these rules and regulations, and to make matters worse, the DNR applies their own interpretation. It's a frustrating challenge.

The notion of filing in Federal Court seems to me a strong possibility, if only to avoid the skewed system we find ourselves under with the State. Arguments for why we might not succeed are also convincing, however. Paul Kent, our Madison attorney, tosses out several ideas that include: a) a compromise offer to provide some sort of fishing opportunity at a location other than at Northport Pier that DNR can accept as fulfilling their needs; and b) an effort for legislative backing to exempt our operation and our piers from WDNR oversight.

Neither choice is a guarantee. Each requires expenditure of dollars, but so will continuation in the appeal process. Our final goal is not only to gain a permit but to have finality to a ruling, so that any future permit submittal wouldn't have onerous conditions attached.

***

Over at Island Pizza for a sub sandwich this noon, the lunch spot was a popular one. Ethan and Margie are working the windows and the oven, and selling out of subs shortly after I placed my order. Pizza slices are flying out the window, along with sodas. It is a good day for that sort of food, and the public is buying.

***

The day turned out to be one of the most pleasant in a week's time. The air is fresher, and I can tell in the look and feel of the traffic that travelers in northern Door County enjoy this day, too.

Several small runabouts are tied up to the wall in front of our office. People, dogs, and bicycles are on the grass, watching, resting, waiting for the next ferry. I've seen several islanders here, too, on bicycle, sitting in the sun and the breeze.

Thursday, August 9 –

Sunny and somewhat humid with light zephyrs in early morning.

Brought the *Washington* to Northport for two gas tankers for Hansen's Amoco. Hoyt and Eric Brodersen are with me. We followed in the wake of the *Arni J. Richter*, the scheduled 6:30 a.m. ferry from the island. We had no cars or people on board, and with an empty ship it was a good opportunity to clean on our way across.

In the pilothouse, I swept and cleaned windows and dusted off the large instrument console. Lunch crumbs and coffee stains, the by-product of spending twelve hours or more a day in a rather cozy space, and dead flies and dead spiders, are among the debris to be cleaned from the work space. There are no salmon trolling boats out this morning along our course, only the ferry ahead of us.

It used to amaze me as a quartermaster in the pilothouse of the

U.S. Naval destroyer I sailed on, out in the middle of the Pacific Ocean for days at a time, no land in sight, how dirt could accumulate daily the way it did. My work group was responsible for ship's navigation and plotting and log keeping, but also for keeping the pilothouse clean. At the close of each watch there was a call over the ship's PA system for "Sweepers, sweepers, man your brooms fore and aft...", the official Naval command to clean work spaces. Because the pilothouse always hosted a great deal of underway activity, the 4 to 8 a.m. watch keeper was expected to do the most cleaning. We would sweep a substantial pile of dirt into a dustpan each morning.

So it is on the ferries. And similar signs of human occupation on the passenger decks, like wads of gum stuck to the deck or the underside of benches, strands of human hair caught in screening that circles the deck, drink containers, occasional gobs of chew dried like an owl's pellet, greasy smudges on windows and doors, and discarded ferry schedules. The pile of dirt found accumulated under the floor mat of a ferry, some days, is enough to grow potatoes, I tell my crewmembers.

As we entered the Northport break wall from dead-calm Death's Door waters, I saw two semi trucks in addition to the two bulk gas tankers waiting for us. We pulled up to the north ramp while the *Arni J.* used the south side of the pier. Glen Wegner in his grain semi, now on his fifth round trip for island grain, is among those drivers waiting. With the recent dry spell, it's a perfect time to harvest grain while it has a low moisture. Ahead of Glen is the 70-ft. grocery semi for Mann's Store. Like clockwork, Monday and Thursday mornings in summer the grocery semi crosses to the island.

Behind these two semi trucks were our tankers. As soon as ticket seller Sami Kahlscheuer processed their tickets, we waved them on board. Grossing near 80,000 pounds each, the first truck put a significant list in the ferry. But that list evened out as the second truck rolled aboard. We raised the ramp and departed for the island as soon as the back set of duals were on deck.

Enroute to the island I kibitzed with the two truck drivers, both of whom are regulars. For many years we've ferried oil, gas and propane to the island for Ray Hansen. We get the drivers' read on what's happening in the Fox Valley, how the Packers are doing, what the price of oil does to their business. How they're often called on to fill tanks at a gas station before midnight when the price of gas is about to increase. And we talk about island fishing, the weather, and water levels.

At the island, I backed the ferry against the south ramp. There was no discernable wind or current, and the morning was picture perfect. The eight boats fishing for bass hugged the channel drop-offs, taking full advantage of ideal conditions.

With a temporary lull in ferry activity, I assumed Hoyt, Eric and I would continue our cleaning project on the *Washington*. I hooked up the portable pressure washer on the passenger deck after spraying for spiders and waiting for the creatures to crawl out from the corners. Five minutes later, spiders hung by threads, ready to be knocked down by brooms and the pressure washer.

Inside of two hours, our tankers were back at the ferry dock, and we loaded them for the return run. I hadn't completely finished my cleaning, but I intended to spend the time enroute to Northport hosing the passenger deck. While Hoyt took the ferry from the island dock, Eric and I cleaned windows and wiped down wet benches. The rest of the day this ferry will resume it's normal run, carrying people and cars.

***

I am in a mild stew, I find. I enjoy the scrubbing and hosing, but I mistakenly haven't communicated my needs and desires for cleaning clearly to my crew, especially to Hoyt. I tend to think others will see the obvious and follow my lead, cleaning and scrubbing, that is, and in this respect I'm not unlike my own father.

If this were not a father-son relationship, maybe I would be more specific and spell things out carefully step-by-step, but I assume he will see and know. There are obviously different ways of doing things, and once in a while we're at loggerheads over the best, or proper method, of completing a task. "Pulling rank" as the Company President or the Old Man doesn't always achieve my goals, either, and in fact may only add to widening the gap.

I can recall my father, stretched to the max, exhibiting body language, facial expressions, showing his frazzled state in many ways other than just coming out and saying what was on his mind. Did I expect I would act differently than my own father as I grew up, not improving on the flaws?

I'm so fortunate to have not only a great son, but a son who is also a great employee and co-manager to work with. Stubbornness creeps in, both ways, and I suspect Hoyt's silence on the matter was picked up from me, passed down from my own father's hat-slamming tirades when the shit really hit the fan. It may have been only a once-in-a-blue-moon tirade, but it wasn't pretty, or fun. As I grew older, college smart-ass age, friends and I called them "Harryisms," the outbursts we saw as amusing blemishes to a man of otherwise fine character and of considerable cognitive and intellectual powers.

So, as I pushed the sponge, squeegeed the benches and emptied trash bins aboard the *Washington*, thoughts rolled through my mind, exaggerated by lack of real communication. The day ended in routine by unloading, mooring, plugging in the shore cord and shutting down the engines for the night. We still hadn't spoken.

Late that evening, less than five hours after getting off the ferry, with one hour's sleep to my credit, Hoyt phoned me to make a special emergency medical trip. I joined him at the darkened ferry dock where the only light came from the engine room entry. We prepared the *Washington* to get underway, this time with the island ambulance on board. A step ahead of me, Hoyt had checked the engines, then went to the pilothouse and warmed up the radar. I untied all mooring lines except one as we waited for the ambulance to arrive, and then, soon afterward, I coached ambulance driver Linda Taylor as she backed onto the foredeck. Hoyt backed the ferry from the slip and swung the searchlight to highlight buoys.

In the wheelhouse it was dark and silent. Instrument gauges glowed dimly and a greenish light came from the radar. The lake and the night were equally black. Only a few lights could be seen on the horizon, dock lights in Wisconsin Bay four miles away and lights on the Northport pier. Off our starboard quarter, city lights of Escanaba loomed in the sky, thirty miles away. Fifteen minutes out, a set of bright running lights overtook us rapidly to starboard. It was the Coast Guard's boat enroute to Northport. Its lights disappeared inside the breakwater for a several minutes before reappearing, heading to open water, back to the island.

The water was glassy calm and there was no moon, but the stars were out in force. Hoyt and I began with conversation about a variety of topics, including the smasher buck seen on the island's east side. While the ambulance crew administered to an elderly island woman on the deck below, we talked about our daily lives, meetings and appointments coming up, and the motorcycle trip his mother and I planned for September. There was also precious silence, enjoying the peace of the run, the thrumming of the engines beneath us, gazing at the lights of the pier ahead as they shone brighter upon our approach.

That peacefulness and the moment of being together — even when silent — is a wonderful thing, being able to work with and alongside, and in awe of, my son. I don't tell him so often enough.

Our trip began at 11:45 p.m. on the 8th of August and ended around 1:10 a.m., early the morning of the 9th. We may have thought we were the only ones on the lake, but that, of course, wasn't the case. We overheard a radio conversation between a yacht and the *Kaye A. Barker*, a 775-ft. ore boat. And we had observed the Washington

Island Coast Guard boat make a run. And, when we moored again at the island, Daniel Nerenhausen was on the pier. He had just returned from an evening cruise, during which his outdrive quit. He had called Kevin Krueger for a tow. Other than that, Detroit Harbor was still.

After a night trip I'm restless. It's not the loss of sleep but the effort it takes to get back to sleep. The rest of my night was segmented by dreams. I dozed off, perhaps around 3 a.m., with no idea of when morning would come until the jackass over at the KKW Ostrich Farm started braying loudly. Did he having trouble sleeping, too? Hay indigestion? Sleep apnea? Or, just being an ass?

Friday, August 10 –

Mid-80s by late morning. Light breeze. Forecast is for more heat with no moisture over the weekend.

Our tourism hasn't suffered, and so we quietly welcome more of the same weather. The lake water has finally achieved a comfortable temperature for swimming, and in the afternoon lulls I can smell the sweetness from the lake, a scent carried by gentle breezes toward land.

During the early morning of August 8, a Coast Guard buoy tender arrived at our pier, having crossed during the night from their homeport at Frankfort, MI. The vessel moored at our dock near the old ferry office.

This Coast Guard Aids to Navigation crew came to Detroit Harbor to replace chain on several of the channel buoys. Nearly every winter we've seen either buoy movement or complete detachment. Chain links wear thin and so do shackles. In addition, at regular intervals of time, the buoy flotation chambers are required to be pressure-tested to ensure no leaks.

Because this crew was one man short, they weren't able to begin buoy work until a fifth qualified hand had arrived, a precaution for working deck winches and lifting the heavy buoys and mooring chain. By the time I had arrived at work this morning, their boat was underway and had pulled the red nun, #6, tested it, and were replacing chain. We appreciate their attention to these tasks because it can mean the critical difference of getting safely in or out of the Detroit Harbor channel during fog, snow or darkness.

Saturday, August 11 –

A warm and still night was followed by a sultry morning. A weather change is coming, and to our west and north rain may fall later on. The early morning sun gave way to clouds and overcast, the type of day when you expect all hell to break loose as frontal boundaries explode with squall lines and powerful thunderstorms, followed by strong NW winds as the front moves through.

However, I remain skeptical we'll see rainstorms based upon the general weather of the past few weeks and the recent weak cold fronts.

***

A public meeting to form a support group for restoration of old light keepers quarters and Coast Guard facilities on Plum and Pilot Islands was held at the Community Center. A draft of a set of by-laws along with applications for non-profit status have been prepared. A board of volunteer directors is required, along with many other volunteers, even though the official transfer hasn't yet been made from Bureau of Land Management (BLM) to Fish and Wildlife, and even when this fledgling organization hasn't yet been recognized as an official partner with U.S. Fish and Wildlife Service.

The meeting at the Community Center was attended by approximately 40 persons, mostly from Washington Island, but nearly a dozen people had traveled from the peninsula, too. Many ideas were floated and membership recruitment and dues levels were discussed.

A nagging question comes to mind with no ready answer: If the buildings and the soils pose problems with hazardous materials or contamination, and if the islands are accepted by USFWS, will the partnering organization be partly responsible for cleanup? A huge liability could befall an organization that has little to no capital, which can do work only through government grants and donations. "Are the buildings really worth saving?" was another question asked. These structures are historically important, but can they be reasonably restored? At what price? Based on initial observations by Rick Bernstein of the Wisconsin State Historical Society, these buildings appear to have uniqueness in architecture and represent fine examples of government light keeping and life saving facilities.

***

The Ferry Line pickup truck was loaded to the gills with sacks of garbage and empty blacktop sealer buckets when Mary Jo joined me for a ride to the Island Exchange, known also as a landfill or recycling center. Town attendants Jeff Stayton and John Furnner were on duty, always helpful to Mary Jo by pointing out or setting aside a relic or piece of furniture they think she'd like, rather than let it go into the dumpster. John once told me, "Mary Jo may not know this, but we've got her on speed dial."

At the most recent yard sale of her objects of art and craft, John stopped by a day early to see what she had created since he would work both days during the sale. And Jeff also came one evening, recognizing quite a few pieces as items they set aside for her weekly visit to the exchange.

I also owe Jeff and John a debt of gratitude for occasionally pointing out a piece of metal scrap, and for helping me load heavy pieces. On today's trip, Mary Jo's sharp eye spotted a heavy iron wagon wheel rim, approximately 3-feet across, hiding under jumbled scrap. Not far away, I rescued cast hubs from an old wooden wagon wheel. The axles had been wooden, but the wheel bearings were iron cones. Looking around more closely, I found four heavy, steel wheels, a matched set perfect for a sculpture piece.

All in all, we had traded in a load of garbage, plastic bottles and aluminum cans, for a wonderful selection of scrap iron pieces. And that's why it's called The Island Exchange.

Sunday, August 12 –

Our front porch roof was wet this morning, from either a very heavy dew or rain last night. As the sun came up the humidity was apparent, and I soon learned that there had been rain around 3 a.m., perhaps all of 10 minutes worth. When it reached the ground the rain must have evaporated quickly, for there were no puddles or even damp grass as telltale signs of rain.

Monday, August 13 –

Once more, sunny and pleasant. Not too warm. The thermometer shows mid-60s to start with and will hit the upper 70s, with a light, fair breeze from the south.

***

More comments from sidewalk observers today. One motorist drove over my freshly sealed surface to gain closer access to the dock and asked, "Can you tell me which ferry Jack Nehlsen's working on today?" I replied, "Do you have reverse on that thing?" With apology he backed his way out.

In the late afternoon, I had a conversation with a man who moored at our sea wall with his family aboard a 50-foot cruiser. I had noted Beaufort, S.C. on the transom, the yacht's homeport, and asked if he had cruised all the way from there. Actually, he said, Beaufort was their home, but the boat was in New Orleans when he bought it. Now, they were cruising the "Great Circle" tour, across the Gulf, up the east coast to the St. Lawrence, through the Trent-Severn waterway (through lower Canada to Lake Huron), and once they passed through the Great Lakes they would head down the Mississippi to the Tenn-Tom Waterway, taking them through the heart of the southland to Alabama and the Gulf once more. This gentleman had been employed, years ago, at Harnishfeger in Milwaukee before starting his own company. At 5 p.m. sharp, and prior to casting off his lines for points further south, he reminded me it was "Miller Time."

Tuesday, August 14 –

Sunny and warmer with an increase in humidity.

The morning clouded over occasionally, and around 10:30 a.m., while visiting with the *Washington* crew at the end of the ferry dock, I swore I felt five or six raindrops. No more than six. After twenty minutes of cloudiness, the skies cleared and the rest of the day was sunny and hot. We should not complain with our 80 degrees when many places south of the Mason-Dixon Line were recording three-digit temperatures, as high as 108 F in some locations.

Our traffic has slipped a bit this week, but just a notch. We kept our fourth ferry moored because there wasn't enough vehicle traffic to justify an extra ferry.

Late Monday afternoon Rich decided to pull aside the *Robert Noble* in order to replace the sanitary water pump. This pump is the equivalent of a pressure system in a home. It provides water from the lake for sinks, for the flushing of heads, and for the three-fourths inch garden hose used to clean the decks. This system is separate from the fire system, but the garden hose is always pressurized and can be utilized quickly and effectively if needed to douse a fire.

We had a new pump and motor in reserve, and the plan was to replace old with new. However, the motor's frame holes and the base foundation didn't match, and the new pump required different piping connections. With engine room operating temperatures near 100 degrees, even the fans won't cool down the iron very quickly, and it's a tight spot with a lack of airflow. Rich, Tully and Ken, who came from other ferries to help, worked until 8 p.m. Hot and tired, they quit for the day.

The following morning Rich tackled the problem again with fresh energy and advice from Stu Fett at Bay Shipbuilding. The pressure switch needed to be piped further away from the pump to prevent hammering, preventing the pump switch from cutting in and out frequently. While they were in the thick of the project, a complete oil change on the engines was undertaken, too.

***

While that project continued, I rolled the remainder of the parking lot next to our offices and striped the parking slots with yellow paint where they had been covered days earlier with sealer.

Where the pavement had read, "Vi's Taxi," I outlined in yellow letters: A R N I. Vi Llewellyn, island taxi tour driver for years, left us three years ago. A tree was planted not far from the spot where she had kept vigil for visitors who looked for her tour for so many years.

In more recent years, Arni Richter has enjoyed watching his ferries from the comfort of his van, the same spot where Vi had parked. Arni hasn't driven recently, a good thing, given his deteriorating eyesight. He had been using the white stripe along the shoulder, the bicycle lane stripe, to keep himself on the road. Now, Chris, his care provider, drives him out once or twice each day to watch the ferry activity and people and cars coming and going. He seemed pleased to learn his name was on a special parking spot, although I don't think he could see the lettering.

Wednesday, August 15 –

The morning is cool and overcast with darkness to the SW. In any other summer, this would be a sign of rain. The forecast is for scattered showers, but mostly to our south and west.

***

I left home on my motorcycle, headed for Sturgeon Bay to have maintenance work done prior to our road trip in September. On board the *Washington* was the Town of Washington's dump truck. As I headed south on Highway 42 for the first 25 miles of my trip, I followed the big orange dump truck with Greg Jensen, town crew foreman, driving. The dump box was piled high with mattresses cinched down with nylon straps. Greg was taking them to a recycling center. For various reasons, including bulkiness and steel springs, mattresses can't be stuffed into the compactor with other cast-off garbage. They require special treatment.

These mattresses could tell us a volume of tales if they could communicate.

We spend a third of each day prone on a stuffed slab designed to give us premium comfort. It's a good thing these mattresses don't talk about our lives: conception; sickness; death; restful peace upon good news; tears over losses and sorrow; fears of the dark, or of the day to come; the sheer pain of forcing ourselves to leave the comfort of bed some days to deal with the rest of the world.

We ferry new mattresses and box springs to the island with regularity each year, and our crew uses the euphemism "work bench" when this freight is called in to the office.

If we knew what really went on with each of the mattresses in the pile on that orange truck leaving the island, we might need to declare them hazardous materials rather than the well-used furniture of humankind they, in fact, are.

I noticed the town's dump truck had no mud flaps over the rear tandems, and rather than chancing a flying stone in the face, I blew past Greg on the stretch of Baileys Harbor swamp where the road is straight for several miles and visibility is good, flying past the A.C. Tap. The mattresses were soon in my rear view mirrors, nothing but a pile of stuffed memories floating down the highway on an orange truck.

***

I said "So long" to Matt Kahlscheuer at 6:30 p.m. as he ended his shift on the *Arni J. Richter*, his college summer now up with the Ferry Line. He's returning to St. Norbert's College in DePere and will practice with the team for the coming soccer season.

Thursday, August 16 –

Cool — only 66 degrees at 9:30 this morning. Clear skies, and a brisk NW wind in the early hours of the morning.

We had a fuel tanker on an early run for Hansen Oil, somewhat of a question with the NW winds, but it went fine. However, as a result of the brisk northerly winds, Charlie Voight elected not to run the *Island Clipper*. His decision gave our traffic, already solid because of the day's freshness, an extra boost.

No rain accompanied the cold front to NE Wisconsin. Walt Jorgenson told Bill Schutz, "This is the driest summer since 1954, the year they put in irrigation on the potato farms." Walt was in charge of the field operations for Edward Anderson. Deep wells were sunk in several locations around the island in order to bring water to the major fields. The galvanized irrigation pipe, 20-ft. lengths, 8 inches in diameter, has been kicking around the island ever since. We bought a number of lengths about 20 years ago when they became available, and sold a few lengths to individuals who used them for culverts beneath their driveways. Kap's Marina used sections of the pipe to support small finger piers.

Our traffic is robust this morning. My theory on this sort of day, more common in the fall of the year than summer, is that after a number of days that are hot and muggy, fresh and cool northerly winds invigorate people. Our crew is happier and livelier, too. The fact that the winds and seas force our ferry captains south of Plum Island is a bonus, a different point of view for passenger and crew. Our traffic numbers are good as the boats slide up to our island dock. Passengers man the rails, ready to rent bikes, visit museums, eat food, shop, drink beer...whatever it is they choose to do

Friday, August 17 –

Cool through the night. Ideal sleeping weather. Dry air and sunshine this morning, in the low 60s as I headed to work on my motorcycle, wearing an insulated sweatshirt for warmth.

Atlas and Evy had joined us for Mary Jo's oatmeal and apple pancakes. Atlas was excited over the pirate float and visited the barn, then the garden. I saw his form behind the row of cedars, bent down over the beans and carrots and peas. When called for breakfast, he came running with a fistful of baby carrots and a beet.

The wind is NW again this morning and stronger than Thursday morning. Today's forecast is for wind to blow through this afternoon. For the second day in a row, the *Island Clipper* is not running.

Approximately 15 years ago, Fridays were the weakest for day traffic. That pattern gradually changed, and as an example of the shift, these past few weeks Fridays have been among our strongest passenger days. Today appears to be another good day, aided by the lack of a competing passenger boat out of Gills Rock. The winds pose no problems for our ferries other than perhaps slowing us down each round trip as the ferry motors around the south end of Plum Island. The Northport stone wall shelters our peninsula landings. Detroit Harbor offers natural protection, perfect in northerly winds.

Saturday, August 18 –

Sunny but cool early in the morning. Clouds in the west indicate a changing weather pattern.

We awoke with one immediate goal in mind: complete the two

floats we planned to enter in the parade at noon. Mary Jo mixed an egg casserole, and as she popped that in the oven, I stepped outdoors to work on finishing touches on the pirate ship float.

***

Evy, Chad and Atlas had signed up their two dogs, Willie and Waylon, for the Fair Day Dog Show at the ballpark across the street from our home. The ballpark parking lot also happens to be the parade staging area. Floats had already begun to assemble at 11 a.m., and our pirate ship entry was among them.

Atlas was the "handler" for his German shepherd, Waylon, who was entered in the Big Dogs and Pet Tricks categories. Waylon is a handsome, purebred German Shepherd with solid proportions and sensitive eyes. He's guarded Atlas since he was an infant, keeping him within his sight, cautious of people or other dogs interfering with his space. Atlas won a blue ribbon for Best Large Dog. When Atlas talked, Waylon talked back in a soft howl, and when Atlas said, "Bang-bang, Waylon," he rolled over and played dead.

The dog show ended in less than an hour, and by that time parade participants had assembled, along with their floats. Some of the parade entries were Tyler, the island policeman in his 4x4 Explorer squad car; the island ambulance; State Representative Garey Bies and his pickup; ladies of the Red Hatters Club; the Deer Run Golf Course float (First Place Float, it would turn out); Landin's Resort; West Harbor Resort; Detroit Harbor Ladies Aid; the Ferry Line float (second place); and a number of antique cars, as well as top-down convertibles for local dignitaries. Arni Richter (96), Rusty Murray (97) and Elaine Reichenbach (90) rode together in one convertible. Riding in Bill Schutz's maroon Triumph were his daughter, Maren, and her cousin. It was Maren's 15th birthday; her cousin celebrated her birthday a few days earlier. They wore the finest of dresses, looking every bit as wholesome and beautiful as the young women in the Rose Bowl Parade, sharing the passenger seat of the sports car, waving to the crowd. A sign "Fair Angels From Heaven" — a take on the parade theme "Fairway to Heaven" — was attached to the side of the Triumph. Following them, Bob Nikolai drove his restored Model A pickup truck, one of several older vehicles he's collected and restored. Other entries lined up behind these, ready to head south on Main Road.

When I arrived at the ballpark at 11 a.m., a car towing a trailer with a canoe strapped to it circled. It was the Landin family resort float, and sitting on the car's passenger side was Sylvia Landin, 99 1/2 years old. I helped the island's oldest citizen out of her car and into the canoe propped on a trailer, where she would reign as centerpiece of this float. Assisting me was State Representative Garey Bies. Together, gingerly, we each held an arm and provided support. I placed her foot in a strategic location so that she could make the difficult step from ground to trailer to canoe. "Mom has her own way of doing it. She's practiced at home," said Joan, one of two daughters accompanying Sylvia that morning. A kitchen step stool helped Sylvia to the top of the trailer fender. Then, pivoting slightly to her left, she swung one leg over the wooden trailer rack and canoe rail to a cement block, and from there she put one foot in the canoe. It required dexterity and balance, and at one point Sylvia kneeled on the hard, narrow rail of the canoe's gunnel. I winced, imagining the pressure that placed on her knee cap. With one foot in the canoe's center, she swung her other leg inboard and sat down, landing on the soft hassock cushion placed amidships. We breathed easier when Sylvia sat calmly in her canoe. Did she know there was still an hour's wait before the parade began? "I'm just fine here," Sylvia said. What's one hour's wait when you've lived so many of them?

Herb Gibson, Marty Bulmahn, Steve Beekman and I marched behind our island's squad car carrying the Colors, the Post flag and two rifles. On our heels were bagpipers Bob and his son Mike Gillespie and Emmett Woods. Drummers Fritz Damler and Jens Hansen kept the beat for all marchers with a snare and bass drum.

From my location, I caught a glimpse of two-year-old Aidan in our front yard with his mother. He refused to get in the little Viking ship and instead wanted to join his cousin Atlas and older kids in the pirate float. And that's where he rode during the parade I found out later.

The many and varied parade entries filed southward, beginning their 10-minute procession down Main Road, past the crowd of perhaps four or five hundred, before turning in at the south school entrance.

By three o'clock that afternoon, most of the crowd except for bingo players had dispersed. The fair was over for another year. The Ferry Line had taken second place with our pirate ship, crewed by Ferry Line grandchildren: Atlas; Aidan; Caitlin (Kim Hansen's granddaughter); Andie Rose (Bill and Carol Crance's granddaughter); and Carson (Carol Stayton's granddaughter). They had done well to stay inside the float during the ride while tossing pirate "loot" to the crowd as little pirates.

***

Summer has passed quickly. Dryness combined with the normal seasonal changes makes wood and field appear ready for fall. Cooler air is now commonplace. It's doubtful we'll see temperatures hovering again in the upper 80s. Hurricanes are forming in the Caribbean, and their impact is beginning to affect our Wisconsin and Midwest weather patterns, too. Flooding is forecast for Minnesota and southern Wisconsin.

On the island, families who've vacationed here for long stretches are beginning to pack their cars for home, preparing for the start of another school year. Tourism businesses lose help from their young workers as a result. Matching the reduction in visitors, Sunday will be our last day of the busy 30-minute summer departure intervals.

With the mass exodus and reduced numbers of day visitors, the pace of island activity will drop, too. We'll begin to see a more relaxed group of older visitors.

Small, puffy, cumulus clouds float overhead set against a strong blue sky, harbingers of fall.

Sunday, August 19 –

The day began with heavy overcast and cool temperatures. The pavement in our drive is dry, and my garden is dusty. I'll have to hand-water to keep the vegetable plants alive. It's a cool enough day for jeans and a long-sleeve sweatshirt.

While visiting in the backyard in the early afternoon we saw and heard a twin engine plane flying overhead, headed south. It was the "bread plane," as Hoyt and Aidan have come to refer to it, the transportation to and from the island each weekend for Brian Vandewalle. He and his marketing and consulting firm in Madison are the quiet forces behind the island's wood-fired, oven baked bread using island grown wheat, and the idea of utilizing excess quantities of that wheat to brew beer and create Death's Door Gin and Death's Door Vodka ... all ideas flowing from the same creative fount. Wood-fired, oven-baked bread made from ground island wheat is then flown to Susan Vandewalle's store in downtown Madison, under the umbrella of Washington Island Brands, LLC, where much of the bread is spoken for prior to its arrival.

This I can say: while it is more expensive per loaf, the bread made by the bakers at the Washington Hotel is hearty, excellent tasting, and it doesn't get stale quickly the way most store loaves will.

Monday, August 20 –

We awoke to heavy overcast once more and news of flooding and mudslides in southwestern Wisconsin, and the worst flooding in Minnesota since the late 1970s, according to the weatherman. There are, surprisingly, a few puddles in our driveway, but when I stepped outdoors, the ground beneath our cedars was still dusty.

I helped Mary Jo load several items, including two chairs, a small dresser and glassware into the back of our pickup truck, a reversal of her normal routine, hauling items from our barn rather than to our barn. We drove to the Twice Around Shop, an island resale shop housed in a building operated by the Detroit Harbor Ladies'Aid Society. A society of women owns the wood frame building, formerly the Evergreen Resort. A bronze plaque mounted on the wall near the front entry memorializes Anna Wickman, Society founder. Charter members included Mary Jo's grandmother, Maggie Richter, and Millie Engelson, among others. (Millie's son, Louie, was famed for explaining at length to inquiring tourists how to get to a location on the island. After detailed instructions, he started over, finally saying in exasperation, "Aw shucks. You can't get there from here.")

It is a small building with a pleasing wrap-around front porch, unchanged in perhaps 100 years, set back from the road and partially hidden to motorists by the grouping of trees on either side of the lawn. We stopped and I opened the back gate of my pickup truck. The porch was filled to overflowing, stacked high with items either recently dropped off or in storage for the next sale. If someone had wished to "pre-shop" these items, they could have easily done so. Proceeds from the sale of these cast-off and pre-owned items is used for worthy, local causes. (One rule, Mary Jo said, is that they do not accept clothing.)

We walked around to the south side of the house and set our items among the collection of treasures. A pair of white, women's figure skates hung from a nail on the porch column. A tattered, original 1950's box with an unassembled plastic model of the lightship Nantucket, still waiting to be put together. A variety of fishing poles, some from cane bamboo. A canvas tent. Folding chairs and kitchen chairs. Garden tools, paperbacks, and so on.

Mary Jo remembered that when she grew up, this building housed the island library, long before the Community Center and the current island library were built. I imagined the stuffiness of this old place, the mustiness of old paper, books shelved in rooms not often opened. Upstairs, Mary Jo told me, there is a room with historical items. Historical? How? It would be a good place for me to stop one day, a place quite strangely I've never been closer than today in all of my 33 years of living on the island. There would be interesting stories from the ladies who make this project the object of their energies. It is open May through October. The ladies do take the winters off.

During one of my early years with the Ferry Line, Mrs. Ruth Gislason stopped in mid-November at the Ferry Line office as she prepared to leave the island for the winter. She and her husband, Lawrence, had operated the general store in Jensenville, near the Washington Hotel.

Arni had worked for the Gislasons as a young boy, delivering ice blocks and groceries to homes by horse and buggy. Son Gene Gislason became a well-known island figure for his heroic role operating a landing craft at Normandy Beach in WWII. Gene continued his career in the Coast Guard, rising to the rank of Captain. He was a completely unassuming man, highly respected by all who knew him and served with him. Ruth, his mother, was a dear woman, equally understated and quiet as her son in her mannerisms. She left with me the Detroit Harbor Ladies' Aid Society "Treasurer's Book," intended for someone to pick up later. The following March we visited Ruth who was then a resident of Scand in Sister Bay, where she passed away before spring came.

The Gislasons were good friends of Arni's parents. Mary Jo and I remembered Ruth because she gave us a pair of hand-embroidered pillow cases as a wedding gift, products of skilled hands during winter's long evenings.

***

The *Arni J. Richter* was sidelined this morning long enough for Rich to change the main engine fuel filters on the Racor filtering system. Each ferry has a set of Racor (trademarked brand) filters, primary filters for fuel oil that flows from the ship's storage tank to engine room. The bowls are of clear, tough plastic, so that with quick inspection one can determine if the fuel is dirty, sludgy, and so on. Since the diesel we purchase is dyed red, meaning not used for highway transportation and therefore not subject to the federal highway fuel tax, it's not always easy to tell if the removable filter strainer is plugged or not. We've installed sensitive vacuum gauges downline from each set of Racors. Normally, zero to three pounds of vacuum are tolerable. When the needle moves toward five pounds of vacuum its time to switch the flow from one canister to the other. Then, later in the day or when time allows, the dirty filter can be replaced with a brand new one, about a 10-minute job best done when the boat is in calm waters. The job is even easier when the main engines are shut down with no danger of introducing air or otherwise interrupting the flow of fuel to the engines. Each main engine and generator pulls fuel through independent Racor filter sets. If the increased vacuum reading is ignored or unnoticed, the next telltale sign is a fluctuation in RPMs, and ultimately starvation of the cylinders for fuel, and loss of power. Since we installed our first Racor sets years ago, our tanks have cleaned up considerably. That dirty, sludgy fuel from the bottom of fuel tanks stirred up on a rough day when fuel in the tank is 20 percent or less in volume, is sucked through the fuel inlet piping. Each engine manufacturer will include a fine micromesh filter on their engines for final filtering before the fuel pump boosts fuel pressure to the injectors. But by then, if it's dirty fuel that's flowing, it's often too late, and the engine can starve itself. Racor filters have macro filtering capability for the larger solids.

Isn't fuel pure and clean as it comes off the truck? Diesel fuel, as it happens, supports a type of fungal growth that lives in the fuel but requires moisture, too. And if it has both, it grows easily, and soon the bottom of the tank has a black, snot-like substance. It will not go away on its own, and actually increases and worsens, so that filtering elements may require change out every few days' running time.

All of this is a long explanation of why it's important to monitor and to change fuel filters frequently. We also used this opportunity today to do some cleaning of the upper decks, pressure washing and hosing down. Later, we made several extra ferry trips to accommodate the rather heavy amount of traffic leaving the island.

Tuesday, August 21 –

It's cool and overcast with breezes off the lake. Traffic slowed down again today. We were busy hauling outbound traffic.

As I watered my garden this morning, I noticed frequent-trucker Al Hiller roll past our house pulling the green tandem Veolia trailers. Al always pulls two boxes at once for greater efficiency. One is light, mostly plastic bottles and glass bottles and tin cans. They're run through a separating process at the Brown County recycling center. The heavy, compacted "wet" garbage, basically everything that cannot be recycled, goes to a landfill, also located in Brown County. For its recycling efforts the town gets a check for plastics, glass and metal. It's a small amount, but it helps to offset costs of operating the town's recycling operation. Ferry transportation charges plus the cost of containers are significant over the year, but burying trash on the island, or burning and then burying trash, an accepted method until the early 1990s, is no longer permitted.

In terms of an enjoyable visit, it was great fun in the "olden days" to visit the island dump, even if it was highly unorganized. This part of town satisfied many individuals looking for old car parts, or those who craved target practice (at cans, bottles, rats and, possibly, seagulls). It was open 24 hours a day. Now, under town management, there are set hours, set procedures, and the place is as neat as a pin. John and Jeff, town landfill attendants, guide residents to the proper receptacles with their trash bags.

North of the dumpster boxes is the metal scrap heap. Quite frequently old timers Vic Cornell, or Warren Jaeger accompanied by Mrs. Jaeger, are found there inspecting items recently pitched into the pile. Vic stopped to show me his recent projects just the other day at the ferry dock. He opened the door to his pickup truck and proudly displayed several aluminum folding chairs restrung with plastic webbing. A continuing hobby of Vic's has been the restoration of these classic lawn chairs of the last century. Vic buys the webbing in large rolls, then re-weaves the backs and seats, fastening loop ends with a screw and washer.

Above all, Vic loves to keep busy with projects, and if you give him an idea, like say, an ice shanty, why he's off and running, hunting for parts and pieces at the landfill or stump dump to build with. In his upper eighties, Vic's workshop is filled with tools and treasures that keep him busy whenever he's inspired to make something useful from nothing.

***

Our crews fueled the two larger ferries this morning at Northport by splitting a tanker load (7500 gal.) between the *Washington* (3000 gal.) and *Arni J. Richter* (4500 gal.). This fueling, with our ferry schedules now reduced, ought to last into the latter part of September. Quoted price per gallon from Semfuel from the Green Bay terminal was $2.30 gal. The product is an "ultra low sulfur" fuel, something that has been rather new in the past few months. Prior to that, we fueled with low sulfur, and before that, plain old No. 2, which is heating oil. Ultra low at one time was hard to find and more expensive, but that picture has changed. It's now harder to find low sulfur.

What's the difference? The ultra low sulfur fuel (30 ppm or less) supposedly creates more power in the cylinder. The sulfur content, however, has a lubricity factor that engine manufacturers in the past seemed to prefer. (One reason why the manufacturers are slow to recommend ethanol products.) I suspect the entire low sulfur to ultra sulfur transition has more to do with EPA clean air limits, with fewer objectionable pollutants in the exhaust emissions.

Wednesday, August 22 –

On board the *Arni J. Richter* I met Greg Thiede who squeezed his small pickup through the narrow stern opening, inches away from a bass boat and a SUV from Tennessee. Greg is the Assistant Door County Sanitarian and his work often brings him to the island for field inspections, to examine new and old waste system installations. I asked Greg a few questions about our own proposed project to enlarge the Island Pizza kitchen. Afterward, Greg talked about his hectic summer as Acting Sanitarian.

First, there was the discovery of a "bug" in the water at the new restaurant, the Log Den, making a number of customers ill. An investigation into the Log Den's well and septic system, both new, showed no initial, localized sources of the problem contamination. Greg's field search spread to the surrounding 33 in-ground sanitary systems within a mile or so of the Log Den Restaurant. Results turned up eight or nine failing systems, and these are now under enforcement orders to update with new, approved systems within one year.

With open limestone strata underlying the entire region, so far there appears no way to point to an exact source of contamination. The Log Den now has the cleanest water around thanks to a brand new $80,000 filtration system, but the owner still faces legal challenges.

Then, Greg hauled out a folder with plastic photo pages. He pointed to at least three examples of steel tanks that he's witnessed after extraction, septic systems or holding tanks from various County locations. One had holes like Swiss cheese in the bottom half. Another had most of its bottom half missing altogether, large enough, according to Greg, "for a bear to crawl inside." It was a dramatic tank exhibit, a tank that had been in-ground approximately 24 years. Other tanks, according to Greg, buried less than 20 years or even less than 15 years, have also had holes rusted through. He said, "Steel tanks can still be used, but we don't recommend them. Concrete tanks are much better and will last a long, long time. Plastic also can be used in most instances."

The rub comes when owners resist the extra cost a new tank brings to an old system. "Why should I put in a new tank when the old one's working fine?" is a question asked. Greg said it's impossible to tell what the condition of the steel tank is until after it's dug up. Once in awhile these steel tanks are still OK, but it's only a matter of time before they will fail.

***

The topic of roundabouts on the evening news, circular intersections that rely on safely merging traffic, brought to mind Mary Jo's uncle, Herman Leasum. Herman was a fine gentleman and our corporate lawyer for many years, also serving as Sturgeon Bay's City Attorney in the '50s, when Stanley Green was mayor. Each had planned to attend a meeting for city officials at the State Capitol, but Herman didn't fancy spending the better part of two days with Stanley in the same car. As a result each man drove his own vehicle, Herman in his large Buick, Stanley in his VW Beetle. As it turned out, while circling the State Capital and the confusing network of roads branching to and from the square, essentially a sprawling roundabout, each was in an accident. That is, Stanley and Herman ran into each other. They got out of their respective cars to confront one another. Stanley was a serious intellectual who wasn't given to much outward humor. Herman was not happy with the situation.

"See," Herman laughed as he recounted his conversation with Stanley, "we drove all this way just to have a damn accident with each other."

Roundabouts seem curious novelties, but not solutions to traffic problems. Soon, if recent news stories are correct, we may have several in Sturgeon Bay to practice on.

Friday, August 24 –

Local meteorologists tell us we had three-tenths of an inch of rain last night. It fell during the early part of the evening, softly, leaving puddles in our drive. Meanwhile, Milwaukee and Chicago had downed trees and flooding.

Our day is overcast, but there's traffic, in what appears to be a weekend build up. The wind is light to nothing at all.

***

Five Canada geese are browsing and lounging on the lawn between my office and the service dock. I would guess it's one adult and four young geese of several months. Early each morning recently they've walked the dock, leaving long, greenish calling cards on the grass and our cement walks. It would be easy to think German shepherds had emptied their bowels, such is the volume, and it diminishes love and admiration for these birds to know they claim our property for their brood.

A few years ago, we counted several dozen geese, numerous adults and their goslings, feeding on the grassy Ferry Line lawn. I would attribute today's lower geese numbers to aggressive swans who reputedly keep other water birds away from their nesting areas.

Saturday, August 25 –

Cool at 62 degrees early this morning. A bit overcast to start with, but by 10 a.m. the skies cleared and the air is much drier, not a cloud in the sky.

On the Hansen Standard Oil dock there are perhaps 15 or more fishermen casting lines, trying to entice smallmouth bass. In the channel opposite the ferry dock several boats are anchored, pursuing the same activity. Other fishermen, especially in the mobile bass boats, head out the channel where they can increase their range of bass territory, trolling the shallows along Detroit Island or Plum Island.

***

Tire marks on our crispy, brown lawn made by customers who parked for Mary Jo's sale in the early days of this month are slowly disappearing after Thursday night's rain. Although it was only a trace, three-tenths of an inch, it helped. There's a slight chance for more rain Monday evening into Tuesday.

***

After manually backing away from the slip and getting squared away with a shove of the boat hook — Chad has the routine down pretty well now — we pointed the *Moby Dick* toward the open water and I hit the starter switch key and the motor took off in forward.

We motored to the East Channel. Atlas was excited and fiddled with all of the fishing gear. He loves to tie ropes too, and by the time we reached our fishing spot and were ready to drop anchor, he had looped and laced the ends of lines through the benches and seats and back around themselves. "Throw the anchor here, Papa," he commanded. "Let's fish!" And we did.

We couldn't get our lines in the water fast enough. By the time our worms hit the water the overcast had come and with it the winds shifted slightly to the NW and the air cooled down. Atlas had on a long-sleever, but Chad and I wore shorts and tee shirts. Then, almost as quickly as it sprang up, the breeze settled, the low clouds passed, and the sun came out brightly once more, and it felt warm again.

Little changed on the underwater end of our lines, however.

My line got caught up in weeds and broke after several casts, and I realized then how weak the line had become over time. It was old, and it had been out in the elements, hot sun especially, for several summers, now. The monofilament had lost all its strength. I pulled out several arm lengths of line from my reel to get at fresh line.

After fishing an hour anchored in the East Channel, the Shipyard Marina half a mile to our NE and Rabbit Point half a mile to our west, we decided to move. The East Channel is known for great bass fishing, and many times when we motored through the shallows there we've spotted large, dark shapes of black bass swimming in the current. But today, I was the only one to have caught a fish, a seven-inch perch that I placed in a bucket of water. Atlas described it as being, "So beautiful," and it was. I think he watches lots of fishing shows on television where every movement brings exclamations of beauty and tremendous fishing accomplishment, all presented to the viewers in hushed, ecstatic tones.

With the action slow, other than the single perch in the bucket which Atlas now had pegged for his aquarium to join his tropical fish Applesauce and Pagoda, we pulled up the two anchors. "I know," Atlas said. "Let's try the bass hole where we caught fish before." He pointed to the spot nearer to Detroit Island, inside Pedersen's Bay. We pivoted on one anchor line in the wind, and pointed west. Then I turned the key switch and we moved ahead. We passed a fishing boat with Butch Young and Matt Foss, who had arrived in the channel a short time ago and were casting about for bass. Atlas kept close watch on the single perch in the bucket as we worked our way into Pedersen's Bay.

Ahead of us two sailboats were moored. One had a large dog on deck, and it kept watch over us as we passed close aboard. A red Lund from Kap's Marina with two men in it were anchored nearby, their fishing lines down in the water. One man nibbled a sandwich as he fished. We waved, but without response. We suspected neither man was excited about having us invade their fishing space. "Wait until Atlas begins talking," I thought. "He'll keep things interesting." We motored until we were just beyond the Lund and cast out the bow and stern anchors over a clear, sandy spot where the thick seaweed wouldn't foul the flukes and cause us to drag.

Here the depth was shallower than our spot in the East Channel, and the seaweed formed a thick mat. If we caught anything here, it would most likely be a goby or a small perch. Our lines were still baited, and it was only seconds before the night crawlers were wet again.

The two men in the Lund were quiet, and I didn't notice their poles move in thirty minutes' time. We had Atlas to entertain us, and he was in constant motion, fishing being only one of his pursuits. He checked on the lone perch every few minutes, dipping it in the net, then back in the bucket. He picked out new lures from the tackle box, based on color and general interest, and asked his dad to tie them to his line.

Finally, after nearly two hours out on the *Moby Dick*, and with the sun shining brightly once again, Chad and I talked about heading in. Our discussion centered on, what to do with the perch? Let the fish go or take it home and fix it for supper? Atlas wanted it for his fish tank.

"Atlas, we either throw it back, or we take it home to eat. He's too big for your fish tank. Besides, he might eat the other fish," Chad said.

"No, he won't. Fish don't do that," Atlas replied.

'Oh, yes they do," Chad responded, and he began to reel in the fishing lines, including Atlas's line with a bobber, while Atlas fiddled with anchor lines in the bow. Atlas's bobber, we thought, was hooked on a mass of floating sea weed, but beneath the gob of weeds was a perch. It was a keeper, from all appearances, larger than the one already in the bucket.

"Come here, Atlas. Wind up your fishing line."

Atlas came from the bow and cranked the reel, and as the line came in he saw the fish on the hook. Excitement started up all over again with two fish now in the bucket. It didn't matter much that the second one floated on its side.

We decided then it would be a good opportunity to show Atlas how to clean a fish. So with Atlas bent over the pail examining the two perch, we left the red Lund and the two men fishing in peace and sunshine.

At home, Atlas watched intently as I scaled each perch with the edge of a sharp knife and then cleaned them. One thing about lake perch, or yellow perch, is that they are a good-looking fish, they're quite easy to clean, and as fish go, not as messy, bloody, or stinky as some fish. It was a clinical operation, and Atlas flinched only when he saw a bit of blood on my fingers. I explained the cleaning process and pointed out contents of the entrails. I located the stomach of one fish and cut it open, and a tiny crayfish popped out, pinchers and all, less than an inch and a half long. Atlas was intrigued. Then I rinsed off the two perch and Atlas carried them in to his Gramma, ready with a pan and butter for the stove top.

All of this reminded me of my 12th birthday when my Dad gave me a new fishing pole, and later we went fishing for perch. We sailed our 18-foot boat down the bay, tacking toward the Sturgeon Bay Ship Canal where we anchored in the wide opening of Big Creek among the tall reeds. In a few hours' time we caught 18 perch of various sizes and tossed the smallest ones back. In the 1950s and early '60s, if you didn't get a dozen perch in an outing, enough for a meal or two, it wasn't worth your time. Neighbors returned from fishing with 50 or 60 perch in a bucket, many of them 10 inches long.

Dad and I sailed back home with our fish on a stringer in the bilge of the sailboat, and we cleaned and ate them for supper. Enough were left over for another meal.

I had wondered if the cleaning process would be a turn-off to Atlas, with the one fish still swimming about happily in the bucket when we arrived home. But here we were at the dinner table within the hour, ready to eat our catch fresh from the lake. I pulled a strip of bones neatly from his fish and held up the classic fish skeleton, minus meat, and then did the same to the perch on my own plate.

"Wait a minute! This isn't my fish. You have my fish." The string of bones from my plate was slightly longer than his, Atlas had observed. Chad quickly changed the subject, and we continued to eat, and each of us sampled the fish, remarking how good it was. The rest of our meal consisted of breaded chicken strips and canned beans. Atlas' eyelids were heavy as we finished supper. Bedtime for the little fisherman was at hand.

Sunday, August 26 –

It was a still night with a nearly full moon. I awoke a time or two in the early part of evening and heard music floating across the still air, over fields and down Main Road from the nightlife in town. A reggae band was at Nelsen's Bitters Club, and another group played at Koyen's. The jack-ass at the Ostrich Farm brayed, perturbed, maybe, by the music and the moonlight.

Monday, August 28 –

At home in the evening, we ate salmon I caught on the fishing trip with Bill Sunday evening.

Bill Crance is a meticulous man who keeps everything just so, in its place, working properly and accounted for. His demeanor is perfectly suited for salmon fishing where being careful, precise, and consistent in your actions pays off. From the vinyl to the teak engine hatch, to the board across the transom with electric downrigger gear, to the handy, homemade tackle box with dozens of lures, Bill keeps everything neat and in working order.

We discussed the wind and wind direction while making the boat ready for getting underway. We decided we'd try under the bluffs of the peninsula first. We bounced across the Door in four foot seas, following the track of a ferry half a mile ahead of us, gaining on it as we also gained on the mainland. Bill dropped in the heavy downrigger weights and set up two poles with large flashers and flies. The pole on the right, said Bill, would be the most successful with its green colored fly and red and silver flasher. The downrigger balls dropped to 80 feet and we settled in, moving with the wind and the two-foot chop under the lee of the headland. An hour passed, and we had a few marks on Bill's graph but no releases. The wind seemed to have settled down, and after a fashion Bill suggested we move to the west side of the island. We pulled up lines and motored back across the Door, this time with wind and seas on our stern quarter.

We arrived off Little Islands south of West Harbor, and upon approaching the 120-foot mark on the graph, we slowed down. Bill again set up the same two poles and same lures, and we began a slow, meandering track toward Denny's Bluff. There were just two other boats on the horizon, and they disappeared around the point of land after awhile. It had been two hours without a bite. We had neared our mental point of giving up. I turned the boat slowly around with downriggers in tow and we headed back toward our starting point, bouncing along in the three-to-four foot slop off Denny's. There were occasional marks of fish on the graph but none went for the bait. Then, just as we were about to resign ourselves to being skunked, the port rod bent deep and then went limp, a solid sign a fish had struck.

I grabbed the pole and for the next fifteen minutes worked to bring in the salmon. The fish immediately stripped yards of line as it dove. I hadn't seen such a stubborn or energetic fish in any of the times I'd been out with Bill. We anticipated a large fish and we weren't disappointed. The long and difficult time I had reeling it in was apparent, though, when we got it in the boat. The hook had caught the fish in the belly fin just behind its head, creating resistance as I tried to reel the salmon in sideways. The fish fought right to the last, when Bill netted it and dropped it into the cooler. The salmon was nearly as long as Bill's cooler, close to three feet long. In a year when fish seemed to run small, this fish would have scored nicely during the salmon tournament.

We cleaned the single salmon in my backyard by moonlight and by the lights of our pump house. It had great silvery color, a female full of eggs, eggs that might be laid, but given the history of salmon in Lake Michigan, they would not hatch. These fish are not native fish, but "exotics" of a sort, purposely planted by the Wisconsin and Michigan DNR for sports fishing. Salmon seem to have less to eat these days, maybe fewer alewives, the once prolific small baitfish salmon were planted to keep in balance.

Monday evening, I prepared hot oil and we deep-fried the salmon, cut into small chunks from one of the fillets. The remainder will be smoked by Tully Ellefson.

Tuesday, August 28 –

We had two good downpours this morning, one at 4 a.m., the other at 7:45 a.m. Each was a solid shower of 15 minutes or more accompanied by thunder and lightning.

***

I downloaded and printed out 63 pages of Coast Guard Navigation and Vessel Inspection Circular (NVIC) 03-07. The subject of the NVIC is Implementation of the Transportation Worker Identification Credential (TWIC) for the maritime sector. It took a fair amount of time, and a fresh stack of paper in the tray to complete the printing run. Now, to digest what it says. Supposedly this was written in a mariner / user-friendly manner, with plainly written explanations of how this new credential is supposed to work, who must have one, and so on. There is nothing simple any more about maritime employment. Congress, through Homeland Security, and now the Coast Guard within Homeland Security, will help ensure our ports and our country is safe from terrorism, thanks to biometric cards.

I have my reading material for the evening.

Wednesday, August 29 –

While aboard the *Carol Ann*, salmon fishing with Bill, he told me when he drove in our yard to confirm our appointment for fishing, Carol, his craft's namesake, asked, "What is that supposed to be?" She referred to the wheel hoops, chain and small flywheel sculpture on the south side of our yard. Bill replied, "Oh, that. Dick gets these ideas and ..." Then, on the way back out, Carol noticed another sculpture, painted in bright colors, the vertical plow discs. "What's that supposed to be, a bird feeder?"

Comments on my sculpture, even though they have no apparent

likeness to anything, and no apparent purpose other than form, are always welcomed.

Thursday, August 30 –

Sunny and warm. No clouds.

Hoyt brought his little pontoon boat, the *"Play Pen"* to the ferry dock to take soundings. He and Rich are out in front of the Ferry Office with a pole, measuring depths. The water is so clear, unlike 10 years ago, that large rocks and imperfections can be seen from the surface.

When traffic built up at Northport, increased by a few large trucks, Rich left with Ken Berggren on an extra trip with the *Arni J. Richter*. Hoyt came to the office to get me, and we motored over to the Potato Dock to examine water depths there.

Oddly, Hoyt noticed a squirrel scramble out of one of many large tires that hang along the steel sheeting as fenders, and it climbed up the short piece of chain to the top of the dock. Seconds later, further down the dock, I saw another squirrel, and climbing out from under the rocks piled off the pier's end was a third squirrel. Although the pier is over 500 feet long and nearly 100 feet wide at the outer end with lots of weeds, seeds, and even small trees, it would be more in keeping to find seagulls or great blue herons there.

Hoyt and I wondered if this was the grouping for a lemming-like movement that would call adult gray squirrels to sea? We wondered if squirrels near the water were peculiar to Washington Island, and if so, was it a result of too many squirrels? When Hoyt was in high school, he and a friend witnessed squirrels swimming in Detroit Harbor. Two squirrels had clung to bleach bottle buoys set out near a channel and were bobbing in the breeze.

The late Jay Hagen, I recalled, told the pilothouse audience one day about fishing in a small boat off the west side as he noticed squirrels swimming out toward him. The fishermen were soon swinging their oars to discourage the grey squirrels from clinging to and climbing up the sides of their boat. Jay was a great storyteller, but this one, he swore, was true.

On our return from the Potato Dock inspection, Hoyt took the end of Kap's Marina dock close aboard. Scampering over the rocks was a gray squirrel, and in the weeds nearby, yet another. If there is no natural predator other than, perhaps, hawks or other large birds, could this be a sign of natural selection, or simply a preference by squirrels to be near a water source in a dry summer?

Friday, August 31 –

The last day of the eighth month of the year began with bright sunshine, no clouds, with a temperature of 58 degrees at daybreak.

The forecast is a good one, and by 9 a.m. our ferries, the two regularly scheduled ferries plus a third, were filling up at Northport within a twenty-minute span. This pattern should continue throughout the day, building in late afternoon or early evening.

Our second shift crews will continue to make trips at least until 10:15 p.m., later if there are still cars in line. Traffic today and for much of tomorrow will be largely one-way, incoming. Sunday will be the big day for two-way passenger traffic, and Monday, Labor Day, will be a busy day outgoing as people and vehicles exit the island and head back home.

The numbers of people this weekend, quite obviously, include the many who consider this their last real chance to enjoy summer water activities and the island. Whether or not they have children in school, the patterns of life change in the fall, and football, among other things, demands greater amounts of attention.

***

Tomorrow will be the funeral of Arne Orman, nephew of Arni Richter. Arne was here in June to assist brother Erik in the burial of their brother Carl's ashes. Arne had helped prepare Carl's burial plot, and the two brothers poured Carl's ashes into the hole. Now Erik is the only surviving brother. It is a particularly difficult situation for family members to ponder what might have been if life choices had only been different. Alcohol had become a crutch for them both. Arne leaves behind Robyn, his wife, two daughters, and several grandchildren.

SEPTEMBER

Saturday, September 1 –

A light cloud cover greeted us this morning. The sun poked through openings in the eastern sky for a time, then disappeared again. Temperatures rose into the mid-70s by 9 a.m., accompanied by more humidity than expected.

Ferries ran late last night making additional trips, but no more trips than anticipated. The last couple of ferries waited to get their loads.

This morning, however, the first ferry from Northport landed with a full load carrying the typical mix of holiday traffic: pickups pulling jet skis and boat trailers, motorcycles, campers, bicycles and passenger cars.

***

Mary Jo and I gathered with approximately 30 others at the island cemetery at 1 p.m. for the interment of Arne Orman. As we gathered and greeted one another near the grave under the shade of pine trees and offered our condolences, Pastor Frank Maxwell in helmet rolled down Schoolhouse Beach Road on his scooter, a drive that bisects the old cemetery from the new. He parked his green Vespa in the shade beside parked cars, then crossed the road and greeted everyone and passed out the funeral programs. He encouraged us to gather close by the gravesite, and after a glance at his watch he began with a prayer, followed by an opportunity for anyone who wished to speak in remembrance of Arne.

Hannes Andersen, in his early 90s, raised his hand. He spoke with wispy voice of his many visits with Arne, including a visit several months ago that followed the funeral of Carl, Arne's younger brother. Through their visits Hannes said he had been made aware of Arne's knowledge of island people and love of the island. At one point in conversation, Hannes had confided with Arne that if God wished to take him, well then, he was ready. Arne replied, he believed the same.

Pastor Frank continued with the order of service, and soon it was Erik's turn as the surviving brother to pour Arne's ashes into a 12- x 12- x 12-inch hole adjacent to Carl's ashes, just three feet from their mother's, Evelyn Richter Orman's, headstone.

The funeral was over in a matter of minutes, and as family members often do at such occasions, especially when they've not seen each other for a time, we visited over the graves and the bit of freshly dug earth and remembered Arne.

Through the service Arni Richter, uncle to the Orman boys, sat in a folding lawn chair not far from the grave, but once the ashes were placed in the ground and the burial service ended, he was helped back to Chris's car at the edge of the gravel drive. Then, as Chris drove her car forward her front bumper struck a low granite headstone. The heavy stone tipped over on its backside and slipped partway under the fender and dragged several feet along the grass. This commotion caught everyone's attention. Tom, one of the cousins of the Leasum family, helped me tip the stone upright, working it back onto its concrete base. Only scrape marks on the ruffled sod were left behind. Tom remarked, "I think this person would be thankful for all the attention. Finally something happened here."

***

Hoyt, who captained one of the ferries that day and could not attend the funeral, later told his mother he dreamed about the funeral the previous night.

In his dream, Hoyt stood at the cemetery with many others, gazing at the hole in the ground dug to receive Arne's ashes. Carl, who preceded Arne in death by slightly more than three months, stood alongside Hoyt and said, "It's getting kind of crowded here." On Hoyt's other side stood Arne, dressed in his best, three-piece dark suit, the same suit he wore to Carl's funeral in May. Hoyt turned to Carl and asked, "Do you mean all of these people who came to the funeral?" Looking toward the ground, Carl repeated, "No, I mean it's getting crowded here."

Hoyt told Mary Jo he awoke from his dream smiling, because that comment was exactly the sort of humorous remark that Carl, or Arne for that matter, would have made on such an occasion.

Sunday, Sept. 2 –

Another warm and sunny day, and breezy. The weather is the finest with blue skies and light, scattered stratus on high.

There's a chop on the harbor and several sailboats are moored tight to the ferry dock, their crews discussing plans for the day over coffee in their cockpits. Traditionally, this day is always our busiest of the holiday weekend, and all signs point toward this becoming such a day.

Everyone I've met is in an exceptionally good mood: our office staff because there is lots of traffic and things are going smoothly at each dock; our ferry crews because conditions are excellent both for good business and safe ferry transportation; and our customers, pleased to be here on the island, drinking in sunshine and blue waters and skies.

For ferry captains and crews, a continually replenished line of traffic narrows their job to the art of getting people, cars, bicycles and motorcycles on-and-off the ferries in the quickest, most efficient manner possible. A shortened turn-around time at the pier is critical, as is making the underway run in the quickest time possible. On days like this the ferry schedule is "tossed out the window" and the four crews load-and-go. Having solid traffic volume on such a beautiful day is a pleasant rarity, and we all realize the importance of such a day. It's good for the whole island.

Despite rapid turn-arounds, past 11 a.m. the ferries begin to lose ground and the line of cars at Northport grew to 50 or more cars, the equivalent of about 2 1/2 ferry loads or perhaps 45 minutes of customer wait time. After each ferry loaded and departed, the same number of cars or more remained in line.

On such occasions, our ticketing staff hustles to keep up with transactions, and answering questions, and directing traffic past the booth in orderly queues and onto the ferries. At times two ferries are loading at the same time. The real bottleneck isn't ticketing, it's in the physical task of parking 18 or more different drivers, instructing each one where and how to park their cars, making sure the load fits, then saving the last few minutes for walk-ons or bicyclists before the ramp is raised. There is added pressure from the ferry that follows as it slides into the harbor, its crew awaiting their turn at the loading ramp.

Monday, September 3 – Labor Day

Today, Labor Day Monday, is an extraordinary day.

It's the national holiday honoring labor, the people who produce goods and services, the solid underpinnings of our capitalistic economy. For tourism-related businesses like ours, Labor Day means a full day's work. Labor Day is also a tourism milestone, marking summer's end, even though the official end of summer won't arrive until Sept. 21st. As days grow shorter we'll have fewer island visitors and ferry customers.

Hoyt and I comprise the fourth crew today on the *Eyrarbakki*, and we'll be prepared to jump into the rotation when traffic leaving the island exceeds 50 or more cars per hour, greater than three ferries can keep up with. Once again, except for the first few and the last few trips of the day, our published ferry schedule will be ignored as crews attempt to cycle more quickly.

"Give us 18 cars," one captain radios to Patty Cornell, island ticket seller. Her job this day is more traffic director than ticket seller. "Hold the camper until last. Send it over to the north ramp." "Give me those three motorcycles before I fill up the stern with cars." And so on.

A lady who forgot her purse on one of the upper deck benches the day before called at the Northport booth to pick it up. She was so pleased to have it returned she brought the crew a case of Guinness.

In all, Hoyt and I wound up making five back-to-back runs with the *Eyrarbakki*. He was kind enough to be my deckhand, deferring to his father, giving me a chance at the helm. Each trip we were full leaving the island but nearly empty on our return. We had time to talk about family and business matters and review the summer. On our noon run, Thor joined us as he began his trip home around the northern end of Lake Michigan and over the Mackinac Bridge to his home in Boyne City.

***

Each trip that morning in the light northerly winds we had observed monarch butterflies sailing south. Most of them floated lightly by in the air. Those monarchs headed directly for our ferry fluttered their wings to a higher elevation, safely clearing our wheelhouse and ferry structure. Occasionally they flew in pairs, but most monarchs flew alone, separated a long distance from one another, so far apart that at first we didn't recognize the southerly flight pattern. Theirs is a seasonal journey south, much like our paying passengers.

I read an explanation of this phenomena only a week ago in an article by Coggin Heeringa, Naturalist at Crossroads at Big Creek in Sturgeon Bay. Coggin wrote that monarchs fly to Mexico and to other points in the deep south, stopping along the way to refuel when the opportunity arises...or when they're forced to ground by opposing winds. Banding has verified this migration, and monarchs from our area have been recovered near Mexico City where they congregate in winter. There are many questions with answers that remain a mystery, such as: How do the uninitiated butterflies know where to go? What directs them? Is there a built-in gene that gives them the required knowledge? How can such delicate, light insects fly several thousands of miles?

An answer to the last question may be their lightness and ability to glide and ride on air currents taking them south. I confirmed this supposition later that same afternoon when I chanced to strike up a conversation with a passenger. This man and his wife came from the Upper Peninsula. "Where in the U.P.?" I asked. "From the Stonington Peninsula, east of Gladstone," he replied.

The Stonington Peninsula! I've passed by it many times by car and by boat. It's a fairly wide and long strip of land that points southward into Green Bay's waters, lying between Escanaba and Gladstone and Little Bay de Noc to the west, and the Garden Peninsula and Big Bay de Noc to the east. Although there is a great deal of forestland on the peninsula, there is also open farmland. I recalled a bit of information given to me by Steve Masters, Executive Director of the Bay de Noc Visitor and Convention Bureau, that the Stonington Peninsula is uniquely regarded as a gathering point in the fall for monarch butterflies.

I asked our passenger about this, and he explained that the annual monarch count (How might such a count be achieved?) was taken just this past week, the same time each year, to monitor the health of the butterfly population. Most monarchs from the Upper Peninsula work their way southward and funnel toward the Stonington Peninsula. From there, most fly toward the Ford River on the mainland south of Escanaba where they follow the shoreline southward. For some reason, perhaps caused by today's light northerly breezes, we were today privileged to observe dozens of monarchs as they continued their journey from the U.P., or perhaps even Canada, taking this water short cut to wintering grounds far away.

Our passenger from the Stonington Peninsula told us he and his wife visit Washington Island each fall. I thought, we should maintain tourism balance and vacation near his home, a short butter-flight away. While it is near to us geographically, this part of the Upper Peninsula remains for most of us a curiously different world. Once the de Noc Indians and other indigenous tribes walked ancient trails alongside the Whitefish River connecting Green Bay waters with Lake Superior, perhaps a journey of not more than two days. For most islanders, I think, the Stonington Peninsula could as well be Wyoming.

In the distance, looking past occasional butterflies and the green of the Door islands, we saw groups of kayaks and powerboats as they crossed the passage, some well beyond Pilot Island. Only avid sail boaters could be disappointed with today's light air.

In the mid-afternoon, the breeze switched to easterly and the colors grew softer with a light cloud cover, dabs of light bouncing from wavelets like an impressionist painting. The softness of the light was a reminder fall is around the corner.

***

Hoyt's phone rang as we approached the half-way point near Plum Island in the early afternoon. He talked for quite some time, animated and laughing. The caller was a contact he had made a few weeks ago who wished to renew his wedding vows on board without his wife knowing the details before hand. Their wedding party of 25 years ago would join them on a recreated honeymoon to Washington Island, and Hoyt, in his official capacity as "The Reverend Captain" would give the blessing and help them renew their vows. Hoyt became a man of the cloth, on paper, online, a year or so ago, after he answered a few questions (none of which had anything to do with character or belief) and paid a fee for the certificate. If this opportunity comes to fruition, it would be his first official ceremony.

***

Traffic thinned by 3 p.m. and our ferries caught up with the flow. By 5:30 p.m., our last scheduled trip of the afternoon, 22 cars were left in line. The *Washington* arrived and got everyone on board. Captain Erik Foss ran the day's last round trip. It was an efficient ending to a busy weekend, concluding the 2007 Labor Day exodus.

Wednesday, September 5 –

I awoke at 4:15 this morning having slept well but unable to fall back asleep. I lay in thought about the day ahead and the days after that when we would be traveling cross-country on my motorcycle, two almost 60-year-olds doing what I would never have guessed we would attempt to do.

We packed our bags last night in a practice run to see if all of our clothing and travel gear could fit into the same bag. It seemed tight, and although we still had the saddlebags available, they would be filled with the things we needed quickly on the road, such as a raincoat, pair of gloves, or a water bottle. Our Yamaha is big, but it isn't a touring cruiser, and it doesn't have protective cowlings or a plush seat like the Harley Electra Glide, or the Honda Gold Wing, or the Yamaha Venture models. No radio. No satellite radio. No intercom between helmets. It would be just us, our few belongings, the bike and the road, a purist's experience except that we would always look for a comfortable motel for a good night's rest, with showers and hot food available.

We're anticipating riding under the open skies of the prairie states, past golden wheat and soy fields, the tall corn of Iowa, smelling super hog farms, and crossing rivers swollen by recent rains. We watched the weather channel as we packed, and the forecast was for light rain on Thursday, then rain all day Friday, ending Saturday. Warm air, record warm air in some places today, then cooling off with below average temperatures. This range of conditions will be a part of our challenge, carrying enough of the right clothing and dressing comfortably for nearly any condition.

Twenty-four hours from now we'll be on the road.

***

We heard brief rolls of thunder early this morning without rain. The clouds passed to our north, probably dropping rain on the U.P. as well as upper Lake Michigan. It will be interesting to see if lake levels dip quickly after early September as they sometimes do, falling lower with each successive northerly high, never to return again to the same level.

***

Humidity aside, the day is bright and encouraging, and our visitors think so too. The late morning ferries brought in good numbers of people for the tour train, as well as several loads of autos. Hoyt and Rich made an extra trip to Northport for the additional activity while I prepared materials for tonight's crew meeting. I also prepared handouts for the 60 or so Midwest Travel Writers who are coming to visit Washington Island tomorrow. As one of several island host companies, we offered to ferry them at no charge, a typical and expected part of travel writing. We hope they will have a good day, an encouragement for the genesis of an island travel piece.

***

At 2 p.m. Hoyt and I loaded the *Eyrarbakki* with 14 autos and several bicycles. Heading into the southerly breeze was pleasant. The *Noble's* crew, Erik and Joel, took on a 45-passenger motor coach and Mack Gunnlaugsson's truck. Mack was returning from his regular run to Green Bay for freight, including kegs and cases of beer and other beverages.

At the island dock, a few minutes before 4 p.m., two Honda Gold Wings pulling trailers waited to board the *Robert Noble*. I spoke to the woman who drove the second bike and asked if they camped, pointing to the two trailers. "No. We do motels all the way. My husband carries our luggage in his trailer, and mine's for shopping!" Not a bad way to travel. They've been all over, including Nova Scotia recently.

***

The day concluded with a crew meeting that began at 7 p.m. Several crew members including Carol Meyer and our Northport ticket seller had just ended their shift.

We covered numerous topics. A good summer season is owed to our good crew, and to positive things happening onboard, and in ticketing, and in the office; everyone's strong support for the Pirate Days theme; safety issues were addressed regarding fuel containers on board — a new policy; dredging; pier permit process bogged down; fall work projects; mechanical items for maintenance on the ferries; and so on.

Since my birthday would occur while I was on a trip, I brought an early birthday cake for the crew baked by Lois Krueger, with a tub of vanilla ice cream. Everyone had a piece, with some cake left over for the next day. I closed the office at 9 p.m. and headed home. My vacation had begun.

Thursday, Sept. 6 –

Overcast with a forecast for rain later in the afternoon or evening. Quite warm. We arose early, excited to be packing and preparing for the start of our motorcycle trip.

Before leaving, we drove refrigerated goods by pickup truck to Hoyt and Kirsten's, but we found that no one was up. Sadly, we couldn't see Aidan before we left! As we backed away after leaving two grocery sacks on their front step, we saw the curtain in Aidan's bedroom pull to one side. We found out later he had watched us from his upstairs window. Mary Jo had tears in her eyes with the thought of not seeing him for many days.

Wednesday, Sept. 26 – Home Again

We are the same two people, but somehow we look at ourselves differently for having made a 4700-mile trip by motorcycle. We're continually reminded of our trip when we meet people who missed us or who wondered how we got along. We think of the fun we had and the enjoyable daily routine that motorcycling a long distance brought to our lives: Washington Island to Wichita; to the Ozarks; to Detroit; to Buffalo; to Albany; then home via the Straits of Mackinac and the Upper Peninsula of Michigan.

We invited Kirsten, Hoyt and Aidan over for spaghetti Tuesday evening and were entertained as Aidan took out Mary Jo's spice containers and pretended to mix up a concoction at the kitchen table. Aidan had grown, and so had his vocabulary. We were happy to see our family again.

***

We may have had more comfortable beds in some of our motel accommodations, but none as familiar. The cool September evenings made us think it won't be long before we turn up the thermostat, but in our upstairs bedroom we leave our windows open, fresh air always being a sedative to promote a solid night's sleep.

Thursday, September 28 –

All of our children are considered "island natives," having been raised and schooled here, but Hoyt and his sister Evelyn are among those, like many of the older generations, who were actually born on the island. Thor's prenatal situation required hospital services, and consequently he was born at St. Vincent Hospital in Green Bay, February 17, 1980.

Today Hoyt turns 34 and soon expects a new son to join his family.

When Hoyt was born, I was stationed aboard the LPD-2 USS Vancouver, an amphibious troop vessel returning from the Western Pacific from duty off Viet Nam, headed toward Hawaii from the Philippines. I received a Red Cross telegram announcing the "launch of a new hull," and I made arrangements to return home soon after the ship moored at San Diego's 32nd Street Naval Base. When I first saw Hoyt, he was two weeks old.

Some of my fondest memories with Hoyt at a young age were doing simple activities, like walking in the woods, fishing, stacking fire wood, making a trip to the island landfill, snowplowing, and taking him for a trip now and then on a ferry with me. It's not a coincidence these are the very things he enjoys today, and they are also activities he shares with his son, Aidan. When the two stop by to visit us early in the morning, they're usually returning from a cruise of the countryside in the pickup truck, and Aidan tells us he saw geese, turkeys, deer or an airplane. A special stop for them is the fire department where Hoyt is a volunteer fireman and an officer. There, in the quiet of the garage filled with shiny, red equipment, Aidan can sit in one of the big fire trucks.

***

Mary Jo was invited for a cake social at Peg Sullivan's at the end of Airport Road. The significance of this party, in addition to being just a pleasant gathering of old family friends and neighbors from the Detroit Harbor area, is that Peg and her family bought the home that Carl and Maggie Richter owned. It is the same dwelling Arni Richter was brought up in, and where Mary Jo spent many afternoons when she was young. Mary Jo has been impressed that her grandparents' old home hasn't been appreciably changed.

These sorts of time warps occur often on Washington Island, I think. People such as Peg Sullivan have made the essential repairs required to keep the buildings in good condition, but it also seems to be her wish to keep things as they were. She has been very kind in her efforts to include Mary Jo with occasional invitations to visit. During one such visit Peg displayed a stack of old books that once belonged to Carl Richter, one given to him as a very young man by another islander with his name and the date of the gift inscribed on the inside cover from the late 1800s. These aren't priceless family heirlooms, necessarily, but they could be considered as such when placed into the right hands.

***

This day was Hoyt's birthday, and we visited Hoyt, Kirsten and Aidan before sunset, arriving at their home just ahead of Arni and Chris. Hoyt was pleased we came over, even though there hadn't been a formal party invitation because he had a volunteer fire meeting scheduled later that same evening.

I presented Hoyt with several gifts I bought in Rapid River, MI. The Knife Works craftsmen there make beautiful knives for fishing and hunting, and besides being sought after as collectible items, they're practical implements meant to be used in the field. We also brought back a tee shirt for Hoyt from the Fort Ticonderoga Ferry, a ferry ride we took just one week earlier with our motorcycle from New York to Vermont as we crossed Lake Champlain. Aidan completed our evening's entertainment with song and dance.

Sunday, Sept. 30 –

Today is our 35th wedding anniversary. Aidan, Kirsten and Hoyt invited us to the Ship's Wheel Restaurant at Kap's for breakfast and afterward, we hiked along the Jackson Harbor Ridges trail. Aidan walked and ran twice the distance we did, taking several side excursions with his little legs running back and forth along the beach, through the sandy dunes and over the rocks. We weren't surprised he was tired by the time we returned home.

I closed the afternoon by picking up sticks and mowing while Mary Jo paid bills and caught up on bookwork...not exactly an anniversary date, but we'd had a great day — and, we recognize we're blessed.

OCTOBER

Monday, October 1 –

Rain fell during the night and through the early morning hours rain continued to fall, steadily and softly, without wind or fuss. Just a gentle watering from the sky. Puddles the size of throw-rugs spotted our drive outside the kitchen window.

***

While I typed, Mary Jo did bookwork...home bills...bicycle rental ...ran errands...and visited Arni.

Tuesday, October 2 –

The morning is damp, gray and foggy. As the early ferry started out the channel on the day's first trip, the captain blew a prolonged blast to let any other vessel know they were underway. A light breeze is blowing, a chance it will clear later on. But so far, it looks as though we may have a wash-out day, two days in a row.

I passed a string of cars headed from the ferry followed by Al Hiller in the Veolia truck. The fog was so thick each driver had headlights on, and when I arrived at the ferry dock I heard the ferry's horn. I couldn't see the end of the pier from the office.

By 9:30 a.m., upon his return from the first run, Joel Gunnlaugsson reported visibility had improved. The forecast calls for fog to lift around 11a.m. We have a bus tour group coming in on that trip, and at least it's not raining. They're walking on board and will tour on the Packer Train, Ed's Green and Gold train purchased from the Green Bay Packer organization several years ago. Normally, the Packer organization guards their logo closely and won't let it be used by others, but since this tram had been used for transporting people from the old Hall of Fame to the old Packer stadium, back when the two were separated by Oneida Street, Ron Wolf approved it's continued use. So rather than paint these three cars red like the rest of his tour train units, Ed Livingston proudly kept the Packer colors and logo.

***

I stopped at the steel building, our 60 x 40 workshop that also doubles for storage of equipment, and visited with Bill Crance. Bill had a section of hydraulic hose clamped in a vise and was attaching fittings.

"Did you ever hold a hummingbird?" Bill asked. He then told me about a male hummingbird that had been in the building, sitting on one of the overhead door supports. This bird may have been in the building for some time because he appeared weak and unwilling to fly. Bill first coaxed him onto a broom, but as he took the bird outdoors, it flew back into the building and sat on a rail attached to a small loft. Bill climbed the steps and approached with open hand. Each time he tried to grasp the bird, it flew a short distance. On the third attempt, he managed to encircle the bird with his hand, gently grasping it around its body, beak and head exposed. The tiny bird was tired out...too tired to fold its wings back. This time Bill walked it across the road to a patch of bushes, at which point it took off.

"There was nothing to it," Bill said, referring to the weight of the bird, not his efforts at capturing it and releasing it outdoors.

***

I gave Hoyt a haircut this evening after work, following a trim on my own noggin by Mary Jo. After giving myself a haircut earlier this summer and receiving mixed reviews on the home front, I offered Mary Jo the chance to improve my look. I think she did quite well. There is certainly a convenience factor in being able to get it done almost any time, any day, at home in our basement. As for my own barbering skills, I learned them from "my old man." Dad cut my hair for years, until part way through high school when I wanted something other than a buzz or a close taper. The Beatles were "in" and so was longer hair, and I wanted mine to look like Paul McCartney's, not Dwight Eisenhower's. Out of self defense I began working on my own head, using a thinning scissors following a friend's suggestion. It worked. At one point I earned a nickname from Chan (Chandler F.) Harris, Advocate Editor, "the Blonde Beatle," in the spring of my senior year of high school as a discus thrower.

At UW-Madison, long hair was vogue. Mine was actually quite short compared to most, with the exception of my UW rowing mates who wore closely cropped hair. A hazing ritual for oarsmen called for upperclassmen to administer G.I. haircuts on a certain Saturday morning in spring, after practice. I was a junior transfer but a newcomer to the crew team. I made myself scarce that morning.

Later that year and the next, as my barbering skills expanded, I gave haircuts to my roommate, David, and to a friend, Leo Burt, who rowed crew with me and was also in my journalism classes. Leo, it turned out, clandestinely joined the radical left and distanced himself from those with whom he was close when he was an oarsman. Before disappearing from sight for these past 40 years, he participated in the bombing of the UW Sterling Hall math building in which a man was killed.

But that's a lot of past. For the most part, there is a simple reason for basement haircuts at our home. Hoyt hates to part with 10 bucks, and so we have a beer in the basement while I trim his hair, and so far, he's not complained about the results.

Wednesday, October 3 –

We had great gusts of wind last night. I'd guess the steady breeze was in the upper 30 mph range with gusts well over 40 mph, and the power went out in several areas of the island. Sticks, branches and leaves were all over our yard and the roadway. By daybreak the wind had settled down and the scheduled gas tanker for the Mercantile's pumps was loaded and ferried to the island. Today we have four buses scheduled, plus several more trucks. One of the long semi trucks is a low-boy with a new aluminum boat for the WDNR at Rock Island State Park from the state of Washington, ferried over on the *Arni J. Richter*. The unit was 75 feet overall, and with the boat on the trailer the air draft exceeded 14 feet, greater than the shipper said it would be. Erik Foss, captain, noted there was 1 1/2 inches to spare between the load and the overhead. As a bonus, the crew managed a tour bus in the adjacent lane.

Later this morning a WDNR truck from the fish hatchery at Wild Rose will bring brown trout fingerlings. This is done annually in spring and fall before hatchery facilities are cleaned for a new batch. We ferry them at no charge for the Island Sportsman's Club, and direct the DNR toward the Potato Dock. There the driver attaches his chute, swings it over the side of the pier and releases the fish.

Our hope is that the small fish get themselves sorted out and find their bearings for deeper water before gulls and cormorants find them a delicacy. We and Sportsman's Club members hope that many of the brown trout return as larger fish, to be caught later, when they're 30 inches long and 10 pounds. There's little in fishing to beat the experience of catching a brown trout through the ice with a light line.

Thursday, October 4 –

I arrived at the Ferry Dock to find Bill Crance and Tully Ellefson pruning cedar limbs near Island Pizza. Tully and I had begun the day before to open up the heavy growth of cedars to sunlight. This will aide in providing access when we begin an addition to the rear of that structure a few weeks from now. This grove of cedars situated on a slight ridge of beach cobble that at one time was the high water mark, the beach line. Years ago, in the early nineteen-sixties, the harbor bottom south of the present ferry terminal was dredged. Spoils of stone, clay and muck were dumped in the low areas near those cedars and later a bulkhead was established, the land on which our office was built in 1995.

It would not be possible to replicate these activities today given state statutes regarding dredging and filling. When we proposed our office building expansion in the late 1980s we went around and around with the DNR about adding to our old office on the pier. DNR said we couldn't build below the high water mark and within the flood plain. We went to a hearing on the subject and were turned down by the Administrative Law Judge. Several years passed, during which time we had forgotten about our application and the opportunity for appeal that was still pending. Then, I received a call from a DNR representative who asked if we still intended to pursue the matter.

We asked about building on an adjacent site in the level, open, grassy space that was seeded dredge spoils. "O.K.," the DNR State's Attorney said, "just build 75 feet back from the steel sheeting. We'll declare the sheet piling as the bulkhead line and you can go ahead and build." That settled the matter rather quickly. DNR held their position (no precedent made for a terminal next to the water) and we were cleared to build in a new location.

So now, here we are in a ferry terminal building opened in 1996, below the high water mark and within the flood plain. To satisfy the flood plain issue, we had to truck in fill, and we sank footings through the old dredging deposits to reach solid, virgin bottom. Once an agreement with the DNR was struck, construction began within months with Martin Andersen as our general contractor.

Friday, October 5 –

The big news yesterday when I got home: Atlas called his grandmother and said, "I'm going to be a big brother!" Evy is now two months pregnant. We couldn't be happier!

***

After emptying trash receptacles at the dock, I prepared the *Eyrarbakki* for what seemed to be a certain busy day. By 10 a.m., I headed out the island channel with Bill Crance as my crew, and by the time we arrived at Northport there were over 30 cars in line. We loaded on the heels of the *Robert Noble*, Erik Foss and Bill Jorgenson as crew, and we wound up leaving four cars. The traffic, both cars and people, has been steady ever since.

***

I visited with Charlie Balestreiri who had worked on details of our ferry designs as a member of the Tim Graul Marine Design offices. Charlie now works for Sea Craft Design in Sturgeon Bay, where several former Graul associates are now employed. Naval Architect Mark Pudlo, also formerly with Tim, is the principal and owner of the firm. Charlie's wife, Patti, is one of two Physician Assistants currently providing care at our Island Clinic through North Shore Ministry Health Care. Charlie commutes to work on Mondays and returns to the island on Fridays. Charlie has an exceptionally good eye for lines and the curb appeal that makes a vessel a pleasure to see and to ride on.

Charlie showed us photos of the trip they had just returned from, to Sicily, where his grandparents came from. In a part of Sicily which is known even today for its fishing fleet of small boats, he found relatives and connections with his past. Balestreiri is a very common last name there. And by coincidence, Bill Crance is also part Sicilian.

On our second trip from Northport, Walt Nehlsen was our pilothouse guest. Walt's grandson, Jack, worked with us this summer. Walter has been the island's Airport Manager for a number of years, and he can often be found at the airport or in transit to the airport on his scooter. He also pilots and maintains his own plane. Besides sporting a John Deere belt buckle, he and son Peter must own eight or 10 Deere tractors between them, plus assorted restored implements. A signature kindness of Walt's is to bring fresh donuts to the crew on the ferry he rides, and today, even though we were beyond the lunch hour, Bill Crance and I benefitted from his generosity.

***

A stuffed turkey was baking in the oven when I got home, one of several dozen being prepared in ovens around the island. It will be delivered to Trinity tomorrow morning where a volunteer crew will place the carved turkey on platters for the 600 or so paying guests who had reserved for Saturday evening's Harvest dinner. Some volunteers bake squash or pies, but Mary Jo prefers to bake a turkey.

Saturday, October 6 –

Light rain fell during the night, more like a steady drizzle, and then the sun poked through around 8 a.m. I heard the early ferry blow its horn through the fog.

Those who saw it said there was the most wonderful rainbow in the eastern sky. I missed it, and soon afterward the haze and fog closed in again, and for the rest of the day the super-saturated air passing over the cooler lake water squeezed out a drizzle. It was warm enough for shirtsleeves, never threatening enough to make people run indoors.

***

We had a family breakfast with our daughter Evelyn's family, then Atlas and I went out to the garden to dig potatoes and onions. He loves working in the garden, digging with his shovel and discovering each potato as it's unearthed. We spent an hour digging and filled a plastic bucket.

When Hoyt stopped by the house, we swapped trucks, and while Hoyt returned to the ferry dock, Atlas and I picked up Aidan for a ride to the dump. The truck cab was tight with Aidan strapped in his bulky car seat and Atlas squeezed beside me in the middle. But then we met Evy and Mary Jo while crossing the Townline Road intersection near Ray Hansen's, and we made room for Mary Jo to join us. The truck cab was now jammed with four good voices for a chorus of the "ABC Song," "Old MacDonald," "Zippitty-doo-dah" and other favorites known to Aidan and Atlas.

I tossed one large garbage sack after the other into the big green dumpster box, then drove around to the metal pile where I parked and threw out an old tailpipe and pallet strapping. Atlas began looking for odd pieces for a sculpture, and together we found several items. He said at one point, "Papa, we have to keep looking. That's not enough for a sculpture. Let's take this." He handed me a hubcap.

From the Island Exchange we took Aidan home for his nap, and then Atlas and I drove to the Open House at the island Fire Station. The crowd of visitors mingled among the fire trucks and ambulance units parked outdoors, and some ate a lunch served in the open bays of the firehouse.

Atlas asked his Uncle Hoyt, "Are there some learning things here?" We ate hot dogs while Atlas waited his turn for the current group of children to move through the training trailer, and we checked out an island ambulance.

Soon it was Atlas's turn to enter the training trailer, where the two training leaders were familiar faces, firemen Joel Gunnlaugsson and Rich Ellefson. He learned what fire hazards to look for in a home, how to call 911, and what to do if you were in a home that was on fire and had to escape. The trailer's rear window provided youngsters practice at turning around and backing down a ladder. In another area, firemen drew water from a portable tank and demonstrated a pressurized fire hose. Atlas was invited to put on a fire hat and jacket and assist holding the hose. He also climbed into the seat of one of the large pumper trucks, perched about seven feet off the ground, an exciting time for a five-year-old.

Sunday, October 7 –

Warm again with temperatures in the upper 60s, and the sun is out. The sky is already showing large patches of blue.

Atlas and I rode our four-wheeler to the Farm Museum at the corner of Airport and Jackson Harbor Roads. We rode shoulders and ditches, with a few short-cuts through the woods.

A few of the things Atlas did: he fed the rabbits and goats; rode in Ted Hansen's wagon, drawn by a team of work horses around the field; made and ate a caramel apple; rode a buckboard with other kids, pushed and pulled by yet other youngsters around the barnyard; pumped water from a hand pump; watched a blacksmith at work and a lady spinning yarn from wool.

When at last we began heading home, we detoured by way of the Mountain Tower.

The last time we climbed the steps up to the tower, Atlas was so far ahead of me I lost eye contact. This time, either out of respect for me or because he was tired, he climbed staying just ahead of me talking as he climbed, admiring the view, stopping at a bench part way up. From the top landing of the tower we gazed out upon the trees changing color and the blue water to the north of Washington Island.

After returning home, I had resumed mowing the yard when I received a phone call from Rich, captain on the *Robert Noble*. He informed me there were at least 75 cars still in line with more expected in the final hour of the afternoon. I headed to the Ferry Dock, started the *Eyrarbakki's* engines and awaited Liz Geddart, Rich's niece, my crew. We loaded 19 cars at 10 minutes to five, and I recognized a few of our passengers from seeing them at the Mountain Tower the previous hour.

By the time we had returned from our overload trip, the sun had already begun to set. Good news: the line of traffic had been "cleaned up" by Bill Jorgenson and the *Washington* crew.

Wednesday, October 10 –

A wet and windy Wednesday hasn't stopped early morning traffic, a drilling rig semi and a dozen other cars and pickups, but traffic in general today will be very light in view of the much cooler air and drizzle.

The wind has switched to the north during the night, and the intensity is expected to pick up from the 15-20 mph of this morning to something above 30, with gusts to 40 mph. At least that is the Mayfor, the marine weather forecast from NOAA Weather for the northern half of the bay of Green Bay. Fortunately, we have no motor coaches on today's schedule. Large busses rock and sway on their soft suspensions, often air bags, and if there is an inclination to get sick on a ferry ride, those swaying vehicles only add to that feeling.

For outdoor work, today is probably the worst weather we've had in many months. Our five-man shore crew is down in the engine room of the *Washington* changing oil and filters. Three ferries now either approach, or are slightly over, oil change intervals. Following the oil change was the task of cleaning the darkened and dingy overhead, coated from light diesel exhaust. The bilge also needs attention. Cleaning an engine room is never high on the list of favorites, but our crew scrubs at least once a year in either late fall or early spring. It takes agility to twist around in tight corners, and our younger crew is superior at this. This job, once completed, the public never will see.

Rich later reported a leaking exhaust connection on the *Washington*, a gasket that needs to be replaced, and also a coolant leak dripping greenish colored liquid onto the white absorption mats under the engines. And the starboard engine hour meter that quit working some 80 hours ago will need replacement.

***

With increasing winds from the NW, rain and falling temperatures, Hoyt joined the 5 p.m. ferry crew as a third crew member, lending experience and support on the final trip of the day. The 4 p.m. ferry had been scratched due to northerly winds in the range of 30-40 mph, the upper end of safe operation for us. The last trip was made to get whatever traffic there was back across the Door. The return from Northport was against strong winds and increasing seas, under heavy cloud cover in the decreasing daylight hours.

Thursday, October 11 –

Skies are a slight bit brighter this morning, and the rains of Wednesday afternoon and evening have diminished. We're back on schedule with our ferry runs this morning, although gale warnings are still up. Considering the drop in temperatures from 75 to 45 degrees overnight, the winds produced by the pressure differences have caused minimal disruption in our business. In all, we cancelled one ferry and pushed back several semis to Friday, including the waste truck from Veolia.

***

I asked Capt. Bill Jorgenson at 11a.m. if the seas had reduced any, and in his estimation the winds and seas were about as great as they had been at daybreak. We're headed off the island on the noon ferry, Mary Jo and I. Although she's a ferryman's wife, and a ferryman's daughter, she's never been comfortable with rough weather. I can only assure her that it is in my best interest, also, to arrive safely at our destination. One saving grace about our ferry runs is that they seldom last longer than 30 minutes, and when we steer to Northport on a day such as this, we're sailing downwind, downhill, with seas on our stern. By late afternoon when we return home, if predictions mean anything, wind velocities should be moderate.

***

Town Chairman Tim Jessen called me to get an idea of the number of bicycles we carried this season, and whether or not that number has increased from prior years. The town would like to widen County W, Main Road to Jackson Harbor, to include a bike lane along the shoulder. The greater the numbers of bikes, the better the Town's chances of getting state or county aid for the island roads. It looks like this year we carried, to date, 3320 bicycles on a round trip basis, plus other bikes that were either inside vehicles or secured to roofs, that aren't counted. And, there are also island bike rentals during the warm weather months. All contribute to the activity along the island's roads, probably one of the more heavily biked areas of Door County in summer.

***

At the Sturgeon Bay clinic, as we waited for our appointments, I overheard an elderly gentleman conversing with the receptionist to make a future appointment. "What day works best for you?" she asked pleasantly. "Don't matter," he replied. "Everyday is the same for me."

***

We returned on the 6 p.m. ferry. Spray from the seas flew into the air as waves rolled by. Although the sky had cleared in Sturgeon Bay and the winds had abated, from Sister Bay north it was still overcast and tree limbs swayed. The conditions, according to Bill Jorgenson, hadn't changed much through the day. He steered a course south of Plum Island to give a better ride, putting the seas and sunset on our stern. A low layer of clouds separated to form a bright slit at the horizon, allowing sunlight to reflect from the underside of the clouds. Brilliant orange blazed against the dark clouds, then reds, then a softer pink light lit the sky, sinking low on the horizon before finally setting. Only sailors, ferry passengers, or the lucky homeowners along the western shore of Door County would experience such a rich sunset.

Saturday, Oct. 13 –

With Janet Hanlin at our front office desk (and also stepping out to the island booth for ticket sales every half hour), and with Kim receiving boat trip slips and stepping forward to fill Janet's shoes, I volunteered to drive the mail van to the post office.

But before I left for the post office, Jim Wilson came in to ask for a small grapple. While casting for bass from the end of the Standard Oil dock, Jim hooked his net, which then flipped his fishing rod into the lake. The pair landed about 10 feet out and 15 or more feet down. Jim told me he could just see the tip of his fishing rod laying on the bottom. I found a piece of light line and then hunted through several boxes to find a small pike hook. With the hook, some wire and line, I fashioned a homemade grapple that might give him a chance for retrieval.

The traffic at Northport had begun to build around 10 a.m., and I had observed Ken Berggren moving about the dock near the *Eyrarbakki*, but not Hoyt. They were changing oil I later learned, a fairly routine process that was slowed because they had to hoof fresh oil from the *Washington* by the 5-gallon bucket in order to refill the *Eyrarbakki's* motors.

The handle on the *Eyrarbakki's* oil reservoir pump had broken, and so the oil stored there couldn't be pumped into a pouring container, the usual and most efficient method to refill each ferry's engines. By 10:15 a.m., engines were topped off, checked for leaks and fluid levels, and started up, and Ken and Hoyt cast off lines for Northport.

On the pier, I collected the four waste oil pails and took them to our 1200 gallon waste oil tank, a collection point for bilge slops and old motor and gear oil. Once each year we call a company from the Fox Valley, and their tank truck comes to the island to pump out our waste oil, which is then either filtered and recycled for use in asphalt plants, or is used in some other industrial setting as a lower grade heating fuel. Or, we store it and burn it later as fuel for the overhead heater in our workshop. As cleanup man, I turned the filters from the recent oil change upside down to drain inside a rain-proof enclosure, after first removing a dozen or more drained filters for my next stop...the Island Exchange.

***

I had a partner along with me today on my ride to the dump, Aidan. He's quite used to the routine of going to the dump with his dad, saying, "Hi, Jeff" and "Hi, John" to the familiar attendants. He's a good little partner, eats his goldfish cracker snacks in silence, quite content to look at the trees, barns, and tractors, describing each as we go by. The Island Exchange was busy. Since we couldn't bring Al Hiller with the empties over on Thursday due to high winds, the dump box was now nearly full and the hydraulic press struggled to make room for more. Once the box is full, that's it. No more garbage is accepted.

When Kirsten and I had seated Aidan in his car seat, he casually tossed his blue plastic blocks into a box of paper I had on the front seat. At the dump, I had forgotten about his blocks and poured the container's contents into the paper bailer. As we were headed up Main Road 20 minutes later, Aidan asked for his blocks.

"They're not here," I said. "They're in the compactor at the dump. My mistake."

Aidan replied, "Get them. Papa, go back."

But it was too late. They were only small plastic blocks, now pressed between sheets of paper and cardboard in the baler. He was disappointed, but one minute later his head bobbed as he sang "Old MacDonald had a farm...." Accepting my peace offering, he settled for lunch at Island Pizza at the Ferry Dock, where his mom would meet us and he could visit "Gramma MJ" in the bike shop.

Monday, October 15 –

Light rain began to fall around 9 p.m., and in the early morning a steady rain could still be heard on our porch roof. The overcast skies and cool air continued through the morning, with more of the same forecast through the day.

By 9 a.m. the rain had stopped and the breeze picked up from the east. We would not expect to see many tourists today.

***

Just before 10 a.m. Erik Foss, on the *Washington*, called from Northport. His engine controls weren't working. A chain on the Morse cable system had parted, visible from the main deck, and needed repair before the ferry could be moved. Rich, Jim Hanson and Hoyt started up the *Robert Noble* and headed for Northport with the aerial "man lift" on board.

The *Washington* arrived back on the island at 5 p.m. with repairs made. The problem was deteriorated chain, bicycle chain, used to activate the Morse transfer system on the overhead of the main deck. Shift commands from the pilothouse, after station, and engine room control heads are each linked by cable to this central set of sprockets, so that every change in throttle position and gear is reflected simultaneously by all three stations.

The chain was weakened from rust and wear despite annual lubrication. Rich, Jim and Tully managed to get new bicycle chain and master links from Northern Door Cycle in Fish Creek, but it took nearly five hours to get one set of control chains properly reinstalled. The other two shift station chains will be replaced tomorrow, with the ferry sidelined until that task is accomplished.

Tonight, Rich Ellefson awaits Rich Hansen to fuel the *Arni J. Richter* with just enough product to hold us for a few days until a bulk tanker can be brought up from Green Bay to fuel both the *AJR* and *Washington*.

Tuesday, October 16 –

When we refer to a dark, wet and windy morning, this is the morning we're referring to. Leaves not quite yet ready to fall have been pushed off their perch by rain and NE winds. By day's end perhaps 50 percent of the maple leaves in our yard will have fallen. Oak leaves will hang on, tough, leathery strips, getting the most out of another one or two months on the tree.

I drove our old Ferry Line dump truck to the dock with chunks of concrete and stone stacked loosely in the bed. The wipers didn't work worth a damn but I drove slowly, and other than one set of headlights behind me (they turned off near the Albatross, headed for the Red Cup) I met no cars on my way to the dock. As I down-shifted into low gear and crawled past the ticket booth, lights from the *Arni J. Richter's* deck and cabins shone ahead of me, and red tail lights from vehicles loading for the 8 a.m. departure glowed as drivers braked. Here it was nearly 8 a.m., but drivers had their headlights on.

Also on the dock, and equally brilliant in the wet gloom, were three of our crew busily unloading oil barrels in the rain from the bed of 'Lil Atlas truck. The crew worked in bright safety orange and luminous safety green rain suits, complete with reflective tape. That was during the light drizzle. By 8:30 a.m., drizzle became wind-driven rain pelting roof and windows.

At 8:45 a.m., rain suits dripping, Erik Foss and Ron Kleckner entered the office from the recently docked *Robert Noble* for respite and to get an update on trucks, busses and other scheduled traffic for later this morning. Ron was his usual, chirpy self, upbeat with a postal carrier's disposition toward the weather. "I used to carry mail in weather like this all the time. You just get used to it and do it. That's why my blood pressure is 110 over 70, every time."

As they left the shelter of the office to walk down the pier to the *Noble*, rain pelted the windows even harder from the east, pure wet nastiness. On the other hand, this is the moisture we looked for in August and didn't get, water critical to help maintain or raise lake levels. Every bit helps.

***

At noon, after a brief let-up, more wet squalls moved across the harbor with winds still gusting from the east. The squalls require skilled docking on the part of our ferry captains. Winds paste the ferry against the tires, and the engines are run hard to counteract the current. Our crew noted the small rocky outcropping on the opposite side of the channel from our pier, an old crib that marked the "false channel" decades ago. This morning, under wind pressure and low air pressure, the harbor levels have raised to the highest in months and the crib is awash. If it would only stay that way, but this is a "bathtub" gain, a sloshing of surface water from across Lake Michigan, wind driven into our little estuary.

***

Duly noting the rain splattering against our east office windows, the steady sheets of water running from the roof, ponding on the pavement, I headed down to the ferry to deliver an envelope to the crew before heading home for lunch. I wore a hooded sweatshirt, fleece vest and hat, but no rain gear, thinking, maybe, I'd be only a few minutes in the elements. The *Noble* crew was about to load a motor coach, and

I stayed to help direct the bus driver as the ferry spun around the dock to bow-load the bus. During those brief minutes while Erik maneuvered the bow to the pier, the rain fell as heavy as any time during the morning, enough to soak my trousers and sweatshirt and fill my shoes with runoff from my pants cuffs. The remedy waited for me at home: hot soup and dry clothing.

Our ferry crews on such days, despite rain gear and boots, can't help but get soaked. Eleven hours is a long day under such circumstances, not to mention the rough seas and windy landings that accompany a rain squall. Tiny rivulets trickle down arms, through small openings in rain suits, down neck and back. And if they've managed to stay dry while out on deck, once they're back inside the tiny 7- x 5-foot pilothouse, the act of taking off wet clothing means brushing against everything that is damp and clammy. It is a long day when your underwear and socks are soaking.

Wednesday, October 17 –

Rather than wind knocking down leaves and rain pelting windows, we awoke to a relatively quiet morning, a bit damp but no rain, and it was mild. By 9:30 a.m. the sun came out and it was quite pleasant, and as a result we saw quite a bit of traffic through the morning, with a good crowd on the Cherry Train. We also had as guests a small group of travel writers accompanied by Door County Visitor Bureau's Jon Jarosh. Two ferries met the traffic demand today, with no extra trips required.

We have a number of people working ashore. The *Washington's* Morse control system with failed transfer chain has been repaired. Jim Hanson installed a new set of forks on our Case backhoe. Tully did masonry work on stonewalls, completing one at the west end of the parking lot and starting another near our ticket booth.

***

We've decided to move forward with a new ramp at the outer end of the Northport Pier. I believe we're forced into this project by the low water we're experiencing and the fact our WDNR permit appeal has taken so long to reach a public hearing. With the prospect of little progress in the next six to nine months on the DNR case, we can't afford not to move ahead.

Thursday, October 18 –

Gloom, rain, and a warm wind from the ESE this morning. Severe weather, including thunderstorms and possible hail are in the mix for this large, moist, low pressure center hanging over Lake Superior, drawing air from the Gulf. Washington Island may be north of the worst weather, but at 9 a.m. winds are blowing sharply and the heavy precipitation is similar to several days ago.

The crew on the *Washington's* early run had the additional task of fueling the ferry by tanker truck at Northport. Our cost per gallon with a bulk tanker (approx. 7500 gallons), including transportation from the terminal in Green Bay, is $2.56 per gallon. This fill ought to hold the *Washington* for the remainder of the fall, with perhaps a small squirt of fuel later to top off the tanks for winter. Full fuel tanks, while penalized by the IRS as "supplies purchased but not consumed" in the calendar year, and therefore subject to inventory and tax, are much better off when they're full. As a result we've been required to declare unused fuel at the end of the season ever since our audit, a practical but ridiculous compromise with the Milwaukee federal office. I've found no other vessel company, large or small, abiding by these same requirements. On the contrary, vessel owners I've surveyed agree, full vessel fuel tanks in winter are best for the tanks and tank contents.

Despite winds that are in the range of 20-25 mph, we're able to make all of our trips, and the 9 a.m. ferry brought in a motor coach tour group. It is a shame these tour patrons won't have sunlight to show off the fall colors...but nevertheless, we're able to transport them with the certainty we will also get them back this afternoon. I can hear them now in our lobby, lining up for restrooms and finding shelter from the rain. Perhaps there will be incidental sales of post cards or sweatshirts!

***

Between 9 a.m. and 9:45 a.m., Hoyt and I participated in a three-way conference call with our legal counsels regarding the Northport Pier permit application. To ensure we have no surprises as we get started, we are advised to let the WDNR Field Representative know our plans, so that later if there should be questions, we have at least proof of notification. I'd consider that type of letter to be a professional courtesy. We hope that the simplicity of our requests to install a new ramp within the footprint of the existing Northport Pier, and to repair or replace a couple of suspect pilings holding up the south ramp apron, will be considered emergency work, and not routine repairs (which may often lead to public hearings, etc.).

Hoyt, who may have more tact in letter writing than I, will author the letter. He has also had the most frequent and most recent contact with WDNR field reps in the Green Bay office. If only the application of charm could guarantee results.

***

While enjoying a cheeseburger at Karly's over noon hour, the clouds began to lift, and by the time I returned to the Ferry Dock the sun had appeared. It remained breezy, with solid whitecaps south of the harbor entrance, manageable for our ferries. A surprising thing, seeing sunshine reflecting from deep puddles on the ferry dock, many ankle deep.

Driving home after work, it was hard not to appreciate the fall colors, even those leaves now pasted to the wet pavement. Color was all around. The sky, clearing in the west, had a few blue patches.

I thought a short motorcycle ride might be a good way to close the day, and so I headed from home eastward on Michigan Road, and soon a glow came over the land. The sun, near to setting, squinted between the horizon and layers of very low, thin clouds. The golden light reflected from the underside of the clouds, lighting up the sky with soft light. Round bales in the Davis field and the farm buildings at the crest of the hill reflected the sun's glow, reminding me of a Monet painting.

Eastward, extremely dark clouds hovered over the lake, with bolts of lightning snapping back and forth. By the time I had turned the corner at East Side Road and motored past Island Camping, a light rain began to fall. I identified five or six different cloud types in the sky, a mix of weather that would make a professional meteorologist scratch his head. The blue patch I had been hoping would enlarge, a sign of a high pressure system filling in, had vanished.

When we sat down to supper 15 minutes later, winds gusted at least 40 mph and rain pelted the windows of our kitchen. Concerned for how the last ferry was fairing, and if they had decent visibility for landing, we drove out to the ferry dock. There we met Walt Jorgenson in his car on the pier, also anxious to see how son Bill and his crew were doing. The rain came down sideways for about five minutes as Tully directed the two-car load off the bow of the *Arni J. Richter*. Then, within the minute, as if a valve were swung shut, the rain stopped and a section of sky revealed a half-moon. Captain Bill Jorgenson said there were numerous lightning strikes near them, and that their marine radio microphone "lit up" from the static discharge in the wheelhouse.

I'm always more at ease when the last ferry is in, safe in the protection of the harbor for the evening.

Friday, October 19 –

It would not seem possible to have another roisterous day after experiencing three out of four already this week, but winds this morning are fresh from the south, about 25 mph. The marine forecast calls for gale force winds this afternoon with rain showers and gusts to 40 to 50 mph. If that velocity is reached, we will likely be forced to suspend operations.

I'm with Fred Hankwitz and Ken Berggren, three licensed captains, so we are loaded with experience on the *Washington* today! It was still dark when I left the ferry office where ticket seller Jason Carr was checking the internet on an office computer before heading out the door to start his shift. Jason will man the Northport booth today. Bill Crance, in one of his many roles, will be in our island ticket booth. Fifteen vehicles waited in line at the island for our early 7 a.m. ferry.

The slop we experienced in the Door came from mixed seas, varied wind and wave energies wrapped around the tip of the Door, its shoals and islands. These conditions continued throughout our four round trips until Rich, Hoyt and Eric Brodersen took over in the afternoon. Their shift will continue into the evening through the scheduled Friday night trips, assuming conditions allow them safe passage. Cancellation of this evening's trips are a real possibility, and in our ferry office through the day callers are reminded of that possibility.

"When will you cancel?" "How will you know?" "At what point will you make that call?"

Repeated questions, each without a definitive answer.

Saturday, October 20 –

My second day as one of the early ferry crew, this time with Fred Hankwitz and Ron Kleckner.

A rich blue tone covered northern Lake Michigan. With the morning sun and 65-degree air, fresh at first from the west at 25 mph, then diminishing, we began to see many visitors arriving at Northport. Three ferries were kept busy hauling in passengers and vehicles to the island, with a reversal of traffic flow around 3 p.m. Our crew onboard the *Washington* made seven round trips today, nearly a July level of activity.

***

We observed more than the usual number of freighters throughout the day today. Our assumption was that many had sought shelter in port, laying at anchor while the winds howled from the south, then the west. Three ore carriers hugged the Wisconsin shoreline this morning, not more than one mile off Pilot Island. A short while later the *Joseph Block* steamed southeast, outbound through the Door for Indiana Harbor, loaded with taconite pellets at the Escanaba ore docks. A "salty," its profile of masts and booms and high bow unmistakably that of an ocean freighter, headed north in the Bay toward Rock Island Passage in the early afternoon. It rode high and looked light, having possibly unloaded tallow or pig iron or some other product at the Port of Green Bay or Menominee, MI the previous evening. The *Maumee*, a gray-hulled cement boat, also steamed north out of Green Bay, leading the salty by a mile or two. With a clear atmosphere and good forecast, ship masters were making the best of improved conditions to cram as many fall trips in as weather and time would allow.

Sunday, October 21 –

The trees in our yard are now yellow, and sunlight reflects from those leaves on the ground. Fallen, flattened, golden leaves.

Before the sun's first rays, Atlas crawled in bed between us and offered a request: "Gramma, let's have a feast." A few winks later and the sun was up, and shortly after that, pancake batter sputtered in the pan. While breakfast was underway, Atlas played with 20-year-old Star Wars toys and action figures, blasting away at a power plant made from wooden blocks. He's given these toys more play time than his Uncle Thor, original owner, now 27.

Monday, October 22 –

Much cooler today and overcast, with the possibility of rain later in the evening.

Tree leaf colors appear rusty when the sun's not shining.

Our ferry schedule reduces one week from today to six daily trips from the current 11 round trips. Not only is it cooler, so that there's little tourism, but the two hours between departure times on our ferry schedule also becomes less attractive to day visitors. Hard to gauge what is the optimum in scheduling, but experience tells us that when a front is pressing against us, blowing in excess of 30 mph, and the temperature gets down to near-freezing, as it will, then we are quite content to complete only six trips per day, and that's sometimes three or four more than we'd prefer. This coming weekend, clocks are set back one hour, so that when our last ferry departs Northport the sun will have already set and the route home will be dark.

Between now and Thanksgiving we tackle outdoor projects with a passion, trying to accomplish as many tasks as possible, especially on the good days, knowing we'll be driven indoors soon by colder weather.

Tuesday, October 23 –

Expecting the possibility of rain, I am elated to instead find sunshine and clear, blue skies, temperatures in the upper 50s, and a pleasant, light breeze from the north.

***

In addition to our permit application for the south ramp at Northport, stalled in legal hassles right now, and in addition to the dredging permits we applied for and received, and in addition to the planned work on the outer end of Northport Pier to build a new ramp there (because the permit process has stalled on the south ramp), we're moving ahead with applications on other dock projects.

If this seems like an endless amount of dock work, it is because of low water and the convergence of several factors at once. The existing steel apron on the south side of the Northport dock has H-piles that have been damaged over time by ice banging against the flanges. This has weakened and bent the supports, and it is imperative we fix this before we carry heavy traffic over the apron. To do this, we need separate permission, aside from the permit application for new ramp and apron supports. We applied for a special "Piling Exemption Permit" and we hope to have a positive answer on the fast track by next week. There is no way this one should be denied. However, given our recent record of discord with the WDNR, nothing would surprise us.

***

Next door to our island property is the former Standard Oil property, owned by Hansen Oil Company, Ray Hansen, owner. Ray has applied for a permit to drive steel sheeting around the dock face on his waterfront, old wooden cribs collapsing with age and deterioration. This is a good time for two things to occur: 1) a settlement of the question of who owns the face of the Standard Oil dock, and 2) a repair of the corner of our slip where the face of the dock has fallen into the ferry slip.

An unusual item surfaced, not an illegality, but an oddity, in that the land transferred to Carl and Arni Richter from Standard Oil in 1943 was never legally transferred to the Ferry Line, and that needs to be corrected. For one thing, Carl has been gone these past 40 or more years. And Arni needs to sign over this sliver of land, an important piece of waterfront, to the Ferry Line.

***

I received a copy of the 2007 Detroit Island Deer Survey completed by Detroit Island summer resident, and also Ferry Line Director, Joel Lueking. This is the second year Joel has done this from a rented helicopter. His findings show that the winter deer population is approximately 60 deer, four times that of the "biological carrying capacity" of that land. Besides browsing on desirable young trees and shoots, the deer herd also enables Lyme disease to propagate with ticks found there. This is a fairly recent phenomenon, deer ticks and Lyme disease on Detroit Island, and it might have been initiated by animals, a horse or a dog, brought in by summer residents. In any case, the ticks with Lyme disease have spread across the island, aided by deer whose warm blood is essential for the adult stage tick to survive and reproduce. An invitation is open to hunters to reduce the Detroit Island population significantly from the density now found there: 60 per square mile.

Wednesday, October 24 –

A few puddles on the pavement in the morning were evidence of a light rain as the cold front came through. When the sun arose, the skies cleared to blue. Our temperature at 8 a.m. was 48 degrees. Leaves on the trees are now somewhere near two-thirds fallen to the ground. The brown leaves of the red oaks are still pretty much intact, and an amazing number of birches have yet to turn golden yellow. Despite these exceptions, the peak of fall colors is behind us, with a few more weeks of gradually fading, duller colors before the tree line is a scraggle of limbs and branches.

***

I rode to Northport on the *Arni J. Richter* at 9 a.m., with Bill Jorgenson, Captain. He sailed south of Plum Island, in the lee of the island, and on the backside of Plum as we passed the *Robert Noble* returning to the island, we ran into increasing swells. Power was reduced and our course was angled to feather through the waves.

At Northport, having seen the progress Joel and Tully had made on a new wooden railing on the property north of Mrs. Eller's home, I made a quick visit to the Northport Restaurant kitchen, now closed. The kitchen crew was in the middle of cleaning prior to turning off water and power to that section of the building.

***

We rolled across the Door until an optimum moment when Bill put the hammer down and turned sharply to starboard, running with the seas toward Pilot Island, avoiding rolling in the trough. The *Arni J.* tends to roll heavily in a following sea, unlike our other ferries which have a square transom and full, hard chine. We were soon behind Plum Island, sailing along smartly in the lee with our load.

***

The breeze let up in mid-afternoon and a beautiful sunset graced the horizon over Door Bluff. Our traffic had been fairly steady during the day, with trucks, bass fishermen, and a few travelers out enjoying the fall colors.

Thursday, October 25 –

Most days start out quite relaxed. On this day, it seemed, there wasn't nearly enough time. I was out a bit earlier than usual to prepare for the 7 a.m. ferry, arriving about 6:20, before a fiery sun rose over Detroit Island. I'd received an early morning call from Mike Kierkoff, Schuh Transport driver, while on his way to the Green Bay terminal. Weather looked good in Green Bay Mike said, and I reported the same: little to no wind, and a good forecast for the day. He would be at Northport for a 7:15 a.m. pickup.

Al Stelter arrived at the Ferry Office door just ahead of me to punch in. Liz Geddert was warming her breakfast in the microwave, and Tully Ellefson was gathering up warm clothing for the day. They would crew on the *Arni J.* with Bill Jorgenson, the second ferry crew leaving the island early, and they would transport the tankers. We would take the regular traffic.

At Northport, after the tankers loaded, a challenging mix remained: three vehicles pulling trailers, five or six autos, and Al Hiller in the Veolia truck.

The bass fishermen, apparently hearing of success of the prior weekend's fishing, arrived with bass boats, mostly the wide Ranger boats. Those boats and several construction contractor trailers filled up our ferry quickly.

At 10 a.m., we again made a trip, returning the empty tankers — flammable vessels and therefore no other traffic could accompany them — on the *Robert Noble*. Enroute, our course took us within a half mile of the ore carrier *Kaye Barker*, headed west through the Door and down the bay, perhaps to Bay Shipbuilding.

***

With the transfer of the parcel from Arni Richter to the Ferry Line, legal descriptions need to be redone. The Ferry Line must Quit Claim this piece back to the Ferry Line, so that it can be included in one comprehensive description of the entire waterfront property. A rather entangled mess and many steps. Among the names of old-time islanders appearing on the property Deed Search were Ole Christianson, who operated a boat yard where we currently land our ferries, and Nor Shellswick, owner of considerable acreage on Lobdell's Point, and J.W. Cornell (Mary Jo's maternal grandfather), who bought land north or the ferry dock from Ole.

Friday, October 26 –

A news item in the local paper, highlighted by Carol Meyer who heard the information first hand: Margaret Young sighted a frigate bird not long ago as it soared above the waters of the harbor in front of their home. The bird's huge wingspan and split tail were unmistakable. Later that day, Margaret's husband, Jim, spotted it again, and he was in position to take a good photo. According to ornithological records this was only the third sighting of a frigate bird in Wisconsin history. The first was in the 1800s, the next was only 10 years or so ago.

I recalled watching these birds effortlessly skim the wave tops as we steamed on a U.S. destroyer from Hawaii to Guam in 1972.

***

My 9:45 appointment at the Pinkert Law Firm followed a quick stop at LeFevre's Tire on the West Side of Sturgeon Bay. My current set of truck tires is original with over 69,100 miles on them. I bought the same style of Goodrich tires to replace the originals at $185 each.

I was given a loaner van by Dennis LeFevre for my morning's appointments in town, a very generous offer. It is a turquoise Olds minivan, and it saved me a great deal of time, allowing me to get to my appointments.

The Pinkert Law Firm, located on Kentucky Street, just a block from Baylake Bank, was begun by Herman Leasum years ago. Herman became Sturgeon Bay city attorney for a number of years, and as Arni's brother-in-law he also handled legal matters for this ferry company. He kindly performed many unsung tasks, with unbilled hours I suspect, because that was the type of person Herman was. Herman's father had a dental practice here on Washington Island when Herman was young, and Charlie, Herman's brother, was an Army physician and a survivor of the Bataan death march in the Philippines.

Herman assisted many island organizations, and he enjoyed his association with island people over the years, even though he was a resident and practiced in Sturgeon Bay, WI. He was the legal advisor for the Island Electric Co-op. He incorporated the Island Medical Memorial Fund in the 1960s, of which I am currently serving as president. And I recall signing the papers Herman drew up for the purchase of our home on Main Road in the cabin of the *Eyrarbakki,* as we headed to Gills Rock in 1976. I was a deckhand that day, and Herman was headed back home on the last ferry of the afternoon.

Tuesday, October 31 –

On our return run to the island, I visited with Jerry Vietinghoff, a marine engineering consultant here to help us pinpoint the source of vibration on the *AJR* starboard shaft. Jerry would have been here last week, but his equipment hadn't caught up with him from his last job on a ship near Nova Scotia. Then, from Nova Scotia he went to Norway for another vessel. Now he's coming to the island, and we hope to get enough data in one day to enable him to conclude with a high degree of certainty what the problem is, or is not.

***

Halloween was observed. A breezy morning with light rain at noon, then a change of weather as clear air and a cold front fills in. By evening, it was quite windy from the NW, maybe 25 kts, with leaves blowing around the yard, but still not a bad evening for the trick-or-treaters. We had Arni and family members over for dinner, including Aidan, Kirsten and Hoyt who had been out trick-or-treating. Arni appeared to enjoy this time with his family, something that used to occur with regularity at his home, but has become rare. He was buoyed by his visiting granddaughter, Brenda, and niece, Linda, who happened to be visiting from San Diego and Denver, respectively. And, Arni had a surprise visit by two special island trick-or-treaters, Lois MacDonald and Jeannine Ronning.

Lois' father, John, was an engineer on a Great Lakes ore boat and one of Arni's best friends, and her mother, Clara, an island school teacher for her career, was a bridge partner of Mary Richter's. Jeannine is related through the Gudmundsen family connection, early Icelandic settlers on the island.

***

Jerry Vietinghoff, Orian Technology, obtained necessary data from two underway trials on the *Arni J.,* and his initial impressions are that the stuffing box gland is not in alignment. He doesn't believe the vibration is caused by either the propeller, the shaft, the engine, or gear box, based on harmonics and his computer model. This is good news as it narrows down the source and eliminates other potentially problematic areas. Now, resolving misalignment, which we thought was the culprit, is possible. But we'll need the shipyard's cooperation. Our crew dropped off Jerry at Northport following the second trial run, about 3 p.m.

Rich, Hoyt and I met with Bob Larsen, Chief Engineer for Marine Travelift of Sturgeon Bay, and we discussed our need for a long, adjustable ramp at the end of the Northport dock. Marine Travelift and Bob have the necessary engineering experience to design a new ramp, and Exactech, a Travelift subsidiary also in Sturgeon Bay, is capable of cutting the steel and assembling the ramp for us. Exactech cut and partially assembled an island ramp we installed in 2001.

NOVEMBER

Thursday, November 1 –

A cold front whistled through leafless trees this morning as dawn broke. A few puffy cumulus clouds were scattered across the eastern sky, and our temperatures dropped into the 40s for the first time in months.

***

A routine morning at the onset turned quickly into a fire drill to rectify a problem with the *Robert Noble* at the Northport ramp.

After admiring the stonework Tully had started near the Island Pizza building, several courses laid and a fresh batch of mortar in the wheelbarrow, I began untangling paperwork on my desk. Joel and Liz came in with the *Eyrarbakki* from the first, early morning run, and tied it up to spend the remainder of their day ashore.

Then, a phone call came from Bill Jorgenson, captain on the *Noble* with Eric Brodersen as crew. He explained that the Cihlar block truck had backed on the ferry, pushing the ferry outward from the shore ramp, and the truck dropped its set of bogey wheels between the ferry and the shore ramp. The truck now straddled the open gap. The ferry's head lines had not been tightly secured before the truck began to back, and Bill said he hadn't yet gone to the wheelhouse to apply more rpm's to the ferry engines to push hard against the tires. The adjustable, hydraulic shore ramp was already in its lowest position, and with low water, the truck's back axles were considerably lower than its front axle.

The heavily constructed truck loaded with cement blocks, maybe 25 tons gross weight, had a fairly short wheelbase of perhaps twenty feet. By backing onto the ferry foredeck, it pushed the ferry out and downward, stretching the mooring lines taut, and the ferry's bow ramp dropped. As it dropped (it weighs in the neighborhood of 1 1/2 tons), cable connections were broken, and now it hung from its hinged connection, more or less straight down toward the water.

The truck's front tires and intermediate axle tires were still on the shore ramp with wheel chocks under them, and the situation was stable.

Joel, Liz and I got the *Eyrarbakki* underway, taking with us two chain hoists, a spool of cable and an oxy-acetylene torch. The seas had begun to subside from earlier that morning which, according to Joel, had forced them to take the southern route around Plum Island. But this time, with only one auto and our equipment on board, we opted to bang into the seas around the west side of Plum Island.

When we arrived and assessed the situation, I was disappointed to find the truck's one set of rear wheels hanging in mid-air. That could prove to be a problem if we couldn't lift the ramp with our chain hoists. The driver had already unloaded the pallets of concrete blocks into stacks on deck while he waited for assistance. There were six cars plus Mann's Store truck with groceries on the ferry, toward the stern, but the foredeck was otherwise clear. With chain falls attached to rings at the outer end of the ferry ramp, we managed to winch the ramp up bit-by-bit to a near-level position. Then, with the driver at the wheel of the block truck, BJ in the wheelhouse, and each of us on mooring lines to control our movement, we slacked headlines to let the ferry sag back. In a coordinated effort, the driver rolled his front wheels and truck about 20 inches closer to the water's edge, holding his rear wheels firm with air brakes on the ferry's deck. This gave us sufficient room to lift the ramp the remainder of the way from its hanging position.

When our chain hoists could no longer lift — coming up against the added weight of one set of truck wheels plus the ramp weight — the driver set down his intermediate axle on the shore ramp. This removed just enough weight from the ferry to lift the bow a few inches. The ferry ramp now overlapped the shore ramp. Bill then forced the ferry forward with the engines, putting us back in a traditional, properly moored position.

All things considered, this incident was resolved with no damage other than a snapped ramp cable that would be easily replaced. One minor injury had occurred when a cable clamp struck Eric on the top of his head. His stocking cap absorbed the hit and the abrasion appeared to be minor.

Reconstructing what had gone wrong, there were numerous deficiencies: an over anxious driver; unclear instructions to crew; insufficient engine power and slack lines...and one that we for the moment can't do much about...low water.

Friday, November 2 –

I'm part of the *Arni J.* crew along with Hoyt and Eric Brodersen, headed to Northport for the early run, then a back-to-back trip to return two empty LP tankers for Ray Hansen. The weather looks good for tankers, with winds forecast to go westerly by late in the day.

***

Our first load was tight. Besides several autos and pickups we had two squad cars, one a county car, the other a state squad car, most likely coming to the island to educate school children about drugs, drinking, driving and to maintain a positive connection with youth. A "DARE" decal was on the door of the state car. Filling our center lanes was a pickup towing a small pop-up camper and two pickups towing bass boats. Those two trailers with 200 hp outboard motors, Ranger-style bass boats, were wide and long. The last vehicle to show, which had been on our reservation board, was a short dump truck from PCI Concrete in Bailey's Harbor loaded with pea gravel. Good thing it was short, because it barely fit in the remaining opening on deck. Hoyt asked the bass boat owners to lower their motors, and that gained us another six inches, enough for the dump truck to get on deck with the bow ramp closed.

***

This is the 18th anniversary of John Fitzgerald's untimely death. I often think about John, his wife, Phyllis, and their family of many children, all girls until at last a boy, John Jr., who is every bit as friendly and willing as his dad. John did tons of dock work for us, building piers, dredging, removing snow and other contract work.

John tackled big jobs in a practical, efficient way. If there was any shortcoming, it was that John didn't watch his own health as carefully as he should have. He seemed indestructible, but then an injury from a swinging beam deeply bruised his shoulder. A blood clot, a heart valve replacement, and doctor's orders to take it easy didn't stop him from pushing himself afterward. John's heart gave out on the ferry *Voyageur* late one afternoon after he had floated two large steel bins fabricated from ship's tank bottoms across Hedgehog Harbor to Door Bluff.

I had photographed him in coveralls with grease smears, sweat and curly hair, hand on hip as his diesel hammer slammed steel sheets into the lake bottom at Northport in 1982 when that pier was extended. John gave whatever was needed to get the job done.

Saturday, November 3 –

Sunny. Cool morning. Light SW breeze. A very fair day for early November. A light jacket or sweater is suitable for most any activity except, perhaps, standing out on the ferry deck while crossing the Door. Underway, it is nearly impossible to get away from the wind. Even full sunshine won't negate the drafts.

I left this morning on the 8 a.m. ferry. Today I am the mail carrier, and I'll drive our mail van to Ellison Bay and back, exchanging sacks of outgoing mail, boxes, and pouches for the incoming mail, all within a time of 25 minutes or less. I can make the run if there isn't much highway traffic and the ferry waits for me. They will!

On my exit from the ferry I thought I recognized familiar faces in line from Manistique, a cousin of Mary Jo's and his wife, Bill and Beth Malloch. I couldn't stop to confirm my hunch until I returned from Ellison Bay.

Seven miles down the highway, I poked my head in the back door of the Ellison Bay P.O. to let them know I was there and not Steve Kalms, our regular mail driver. Gloria Johnson, postal assistant for many years who has outlasted the careers of many Ellison Bay post-masters and rural route carriers, answered cheerily as she sorted the northern Liberty Grove mail. I wrestled with one of two carts, both heaped with island-bound mail. After unloading the smaller cart, I rolled it empty toward the building. Then, island outbound mail from my van got tossed into that empty cart. Already 12 minutes into my routine, I transferred the rest of the incoming mail from a cart stacked 6 feet high into my van. By the time I'd finished, mail filled the entire back section of the van to the front seats, level with the windows. I slammed the rear door closed and hit the road for Northport.

Onboard the ferry was my sister, Helen, and my mother. They would be our weekend guests and would attend Aidan's "golden" 2-year old birthday party. I found Bill and Beth Malloch in the passenger cabin, and Suzanne, Kirsten's mom (Hoyt's mother-in-law). Sitting at the cabin table was Tim Sweet, leader and exceptionably able volunteer of the Rock Island Friends group. Tim has placed energy toward the formation of a new group, the Friends of Plum and Pilot Islands (FOPPI).

A unique connection was made between Bill and Beth Malloch and Tim Sweet. Always on the alert for capable docents on Rock Island, Tim learned Bill's grandfather was a lighthouse keeper on Rock Island years ago. A photo of Bill's grandfather in lightkeeper uniform hangs prominently on one of the lighthouse walls. Would they consider being docents, spending a week living in the lighthouse on Rock Island?

Tim Sweet spoke briefly about the docks at Plum and Pilot Islands, their present state of repair and the wisdom of putting first efforts into fixing them up for safe and reliable small boat landing. Ice and seas have ground away ends of the large timbers on the Plum Island pier and breakwall arm, and at Pilot there is only an isolated section of cement pier, barely adequate for even a small boat to properly moor.

***

It's hard to be more proud of a son, Hoyt, daughter-in-law with baby soon-to-be, Kirsten, and a two year old grandson, Aidan. The party was a very lively affair with friends and relatives and their children having fun, with children running loops around the kitchen, living room and front room. At the center of focus and having only one other birthday as a yardstick, young Aidan Hoyt Purinton was a great host. He gave hugs, thanked people, and was far more engaging than one might have hoped, considering the noise, confusion, and his missed afternoon nap. He is a pleasure to observe.

We took a ride before dark — Mom, Helen, Mary Jo and I — to Jackson Harbor. The evening glow settled upon the back roads, typical of late fall. In the State Park lot were seven pickups with trailers. Visiting bass club fishermen were hitting it hard along the island's northern shore while the calm waters allowed. In the harbor between the state and town docks lay the exposed remains of the *Iris*, an abandoned schooner. State Historical officials and divers refer to this as a 'shipwreck,' but it is, in fact, a hull that was abandoned, cast-off, no longer fit for sailing. In my mind this relic is akin to finding a rusted-out pickup in the woods, with questionable historical importance. In any case, remains of this hull can be accessed easily from shore in flip-flops, no flippers and snorkel being necessary.

Sunday, November 4 –

In the air this morning is a tension of weather soon to come. Current conditions are a cool 34 degrees with frost on the windshield, absolutely calm on the water, not a ripple.

I drove to the ferry dock to address unfinished work before Mom, Helen and Mary Jo stirred. I had awakened at 4:30 a.m. (our clocks had been set back one hour before going to bed) and after reading awhile, I drove to the dock.

Joel Gunnlaugsson arrived early, too. He and Rich Ellefson were preparing to get the *Arni J.* underway for Bay Ship this morning, rather than wait 24 hours until the weather turned. The regular early crew came in shortly thereafter, as did Patty Cornell, island ticket seller.

I made copies of the vibration report just received via email from our technician, and prepared my own files for leaving early Monday morning. The weather on the NOAA near shore forecast predicted gale force winds of 35-40 mph with gusts to 50 mph Monday, then cooling and swinging NW, increasing slightly to 45 mph gales, with gusts again to 50 mph. Snow flurries were part of the forecast mix both Monday and Tuesday. With such wind velocities predicted, our ability to make trips could be hampered and service discontinued for a time.

A number of customers also knew this, and they had decided to leave the island early to avoid missing appointments. One was Joe Elmore who boarded the early ferry with a trailer filled with prized cattle, two bulls and several cows with calves. A part of his load was headed for a national show in Louisville, KY, Tuesday. Other travelers had heard of changing weather and they exited the island while traveling was good.

As it turned out, Sunday proved to be a fine day, calm in every respect even up to sunset. In fact, it is hard to fathom gale force winds and snow flurries with icy winds within 24 hours when it is so moderate at the moment.

Monday, November 5 –

The switch from daylight savings time to standard time, "falling back one hour," makes it easier to get up early, and so this morning I rolled out of bed to shower at 5:20 a.m., packed a bag just in case I didn't get home, and rounded up gear for my trip off the island.

Strangely, the wind had remained calm all night, and our current early morning weather gives no hint of what forecasters say lies ahead. The barometer is dropping, however, and just past daybreak treetops began to sway. According to our computer weather report, the Upper Peninsula is already getting plenty of wind, and the low is sliding over Lake Superior. They will get snow tonight, up to a foot in places.

***

Winds increased from nothing at daybreak to 25 mph by the time we cleared the harbor entrance light on the *Robert Noble*, on our way to the shipyard in Sturgeon Bay. To the west, clouds were dark with impending rain, but to the east there was a sunny hole in the sky pouring down golden light on Pilot and the far end of Detroit Island. This would be the day's pattern, dark patches and open skylights, with ever-increasing winds.

***

On my way into Sturgeon Bay, I phoned Rich. The yard tug had just opened the doors to the flooded dry dock, a very small graving dock that is the oldest piece of equipment on the property. The *Arni J.* was about to depart from its berth for the dry dock. Winds by this time were blowing a steady 35 mph. Over at the far pier was the *Spirit of Chicago*, a 4-decker dinner cruise passenger vessel that had arrived at Bay Shipbuilding during the night. She was scheduled to enter the single section of floating dry dock (the other section already held Milwaukee's *Lake Express*), but side winds and the high sail area nixed docking operations.

Rich made an excellent entry to the dock opening by coming in high and settling down with the wind, then gently nudging forward inside the protection of the dock walls. The dock walls allow approximately 10 feet on either side of the ferry. The AJR stern settled down with about 20 feet of stern still hanging beyond the gates, and some paint was scraped from the starboard rail, but the ferry was safely inside the dock where it could be finely adjusted with cables and winches. By the end of the hour, large pumps had begun removing water from the dock, a process that would take nearly five hours.

While the dock was being pumped dry, Joel and Rich were more or less captive on board, and they began planning the work to be undertaken once the ferry sat squarely on the blocks and the dock floor was dry.

I drove to Two Rivers with my company pickup to get the repaired *C.G. Richter* propeller and two refurbished *Arni J. Richter* stern bearings. It would be 2:30 p.m. when I got back to the yard, having driven through both sunshine and rain.

On my way to Kahlenberg Bros., as I passed through Kewaunee, Rich called me with a new problem. A rubber strip from an oil seal on the rear output shaft of the reduction gear had begun to work itself out between the shaft and the gearbox. This newly discovered item might be a sign of an output bearing beginning to fail. Conversation with Twin Disc reps at the Palmer Johnson Power Systems in Sun Prairie confirmed the gear could, or would, fail in the near future, with the possibility of further damage to the gear. The kicker was that the gearbox package weighed in at 4500 lbs., and it would have to be removed intact and driven to the Sun Prairie shop where trained technicians with proper tools could press on new parts. This new problem added significantly to our current project scope, and to the shipyard labor and cost of both removal and reinstallation besides the cost of the overhaul.

At home, the day hadn't improved. Our ferry crew made trips despite gusts into the 40s, but in late afternoon the decision was made to cancel the last trip. The three of us would spend the night in Sturgeon Bay rather than head home. Tuesday's forecast called for even greater winds, this time from the NW rather than the west.

We were certain the reduction gear needed to be removed and repaired because we couldn't afford a mid-winter breakdown when equipment, manpower, and a means of transporting a heavy gear would be very limited. A winter gear failure could have the potential of curtailing island commerce for a number of weeks. As it was, if we got the gear to the Twin Disc shop right away, we might have the gear back in the ship in 10 days.

At the Kahlenberg Bros. shop I waited awhile for the shipping/receiving manager to return from lunch break. Meanwhile a computerized lathe operator located the pallets with our prop and bearings. Among the deep warehouse shelving parts were props of all shapes and sizes, bronze and stainless. Once known for manufacturing slow-speed diesels crafted by hand, Kahlenberg is now a major supplier of ice class propellers, air horns, and machined castings. Their biggest machined casting customer currently is the Manitowoc crane division, just a few miles down the lakeshore.

I signed the receiving slips and inquired about our new shaft machined by the Kahlenberg shop. The 18-foot Aquamet shaft had already been shipped to Badger Roll in Green Bay, a shop with finish machining capabilities. They would fit the propeller shaft to the coupling.

❊❊❊

Back at Bay Shipbuilding in the late afternoon, I met with Rich and three Bay Ship representatives, including General Manager Todd Thayse, head machinist Steve Krauel, and new construction supervisor Steve Propsom, project manager when the *Arni J.* was built. We discussed the vibration problems and a game plan to determine cause and eliminate non-factors. We now had the gearbox situation to address as well. Number one was to get the ferry repaired. Second, determine cause, if possible.

Another late afternoon wrinkle popped up. When I spoke with Hoyt to see if there was a chance the ferry would run anymore that day so that we could get home, he informed me Kirsten had begun light labor, the start of regular contractions. Would she hold out on the island with no chance of leaving during the night, or would they opt to get off while they could on the last ferry? They chose to stay home.

❊❊❊

That evening the Maritime Inn on 14th and Egg Harbor Road

became the Island Annex, with many familiar faces popping in and out. Rich stayed in Egg Harbor with his wife and children, who were on their way back from delivering niece Liz Geddert to the airport. She would return to her home in British Columbia.

Larry McCarren's Locker Room show that evening featured Brett Favre as guest, perhaps the NFL's single-most popular figure, all the more interesting because of the Packer winning streak and Brett's top-caliber play this season. We watched on the large TV in the lobby along with some of the Maritime Inn staff.

Tuesday, November 6 –

Winds whipped across the shipyard, sending up swirls of dust at velocities advertised. I had called Hoyt at 6:45 a.m. at his home on a ridge in the center of a field, an excellent place to gauge the wind. The ferry would not make a trip that morning, he said, and maybe not all day.

Rich was already there when Joel and I arrived at the shipyard. We were ahead of the team of machinists who were scheduled to remove the starboard propeller from the *Arni J.* When the 7 a.m. whistle sounded, yard workers leaned into the wind across open stretches of pier, one hand on their hard hats, the other holding a bucket of tools or walkie-talkie. An outside job on such a day can be brutal, and the 39-degree temperature was not forecast to rise through the day.

One of the machinists told me, "You know, I'd rather work in the cold than in the heat. At least you can dress for it. In summer you might have to crawl into a small, enclosed space like a tank where the temperature is over 100 and there is little air movement. And you're already down to the fewest clothes you can wear."

One problem this morning: the bottom of the dry dock had gained a foot or more of water from leakage overnight. No work could begin until it was pumped dry, so the entourage of workers instead trooped to the *Arni J.'s* engine room. There, Rich and Joe Weber, foreman, discussed ways of getting at the gearbox, how best to remove it. A plan was formulated, a step-by-step process everyone was clear on. One goal was to disturb as little of the overhead insulation and main deck plating as possible.

***

I went over to the *Spirit of Chicago* to visit friend Oscar Fittipaldi. His crew had fashioned makeshift sleeping quarters on air mattresses in the vacant dining and entertainment spaces. They didn't have a very good night on board as mooring lines popped and the vessel bumped and ground against the windward side of the steel pier.

I invited Oscar to come over to visit our crew and to see our ferry. From Argentina, Oscar is the marine manager who oversees the Spirit fleet of three cruise vessels and several Rocket boats, go-fast passenger boats, all operating from Navy Pier in Chicago. We spent an hour or so in the *Arni J.*'s engine room talking shop, explaining how our ferry was arranged. We earned several very nice compliments from Oscar both for style of layout and cleanliness of the engine room, comments well received by Rich and Joel who do much of the actual work to maintain the ferry in top condition.

***

By late morning the starboard propeller was removed from the shaft and strapped in the back of my red pickup truck, and I started for Metso, a company in Neenah that specialized in spin-balancing. We would spend even more dollars here to construct an arbor to fit the prop hub, necessary for Metso to conduct a dynamic spin test for us. From that testing we would be able to tell if the prop was a source of vibration or not.

The Metso shop is adjacent to the Kimberly Clark headquarters, just off Hwy. 41. I backed through the airlock door and under an overhead crane. When the hoist picked up the prop, the readout showed actual weight of 1700 lbs.

***

At the Maritime Inn that evening, we again saw familiar faces as people returned from travels and learned the ferry had shut down. No one was surprised, but the question that followed was, 'What about tomorrow?'

Forty degrees was today's high temperature, and the television news reported Gills Rock had steady winds of 46 mph.

Wednesday, November 7 –

Winds dropped during the night and dawn peeped through a partially cloudy sky. Ferry trips are assured today, and in fact two ferries will shove off early from the island to catch up on the traffic backlog, getting people on their way as quickly as possible. Joel and I drove to Northport, after meeting Rich at the filling station north of town to exchange last minute information. Rich would stay another night monitoring the *AJR*'s progress.

At the Northport freight garage, Joel and I encountered three carts loaded with food products and a stack of some 40 UPS and FEDEX packages. We loaded the packages in our truck and towed the carts down the pier to the ferry. Patty Cornell noticed our plastic trashcan was missing from its location near the beach. Only the heavy metal lid lay on the ground. After searching, we spotted the can pinched between stones of the south breakwall, its paper and trash contents strewn throughout the 6-foot tall phragmites that grew along the beach. Two groups of misplaced items: the trash and the invasive phragmites. Patty and I patrolled the beach and reclaimed 90 percent of the litter, but we think a small portion sailed east on the gale winds to Beaver Island or Charlevoix.

Rich remained at the shipyard to monitor work progress and to answer questions regarding preferences on this or that, what methods to use for determining alignment, and so forth. Yard machinists will set up a wire today to determine if the stern tube and original machining was on target.

Our new propeller shaft, now at Badger machine shop along with the old prop coupling, was double-checked for straightness. Questions arose as to how perfect the alignment was and how straightness ought to be measured. Yard machinist Terry Gunnlaugsson, with family ties to Washington Island, accompanied Rich to Badger in Green Bay to observe the measurements.

***

When the 8 a.m. ferry from the island arrived at Northport, I met it on the pier. Today was my scheduled day to drive the Island Community Van, and so I slid behind the wheel and drove behind the line of traffic that snaked down that first stretch of Hwy. 42, headed to Sturgeon Bay. I would see many of these same cars and drivers on the streets of Sturgeon Bay later that day, some of them several times. The Ferry Line has for a number of years given the Community Van a pass, with each senior passenger paying their own fare.

One of my passengers today is Dave McCormick who was born on Plum Island when his father was stationed there in the Coast Guard. That was in the early 1940s. Today, giving birth to a child on Plum Island seems strange and remote, but at the time, servicemen were permitted to build and own a home there, and they raised their families on this island.

While parked at places around town such as at WalMart, I met several familiar faces, including Tim Weborg's of Gills Rock. Tim, walking gingerly, had recently had all of his toenails yanked, he told me. A fungus had set in and the medicine to cure it was a danger to his liver, so he chose pliers over pills. His description of the procedure made me queezy, and Kay (Koyen) Polster, who was also present, excused herself rather than hear more. Then, while waiting for my passengers who were shopping, I spotted "Stan, the Frito Lay Man." For years, Stan met our ferry weekly at Gills Rock, and later at Northport. In later years, before retirement, Stan drove his delivery truck on the ferry with large orders for Mann's Store. He was always friendly and always happy to fill orders. Before Stan departed, he zipped open his jacket and proudly showed off his burgundy red Ferry Line sweatshirt with the *Arni J. Richter* monogrammed across the chest.

***

Because we had extra time on our return north, I took detours with the Community Van as we neared Gills Rock, roads my passengers had probably never driven on. I pointed out the Garrett Bay boat launch. We drove the shoreline around Hedgehog Harbor and then swung into Gills Rock. At the old ferry dock, the newly-surfaced parking lot had stones strewn about. Seas driven by exceptionally strong westerly winds the night before had carried stones around the Shoreline Marina pier, then huge waves flipped several bushels of them onto the parking lot. Some stones were 6 inches across.

***

While we waited in line for the 5 p.m. ferry as traffic filled in behind us, I visited with Larry Young, a motorcycling partner and an island carpenter. Meanwhile, the *Robert Noble* pulled into the landing and unloaded, and I missed my chance to say "Good luck" to Kirsten and Hoyt. They were headed to Green Bay, finally, to the hospital. There, in the next 48 hours, Kirsten anticipated giving birth to a new baby boy.

Thursday, November 8 –

It is cool, in the upper 30s. A light sleet fell the night before and the pavement was wet. Mary Jo is staying at Hoyt and Kirsten's home with Aidan while they are gone. We'll keep that arrangement so that Aidan sleeps well and can maintain his routine. In the morning, Mary Jo and Aidan will come to our home so that she can work while he plays.

***

Rich stayed at the shipyard another day. In fact, he was there until around 11 p.m. Second shift machinists had the task of preparing and moving the reduction gear from its foundations and lifting it through the access hole in the main deck. There are snags to every project, and this one was held up because the main engine exhaust line was smack in the way. Instead of an easy unbolting process, the pipe ran aft through the bulkhead and had to be cut off. Entering the compartment aft of the engine room, Rich tasted diesel soot, and he discovered several failed gaskets and a crack in the small generator silencer. More items in need of repair.

I played with Aidan after breakfast and then headed to the ferry office to prepare for my return to the shipyard. Tully and Joel, in from their run on the early boat, hooked up our double-axle trailer to the red pickup. I would drive it to the yard, leaving on the 10 a.m. ferry. The reduction gear could then be loaded and secured at Bay Ship, ready for Joel to tow it Friday to Palmer Johnson Distributors in Sun Prairie for the repair. I would park the truck and trailer in Mom's driveway in Sturgeon Bay, rather than driving it back to Northport, and Joel would thumb a ride down in the morning.

***

Rich updated me on the events and the status of equipment of the prior 24 hours. Most notable was recognition by the Bay Ship machinists that we had a problem with shaft alignment. This was determined after shooting a line through the stern tube bore that replicated the ideal centerline of the propeller shaft. The center of the actual bore and ideal shaft centerline were off by significant thousandths.

We met with several foremen in the machinist's trailer in the early afternoon, and the consensus was reached that reboring was necessary, starting with cutting off the inboard flange of the stern tube and reattaching it squarely. Cost, time, and results all needed to be weighed carefully. We further consulted with Jerry Vietinghoff, our vibration engineer expert, to see if we were on track with our combined ideas. He supported beginning anew with the boring process, using the reinstalled reduction gear (maybe a week hence) as the target.

***

Later that afternoon, while Rich and I discussed stern tubes and shafts, reduction gears and tolerances on our drive home to Northport, we learned that at 2:45 p.m. Kirsten had given birth to Magnus Foster Purinton.

Grandson #3 has dark, curly hair. He weighs 8 lb. 6 oz. Both Magnus and Kirsten are doing well, as is proud father, Hoyt. The name

Magnus is a strong, traditional Icelandic name.

***

Mary Jo and I celebrated privately as grandparents while trying out the name of his new brother with Aidan. "Magnus" came pretty easily from his lips, but we don't think he has an idea yet as to what this might mean. He took umbrage at the departure of his parents, and since they've been gone he's said "No" when asked if he wanted to talk on the phone to his daddy or mommy. I think he senses being left behind for a few days and might be making them pay, in his limited, but effective, way.

Friday, November 9 –

Cool and damp, around 40 degrees with overcast and a light breeze. There will be a tanker of gasoline later this morning, and Ken Berggren and Tully will double back for it after their scheduled early trip.

I turned the heat up and had coffee on when Aidan and Mary Jo came over to our house. He's a great sleeper, and last night once again he put in 12 hours in his crib before stirring. His energy is high, and he's busy with breakfast, toys, following his Gramma and me around the house, and watching squirrels out the window. His vocabulary ranges from "limousine" to "pepperoni."

When he goes down for his nap, he insists on taking with him his toy plastic hammer and drill, and a paintbrush. He slides them underneath his tummy and tucks his hands in and sleeps that way, dreaming perhaps of a day when he can knock together some structure of wood, or paint his way into the ferryboat painter hall of fame, like his grandfather. For all the fancy and sophisticated toys he has, these are his favorite at the moment.

***

At 3:50 p.m., as the afternoon wound down and the last ferry of the day loaded, Gay Hecker at our front desk fielded a call from a tearful woman, asking her to, "Hold the ferry. I need to get my pet to the doctor!"

As it happened, the ferry at 3 p.m. had just left Northport with a full load. So Ken and Tully fired up the *Eyrarbakki* as an extra boat and headed toward Northport, followed minutes later by Erik Foss aboard the *Robert Noble*, with a load that included a frantic pet owner and a sick pet.

Saturday, November 10 –

Calm this morning. Cool. Upper 30s and overcast again for the fifth day in a row. This is November gray. Temperatures vary less than five degrees from night to day.

***

Hoyt and Kirsten returned home from the hospital on the 1 p.m. ferry from Northport, little Magnus' first time on the island. I followed them and we arrived about the time Aidan awoke from his nap. He said very little and was unusually cool toward his parents, standing behind Mary Jo on the couch rather than jumping in his dad's lap. In the course of the next thirty minutes, though, he began to show interest in his new brother, and soon he was on the floor, helping by carrying a diaper to his new brother, the beginning of adjustment.

Tom Wilson Appreciation Dinner at Karly's,
Saturday evening, November 10

How could 200 people at Karly's for greeting and celebrating Tom Wilson's 33 years of dentistry be taken as anything but a genuine out-pouring of friendship? It made me proud to know Tom, but also proud to be a part of a community that showed its appreciation easily.

Thanks to Jens Hansen, too, for the idea, the promotion, for heading up a committee of volunteers, and for being emcee on one of the most entertaining evenings I can remember. Hamilton Rutledge, son of island doctor Paul Rutledge who retired in 1975, the man who was greatly responsible for introducing Tom to an island dental practice, set the tone. He wore a bloodied patient's dental bib around his neck as he began with, "It's a good thing the Writer's Guild Strike hasn't af-fected Washington Island." Ham's humor, and the skits and jokes that followed, rivaled the best of Saturday Night Live.

Clever and appropriate table settings of dental floss; clacking teeth; dental patient bibs and bags of Cheetos (a favorite lunchtime snack); enlarged photos of toothy island smiles (Guess Whose Teeth These Are?); Bob Wagner in Tooth Fairy costume, pack of smokes rolled in his tee shirt sleeve; proclamations and letters speaking to Tom's loyalty to his job and his patients, and his dedication to cross-ing by ferry to keep his practice going; and a side-splitting skit with Jens Hansen in the role of Dr. Tom and Celia Hansen as his patient.

Tom laughed and perspired his way through the evening, enjoying himself but dreading the thought of speaking. He enlisted a stand-in, his oldest daughter, Erika, who skillfully delivered Tom's "Top 10 List of Reasons Why Tom Likes Dental Practice On Washington Island." At the very last, under duress, Tom took the microphone and insisted he was **not** retiring just yet, and that he would continue to visit the island with his same regular office hours.

Monday, November 12 –

A balmy 48 degrees at 5 a.m. when I went outdoors to get into my truck. Unable to sleep and choosing not to try, I headed to the ferry dock to get work done prior to the start of the day. We had two LP tankers scheduled for later that morning, covered by the early crew of Bill Jorgenson, Tully Ellefson, and Eric Brodersen after their early run.

Even though the official day for celebrating Veterans (or Armistice) Day was the 11th, on Washington Island our Legion Post chose to have our program at the Community Center this morning so that school children as well as community members could attend. Typically, 150 to 200 people are at the program. Giving the address this year is Guerdon Trueblood, an island author, Hollywood movie screenwriter, and amateur pilot. Guerdon has owned several planes, including a bi-plane. His most recently published book is about the role of U. S. airmen in the Spanish Civil War, an air action leading up to WWII. Guerdon's topic of address this day was his grandfather, Billy Mitchell, one of the nation's most decorated airmen, and the man for whom Milwaukee's airport is named.

Guerdon explained how Billy Mitchell was an influential and significant wartime figure, through his personal record of service and through his innovations in air warfare. Billy Mitchell's home was in Milwaukee (in Brookfield, really) and as a young man Guerdon met famous people who were entertained by the Mitchells at their home, including Charles Lindbergh and Jimmy Doolittle.

***

"It will come down. It's just a matter of time. I know it will have to come down."

Those words, or words very similar to those words, were uttered by Guerdon after the Veteran's Day program had ended and all but a few people remained in the gym. His words referred to the Wilson and Carol Trueblood Performing Arts Center facility, known locally as the TPAC, and the suspect walls of cement block supported in recent months by steel angle bracing. The mortar used, according to Guerdon, was subpar, and as newly laid mortar froze each night the moisture that would normally cure properly froze rather than chemically set. An ingredient to prolong the cure process in cold weather had been purposely omitted, Guerdon claimed, for the reason that drips along the building's face would stain the glazed blocks. "Only the rebar is holding it up," he said, referring to the 30 ft. or higher walls of the audience chamber. Rebar was to be inserted inside the hollows of the blocks, vertically, to increase lateral strength of the walls.

Guerdon may be right on target. By starting construction at the onset of winter and laying block walls during a long stretch of sub-freezing days, the architect, builder, and citizen's committee took great liberty in attempting to produce a product with structural quality.

The TPAC Board steers a private, non-profit organization, and thus far they have not shown interest in enlightening the public as to the extent of the problems or possible remedies. It would be a hard task to generate funds for the operation of a "lemon" building, and so their silence may be understood. Worse, I think, is the speculation that occurs when the Board isn't more open with the public.

Why should Guerdon care about the TPAC? He is a proud Trueblood, and he's not at all happy his Uncle Wilson's name is on a flawed structure.

Tuesday, November 13 –

Mid-30s this morning and still. Frost covers some of the golf course grass, my truck windshield, and our porch roof. With the help of morning sun, temperatures are supposed to reach near 60 degrees by noon.

Rich stayed in Sturgeon Bay again last night, riding herd on the multitude of details and problems that keep increasing with the *Arni J's* repair list. The propeller I dropped off at Metso last week in Neenah needed to be "blue-fit" to the propeller shaft. First, Rich hauled our new shaft, with the completed, machined coupling from Badger Roll to Metso. Then, because Metso could not get the proper fit on the shaft taper, and their shop schedule didn't have extra time, Rich trailered the entire set of items back to Badger in Green Bay from Metso, dropping off the prop and coupling at Badger at 6 p.m. where shop machinists waited to start our job.

This was a tremendous amount of running around, hauling parts here and there, and coordinating work between the several shops, all the while keeping Bay Ship and me informed on what was happening. Rich has been excellent at chasing down the "snakes," as he calls these unforeseen glitches.

Other "snakes" popped up in the findings of the Twin Disc people who began to disassemble our gear and inspect the bearings and parts. The forward carrier bearings were found to have wear beyond normal for 8000 hours. Bolts holding the heavy bull gear, a major clutch component, had shown signs of losing torque. These are tightened to spec from the factory, and such bolts loosening could lead to catastrophic failure down the road. How they might have loosened is conjecture, but shaft vibration working forward through the two major points of gear contact may be one cause.

***

Two CAT field mechanics in the *AJR* engine room were nearing completion of their tune-up on the two engines when I arrived, setting valves and replacing oil seals on the starboard engine crankshaft. The engine room still looks like a disaster with the equipment torn apart, but Ken Berggren's cleaning work on Monday helped in getting it back in shape. There will be even more dirt, dust and grease before the shipyard work is completed.

Rich and I returned to the island on the 1 p.m. ferry from Northport. Our meeting with Todd and Hoyt on the conference phone went well, in that our concern for getting the ferry back to where it should be, and our interest in the shipyard taking a share of responsibility for the realignment, seems to be supported by the yard.

The starboard prop was determined to be in balance, helping to further narrow down the possible cause of vibration. It appears we are now on track to get the boat fixed and back in service, with a remedy that will last.

Wednesday, November 14 –

Sunny and warm with a good breeze from the SW. The prediction is for 30-plus mph from the west, and by 9 a.m. it is all of that. Our ferries are making their trips, however.

Rich, Joel and Tully broke ground this morning for the Island Pizza addition foundation. Weather and time are closing in on possible cement work before it gets too cold. Employees taking time off for deer hunting will disrupt work over the next week.

Thursday, November 15 –

After a visit with Warren Clark, our Principal Financial Advisor, Mary Jo, Warren and I went to dinner at KK Fiske.

In the dining room, the only public dining room open that evening on the island, four tables were taken. Harvey and Dave Jorns, brothers and frequent visitors to the island with their well drilling rig, were just finishing supper as we sat down. Barry McNulty and John Moore were about to begin dinner, and shortly afterward, Rodger Schuettpelz, installer of heating, ventilation and cooling systems on the island, sat down. We chose a table in the middle of the dining room. There is no such thing as private conversation at an island restaurant, and so we kept our topics to current events, island history and such.

For Warren's benefit, Mary Jo and I recalled the winter of 2003, the same year the *Arni J.* was being constructed at Bay Ship, and the day when our well pump went out in early January. The shallow well foot valve became stuck, and we couldn't pull it up or push it back down. We had no water pressure. I called Harvey Jorns to ask his advice on what to do. Drilling a new well was out of the question because ice had just begun to form in the harbor and it would be late April or early May before they would return with their drill rig. We carried water for cooking and toilet flushing for the next four and a half months, bathing and washing clothes at Hoyt and Kirsten's home. I learned to like not shaving or showering every morning. We quickly established a routine. I brought pails and containers of water home every day from the ferry office, but we were otherwise still quite comfortable living in our home.

Harvey and Dave had the drill bit spinning within minutes of pulling into our yard that spring, and within two days, by May 17th, we had our new well. The pressure and thrill of hot water in our own home quickly faded with the arrival of many people who helped celebrate the christening of the *Arni J. Richter*. Our mini-ordeal had ended just in time for a community celebration to begin.

When Jorns Well Drilling comes to the island, generally in the spring and again in the fall, they have a backlog of a half-dozen wells or more to drill, a two week process. It's a pleasure to watch these brothers work, no speaking required. Each knows his job and gets to work, letting the loud noises of their diesel drill rig and compressor motor and whirring drill bit do the talking. Efficiency is their middle name, and that applies even to their dining routine, according to Marianna Gibson, where they stay when they're on the island. For years, when the West Harbor Resort kitchen was up and running, Marianna filled a standing order for breakfast of so many eggs, fixed just so, with coffee and juice. No variations. Ever.

When many activities in life seem to change drastically, it is a reassuring thing to have professional people like Harvey and Dave Jorns get right down to business. We've also appreciated their business on the ferry over the years. Their drill rig is one of the heaviest (and also top-heavy) pieces of equipment we haul, and it takes special consideration for loading. They have been most flexible and cooperative in that regard.

***

I hauled bikes from the dock bike rental for winter storage in our barn loft with Jim Hanson's help this morning. Jim was reminded of a couple with a tandem bike on the ferry this past summer. He asked the woman: "Who steers, you or your husband?" Her answer: "He steers, but I tell him where to go."

***

Rich started early this morning with the backhoe and has a large trench dug for the new addition behind Island Pizza. He hopes to get a cement truck from Martin Andersen later this afternoon to pour footings, then prepare forms for the walls tomorrow for another pour early next week. Daytime temperatures are supposed to stay up in the 40s into next week, although the nights will be in the low 30s. This is mild weather, considering what we could be experiencing for mid-November.

Kay Miller of the DC Zoning Dept. was here this morning to give us the formal OK on the Island Pizza addition. All permits are in order.

***

Rich received an email, followed with a phone conversation from Bob Lenius of Badger Roll regarding our propeller. Our prop tested "Good," that is, well within the limits of acceptability, with no imbalance that could conceivably produce wobble or shaft vibration on the *Arni J. Richter*. This is a helpful finding, further reducing cause for an alignment problem.

Our reduction gear may be ready by late tomorrow, and Joel will travel first to Green Bay for the shaft and prop, dropping them off at the yard, then to Sun Prairie to pick up the gear. Joel hasn't hunted for some time and doesn't care if he's on the island for opening morning of deer season or not.

***

The frost footing was poured in mid-afternoon and finished shortly before quitting time. Rich and the crew had knocked together forms for the cement, and the truck came shortly afterward. The timing will be tight for cement work on this project. Below-freezing weather will shut down the local cement plant until spring. There is often a scramble to pour that one last slab, that one last foundation, critical for construction crews who need to close in a structure and keep working through winter.

Friday, November 16 –

Mary Jo had an appointment in Green Bay, so we both arose early as she headed off to catch the 7 a.m. ferry.

I made coffee and skimmed the 2007 WDNR Deer Hunting Rules: official time of sunrise and sunset; special Deer Herd Control Unit rules; which tags to use for what deer sex to field mark them. Like most activities, rules for deer hunting have increased in complexity. As a hunter you hope you've read the fine print correctly.

On this day prior to opening season, I headed to the basement and collected my muzzleloader, back tag, jacket and ammunition, plus other gear for my tree stand. Then I headed outdoors into 34 degree air, calm but bracing, with the intention of walking to my stand in the woods and setting up for the following day. Tomorrow morning when I walk in, it would be dark and I would be feeling my way among the trees and over crevices in the rock ledges.

***

The Friday before opening weekend, incoming hunter traffic is always heavy. Two ferries left early this morning to get a jump on the line of blaze orange jackets in pickup trucks. We're pleased weather is good today because more than a few times in the past we've had winds so strong our service was curtailed, making many unhappy hunters. That's like leaving people on the pier on Christmas. Maybe worse.

Opening morning of Wisconsin's deer hunting season is a sacred date. Hunters plan all year, take time off work, buy hunting gear, travel long distances, pay a ferry fee, and stay in an island motel, just to be ready for that moment. But most of all, it is the extreme urgency to be in the woods when the sun comes up on opening morning, a time when deer are still unaware of hunters hidden behind tree and rock. By the close of opening weekend a high number of bucks and does will have been eliminated, and the remainder of the deer are scattered, their senses sharpened.

During my first year with the Ferry Line, when I was still an unlicensed deckhand, we made two trips to Rowleys Bay to pick up hunters, forced by strong northwest winds to find a protected landing site. At this time the Northport pier hadn't been lengthened and there was no breakwater for protection. Our only option was Rowley's Bay. I was onboard the *Voyageur* and we followed the *Eyrarbakki* into the Wagon Trail pier. The fourteen mile trip to Rowley's Bay was challenging as we searched for bobbing navigational aids and sailed in and out of snow squalls. Then, once moored at the narrow pier, we loaded cars over wooden planks through the ferry's side gate. There were more cars in line than we could carry, and we asked drivers in line to park their cars because we wouldn't be coming back for them. Their choice was to stay and wait, or park their car and bring their gear and come with us. Many did just that. The passengers who boarded toward the last found no room left in the tiny cabin, so they huddled together against the freezing cold and sleet as we pitched our way into head seas toward Pilot Island, eight miles off our bow. Because of head winds, this trip often took two hours on our return. The blunt, squared bows of the ferry occasionally slammed against the short, steep waves, sending showers of spray over the entire ferry. With deteriorating conditions and waning daylight, we tied up after just two round trips.

Saturday morning, with the winds greatly reduced overnight, two ferries made their way into Northport. We loaded up hunters, cars and gear and soon were rounding the south point of Plum Island. That year, and I think it was 1975, the Plum Island fog signal had been permanently shut down. Several large bucks were known to inhabit Plum Island and the herd was growing. For the first time in decades, absent the loud foghorn blasts, the deer had begun to thrive. Looking toward our ferry as we approached the south end of Plum Island, poised above the rock ledge was a 10-point buck. Swimming in the water below was a smaller rack buck with a doe, chased into the water by the larger buck, apparently. Drooling hunters on board gaped at the bucks, taking photos of the scene and wishing for a similar opportunity in the upcoming hour as they made their way into island forests.

***

We're fortunate to have a number of ferry crew who are not hunters. And for some of our crew who do enjoy hunting but aren't fanatics, opening weekend isn't important as long as there is time available in the woods during the week.

This is an important week for the island, too. Motel rooms are filled, taverns and restaurants are busy, and the Thanksgiving holiday during the same week attracts many visitors for an extended weekend, people who just enjoy sitting by a wood fire.

Sunday, November 18 – Second Morning of Deer Hunting

I entered the woods at 6:15 this morning with the temperature a few degrees warmer than yesterday. My single shooting opportunity Saturday had resulted in a miss. On this still morning the conditions are right for listening, and the direction of wind has shifted from north to southeast, a better direction as deer approach the ledge upon which my stand is located.

I'm dressed this morning with an extra layer of clothing, and I carry a handkerchief for my dripping nose, alternating its use with the back of my knit glove. By 7 a.m., I peeled off the vest from under my parka because I was too warm. A pinkish sunrise lit up the top 30 feet of treetops in the woods. For each minute the sun rose, details of the forest floor came into sharper focus: the scattered stumps, mossy boulders, and fallen trees and limbs became identifiable objects in the landscape, not shadows. But there was no deer movement across that canvas.

***

Maples and beech trees dominate this forest, and the first limbs are often 30 feet off the ground. It's amazing any trees at all grow here, but in fact the maples are quite healthy, sending down roots into crevasses and through thin soil as best they can to gain a solid hold on the earth. Sunlight has difficulty penetrating to the forest floor, and as a result there are few younger trees and almost no undergrowth of shrubs or bushes. There is plenty of moss, soft springy green patches on nearly every rock, and even vertical faces of cliffs where sunlight seldom shines.

***

The land on the east side of the island rates among the poorest of Door County's soils for farming. Here hardwoods were cut and cordwood was shipped down the lake to fire boilers and home fires. Cedar swamps abut the stands of hardwoods, and there is no gentle transition. Craggy, rock-strewn acreages such as this can change to sandy or gravely soils within a quarter mile, places where the ancient high lake levels deposited beach sediments.

Despite the rockiness of the east side, early settlers made homes here. They were among the poorest of island farmers. Old barbed wire fencing runs along the north line where old cedar posts are visible, scattered, lying on their sides, victims of an encroaching forest. Progress in this case seems to be the cessation of farming and the wild growth of neighboring timber. An old gate where rails slid aside to open the pasture for cattle or farm vehicle lies rotting near the corner of the 20-acre piece.

***

9:30 a.m. – A single deer walked along the lower edge of the terrace, and the shuffling hooves caught my attention. I held my gun and waited until I was certain the deer's head was behind a tree, then brought it to my shoulder. I clicked the safety off and waited another few seconds. The deer resumed its slow pace, nose to ground, most likely a buck sniffing the trail for a doe. He was unaware of my presence, 80 or more feet away and 20 feet above him. I pulled the trigger and the powder ignited. When the smoke cleared, the deer lay in the same spot I had shot him. His horns were now visible, a small set of five points total, but a deer in very good physical shape.

Half an hour later, I had tagged and field dressed the buck. Warmed by my efforts and with bloodied hands, I skidded it up the first ledge, a height of 15 feet or more. There, I caught my breath for a moment, then went back for my gun, and the heart and liver. Arni enjoys venison liver, and I find there are few sandwiches that compare to boiled venison heart. The liver and heart are in a plastic bag, my sandwich bag from Saturday's hunting session.

There is an adrenaline pick-up when the hunt is on, the shot is made, and the mark is hit. Strangely, there is also a lift from the act of field dressing, dragging the deer carcass toward home, and the thought of the meat being processed into something not only edible, but very tasty and healthy. The blood on my fingers is soon dried, but there is no snow to wash off my hands.

This deer will do justice to our dining table. In the parlance of the WDNR, the exercise I just went through is called a "harvest," the politically correct term for legally hunting, killing, tagging and registering a deer. Any way you care to look at it, the deer herd needs to be reduced and thinned, brought into manageable numbers for the land that supports them. Most people, even non-hunters, can see that reasoning.

I had completed an even loftier mission than just shooting a deer, it seemed. Was I helping save deer from themselves, or just enjoying the hunting? Maybe, both.

Monday, November 19 –

Strong southerly winds blew rain as the *Robert Noble* pushed against the tires at the island pier. It was 7 a.m. when Orion Mann backed the 25-ft. Mann's Store truck down the center of the deck to complete our load. Bill Crance, dressed in a bright orange rain suit this morning, this time not a hunting jacket, cast off the bow lines and raised the ramp.

I joined the crew in the pilothouse, Joel Gunnlaugsson, Bill Crance, Jason Carr along with Paul Swanson. Our talk was mostly about hunting once we squared away for Northport, stimulated by the sight of two large bucks strapped to the top of a SUV parked just forward and below the wheelhouse.

My goal this day was to pick up our gear from Palmer Johnson Power Systems located near Sun Prairie, but it would be 4 p.m. before I had the marine gear loaded on our trailer with paperwork signed. I headed out on 151 north in rain and fog for the drive back to Sturgeon Bay.

I had driven 400 miles for the day when I pulled into the shipyard to find awaiting machinists ready to unload the gear and begin the process of lowering it into the *Arni J. Richter's* engine room. A crane lifted the 4500-lb. gear from the trailer and set it on the ferry's vehicle deck. From there, the crew used two pick-points and chain hoists to position the gear over the hole and lower it into the engine room. By morning it would be mated to the engine.

Tuesday, November 20 –

A frosty but clear morning as I left my motel room at the Maritime Inn and headed to the shipyard, stopping for a cup of coffee along the way. It was 7:15 and the yard had just come to life as the sun came up.

I checked in with machinist Terry Gunnlaugsson, then headed across the bay to Schartner's Implements on the west side of town to borrow their trailer, longer than ours and better suited for the 19-ft. box with shaft.

Badger Roll is located just off Webster on Green Bay's east side. Their building is large enough to house machining equipment and the heavy hoists necessary to work on rolls from the paper industry, a primary part of their business. After backing the long implement trailer through one of the panels of their overhead door (sorry, fellas) I met John Sherman who is a salesman and engineer for Badger, and we sat down to discuss dynamic balancing. John called it, "Balance Info 101," and he took me through their testing procedures, complete with a paper visual, explaining both the process and how to read the test results. Although a small amount of material was ground off one of the blades to bring the whole into balance, it was a relatively small amount. Near-perfect balance, at our better-than-ISO standards, was achieved with a comparatively few cycles by the operator.

I spent the remainder of the morning with Stan Lenius, son of the shop owner, who loaded the shaft, prop and armature on my trailer. I chained down the shaft box as he loaded the wheel. Presses, lathes and other large machines, many of them still manually operated, fill the large space, with a 40-ton overhead crane on rails to lift heavy pieces such as 20-foot long paper production rolls.

Wednesday, November 21 –

The day is overcast and in the upper 30s, with a light wind from the north.

Hoyt brought his scuba diving gear to the dock. When Joel and Ken return from their trip with the *Eyrarbakki*, they will take up position inside the ferry hull up forward, ready to release the old and receive and fasten the new transducer. Meanwhile, from the exterior, Hoyt will insert the transducer sensor. The exchange from old to new should take only seconds, and, with care, not much water will enter the hull. This through-hull fitting is located about four feet below water level, so there is pressure and there will undoubtedly be spray, but it can be checked with a rag or by hand. Water temperature is in the mid-40s and Hoyt is wearing a dry suit that will help him to stay warm.

By 11 a.m., the new transducer is in place and wired. Joel reported the unit works perfectly. At a time of year when our last trips of the day are in the dark (and sometimes in snowfall) and the water is at its lowest depth, having a functioning depth unit is important.

Thursday, November 22 – Thanksgiving Day

North winds blew hard all night but tapered off by sunrise, but it is still a stiff and cold northerly wind. The temperatures were in the upper 20s this morning, and tonight the low will be in the teens, the coldest yet this season.

Hoyt and I worked in our garage until past nine, skinning the three deer that were hanging, cutting and processing the venison. He is deft with the knife, boning the carcass as it hangs, removing larger sections like a haunch for me to cut up, package and label. He is twice as fast as I am, and agile, not only with the knife, but able to get down on his knees to work on the forelegs and neck of the upside-down deer.

Bill Crance told me his preferred method for a deer carcass after butchering. He hangs it from a tree limb not far from his house. "You wouldn't believe the birds we see landing on it. They pick it clean by spring time." The sight of a hanging deer skeleton may be off-putting to a first time visitor, but Bill and Carol's home is set well back in the woods, out of view, and they do enjoy seeing wild life. Hunting is important to Bill, but so is the entire spectrum of observing nature up close. The Crances entertain fox, raccoon, squirrels, turkeys and other wildlife that they feed on corn, apples and other items tossed out for them. Bill, with Carol's help, was at one time a taxidermist who started the Illinois Taxidermist Association years ago. He appreciates and knows more about these animals than the average hunter.

***

Ken Berggren and Jim Hanson are the early ferry crew, and I met them as they came in from their first trip. A half load of cars was the payload. They're now "winterizing" the *Eyrarbakki* for the colder temperatures tonight. They accumulated spray as they came home bucking against the northerly winds. Freezing spray, too, changes the operational picture as we get into winter weather. If a water line is not properly drained and freezes solid, then splits, a mess can ensue. The defect might not show up until after it thaws.

Saturday, November 24 –

Windy and blustery this morning. Very wintry out our bedroom window, with a light snow covering the ground and swirls working their way across the pavement from the southwest. The temperature is 27 degrees at 7:30 a.m.

***

Joel and Jim are back from their early ferry run, bringing with them *Press Gazette* newspapers for Mann's Store and a cart loaded with Do-It-Yourself hardware for Lampert's Home Center.

Today will be fairly routine for ferry traffic, with hunters beginning to leave the island for home. Joel said the WDNR warden Mike Neal came over this morning, the first appearance of a conservation warden this season, as far as we know. Word spreads quickly when a warden visits the island, but for the hunter who does everything by-the-book, the presence of a warden from time to time should be welcomed.

Typically, on this last Saturday of the hunt, a group of islanders will head over to Rock Island or to Plum Island by small boat. Both islands require a good number of people to cover the territory. A sight that makes me uneasy are the small boats loaded with hunters and their gear, heading out in sea conditions that are anything but ideal. A wave climbing over the gunnel or transom could easily swamp a small Lund with its heavily-dressed occupants. The water temperature is probably in the mid-to-upper 40s and except for our ferries, there are few rescue options available.

***

Today our Board of Directors meets at 1 p.m. Our meetings often last three to four hours, but I have hopes we can get through our agenda in two hours. Key topics today include: management compensation; 2008 tariff; financial report and upcoming projects; Northport Restaurant season wrap-up. Our Board of Directors includes Ed Graf, Bill Schutz, Hoyt and me from the island, Joel Lueking, Chicago, and John McClaren, Baltimore. Joel will drive up this morning, and John may participate by conference phone.

Sunday, November 25 –

It's overcast but warmer today. By 10 a.m. the sun shone and the sky cleared with bright blue from horizon to horizon. Light snow on the ground from the previous day melted. This will be a Sunday without the Packers. How shall we use it?

Monday, November 26 –

There is no wind this early November morning, and the temperature is 33 degrees. Two LP tankers are scheduled to come in for Hansen Oil, and later the early crew will double back to pick them up at Northport.

***

From here on through the end of the year, each day with above-freezing temperatures is a boon to construction workers and outdoor contractors. Work might continue regardless, I suppose, but a greater range of activities and better quality work can be achieved when it's above freezing. Our crews are adjusting to the change in weather, too. Each ferry carries a product similar to Ice Melt onboard, but it's made from limestone, a natural by-product that can be applied ahead of time to decks. It's impossible to avoid spray on deck when wind and seas are up.

Tuesday, November 27 –

There are gale warnings with gusts to 45 mph posted for the open lake on the NOAA Marine Weather, posted for 6 a.m. to 2 p.m., then diminishing to 30 kts from the NW in the afternoon. That is all the wind we would care to handle.

We can easily guess wind velocities this morning. Gusts of wind rush through the maple limbs in our yard. A large, dead oak limb lays where it fell alongside the driveway. Water in the upstairs toilet bowl dances under varied air pressures as winds pass over the roof vent. Our American flag has several new wraps around the staff. And leaves from near the ballpark are racing one another across Main Road, looking for a new resting spot in our yard.

Our ferries will struggle with wind velocity and direction. As a result, all morning trips were cancelled.

***

I bundled up to head out to the dock at 8:30 a.m. wearing flannel-lined jeans for the first time. I think this means winter instead of fall. My route deviated around Green Bay Road to see what the winds and seas looked like. In Figenschau Bay along the shallows there were signs of ice building up on mud flats, with iced marsh grass laying down where winds sent spray toward the cold beach. There are few vantage points better than the Potato Dock for observing the seas, and I spotted a set of tire tracks before me in the light snow. Walter Jorgenson, early riser? The seas to the west, toward Door Bluff and Northport, were white with breaking waves. Seagulls hugged the beach stones rather than take to the air, and alongside the dormant *C.G. Richter*, tucked into the corner against the sheet piling, a raft of black coots paddled parallel to shore.

At the end of the Potato Dock, spray flung by the winds had already glazed the rocks and weeds. Gusts were strong enough to buffet my truck. Making a call on the ferry trip is easier when winds are strong and the temperatures are below freezing.

***

Another sign of a continuing drop in water levels brought to extreme by the sharp northerly winds: the pile of rocks across the ferry channel, the old "false channel" crib, is exposed by nearly two feet. There are more rocks exposed on this crude water level gauge than I've ever seen. Our ramps are now at their absolute lowest limits. Only by cutting away part of the pier or digging several feet lower into the dock surface can we hope to lower the ramps, not a practical solution for this late time of year.

Water depths are more ticklish around the entrance light. At Northport, when the *Arni J.* is back in service, we'll have to be cautious to avoid scraping bottom. Our contractor, Mike Kahr, is still working on the marina at Chambers Island, and we've stated our need to get dredging done before ice covers the harbors.

***

By 1 p.m., following a morning of many inquiring calls and several in-person stops at the dock, we decided to hold off a bit longer in making a ferry trip. The forecast is for the winds to drop after 3 o'clock., and we'll set our sights on making a trip from the island at 4 p.m., hoping to get all traffic off the island, and incoming traffic at 5 p.m. from Northport. This trip will return in the dark, and we are hoping the velocity will be down enough that deck icing won't be a problem.

Harvey and Dave Jorns are in line with their two trucks. They've completed their list of wells to be drilled for the fall. The last well was in an open field, Harvey said, subject to wind and cold, and their truck's water lines started to freeze up. We'll get the smaller and lower pipe truck on board when we run today and transport the bigger, heavier drilling rig tomorrow. (Winds are forecast to be 30 mph from the south tomorrow...not a major improvement.)

***

At 3:30 p.m., with a downward trend in wind speed, our crew is loading the ferry for a single trip. Those who need to get off the island will be able to do so, but undoubtedly there will have been missed appointments and flight departures.

The U.S. mail is going across, too, and we'll bring back island mail so the post office crew can get an early start with sorting Tuesday's mail on Wednesday morning. Rich Ellefson, who departed around 8 p.m. last night on a special ferry with his grandpa Dick Ellefson, is returning to Northport. He'll have a chance to organize the freight dropped off there during the day. The air temperature is 21 degrees as the sun begins to set.

Tomorrow's forecast predicts 2-3 inches of snow with winds out of the south at 30 kts. Thursday gusts are forecast to be back up to near 40 kts, from the west. There is little relief from the wind.

Wednesday, November 28 –

We listened to the NOAA weather this morning on the "Weather Cube," which is pre-tuned to NOAA and marine weather forecasts. To get a better picture of what's going to take place near Washington Island, it's prudent to blend forecasts of the UP weather with the Green Bay weather. I also give great weight to the marine off shore and near shore forecasts. Wind speeds are almost always greater off shore, and from a practical point of view, we are an off shore land, subject to the fall winds that seem to blow relentlessly each day. Gale winds yesterday from the north; today, from the south; tomorrow, from the west; Friday, back to the north.

Nearly every forecast includes the words "blustery winds," which, I guess, means a wind that rubs your nose in the cold.

With no break in weather soon, large trucks for today and tomorrow are cancelled, including the Veolia waste truck. Harvey and Dave's well drilling rig is on the island dock, still, and it may be several more days before we dare load it for the trip across. We will do well to make the regular runs with auto traffic.

Snow is also in this morning's forecast, with greater amounts north of Menominee, MI and inland. Flurries began to fall around 11:30 a.m.

I've made the trip to the dock twice, with a short run back to the clinic to get checked out by Patti Balestrieri who is on duty this week. It's great to see smiling faces, Janet at the reception window, and Patti, when you're not feeling well. I'm over the fever, but have clammy skin despite being well-dressed and having not done any hard physical work today. It's a classic case of flu, Patti tells me. Try a few more days of rest and see if it runs its course, she ordered. Stay home and don't transfer the virus-fed cold to co-workers.

As I left the ferry dock three of our crew were on the roof of the Island Pizza building, laying shingles. Amid gusts of wind, one man held the shingle for the other who fastened it down. The third man kept the supply coming. Rich is home on the island for a breather, taking the day off. In exchange Hoyt went to the shipyard to observe the boring process on the *Arni J.*'s sterntube.

Thursday, November 29 –

It's only 18 degrees and our treetops are swaying smartly. In the words of nearly every observer and describer of our region's weather, it is blustery. A "kick-in-the-ass" blustery, today.

Mary Jo left for an appointment in Green Bay this morning, and caught the first ferry. Hoyt will also be on that ferry, heading to Bay Ship. Crew members are Erik Foss and Ken Berggren.

After breakfast, I sat down to begin work on my computer at home. The flu is still with me, although I sense a bit of improvement from yesterday, especially in joints and muscles. A tightness still grabs at my windpipe, and I cough dryly when I breathe deeply. This flu is not fun, and I've had symptoms now for a week.

At 7:45 Mary Jo called from onboard the ferry. She wasn't doing well. The early ferry, she said, was still enroute to Northport, running slowly, bouncing in seas that she described as "8 to 10 feet." Then she thought they were nearing Northport and that the seas were finally flattening a bit. Hoyt sat with her in the car for a while to give her support. She's never liked windy days on the ferry, and today she had put all of her faith in TV weatherman Tom Mahoney, who said, "25 mph winds...," Probably correct for some corner of his viewing audience, but in the Door, especially with WNW winds and cold air, figure another 10 to 15 miles an hour. Eric had estimated the winds were nearer to 40 mph, she said.

A decision made by the crew, and one not frequently made, was to cancel the 8 a.m. ferry from the island, holding the first ferry in at Northport rather than returning, until conditions improved. Later in the morning if winds abate, they could return with the island mail, with freight and passengers, and then wait to see what developed for the afternoon. One forecast indicated winds would subside. Like many people on board the early ferry, Mary Jo was hoping to return home later this day.

***

Few birds enjoy wind and cold as much as crows, it seems, and a flock of them have been on the golf course and in our back yard, even in the ashes of the fire pile. My guess is the seeds and remaining pulp of old gourds dumped on the burn pile are what attract the crows. Crows are an odd, different bird, not as competitive as gulls who swipe lunch from other gulls, but they are sociable and follow one another, walking about on the ground as much as flying. Why crows are even out this morning is a mystery...but then, where are they supposed to be, if not out?

The blue skies and few light clouds would indicate a great day coming up. But for our ferry crew and travelers it will be a trying day requiring patience. Temperatures are too low to fool around in breaking seas. An iced deck would take hours to melt or evaporate back down to bare steel.

***

At home, I've been reading and rereading the WDNR reply brief on the Northport Contested Case Hearing. It is a depressing read to know there is such little understanding of our operation and the work that we do to make daily ferry trips a reality. The DNR authors — and I have to ultimately put this on the Secretary of the DNR as well as the Governor — singled out our company and this permit application, to impose their will for public access.

I prefer to call it coercion, or blackmail, if you will. Yet, arguments aren't won by discrediting our opponents. The judge is one who has heard our case before in 1999, with essentially the same arguments, and it was he who encouraged the DNR to condition or pressure us if the permit on the pier was ever reopened. We expect little-to-no objectivity from this Administrative Law Judge.

My morning's work will be to outline a few of the key arguments from a layman's point of view, and later confer with our legal counsels to see what their thoughts are.

***

Just received in yesterday's mail was a solicitation letter from the TPAC. I appreciate that at long last a mention has been made of the structural problems of the building. It's still not easy to interpret what has gone wrong, or what the actual remedy might be:

"...we expect to have a new wrapper system constructed around the building to remedy the water penetration and related problems. At this time there are design, engineering and material issues being finalized and the contractor plans to begin construction early this spring at no cost to the TPAC."

What sort of wrapper?

It is a question for me, then, of whether or not to support a facility with major structural questions through an end-of-year donation, or put my money toward other worthy island organizations.

Friday, November 30 –

Another windy morning with cold temperatures. It's the coldest island morning so far at 15 degrees. Upper Wisconsin and Michigan have recorded single digits overnight. Hard to judge wind speed today, but it appears to be in excess of 25 mph, probably NW, (I think it might easily meet the "blustery" criteria once again), and that is too much wind to handle, for the seas and for the spray and icing on deck that it produces on a crossing even as short in duration as ours.

Yesterday, Mary Jo told me she didn't think she had ever experienced waves like that before. It took a long while to back cars off the ferry at Northport, she said. Mann's Store truck, in the center of the deck, had been fastened down with chains and binders to pockets in the deck. When it came time to drive off, the tires spun and slipped before the truck climbed up and out of the "hole" from the ferry up the sharply inclined ramp.

***

Hoyt and Rich had planned to return to the shipyard this morning. All day yesterday the yard crew enlarged the pre-drilled holes and fitted the output flange to the reduction gear, and reestablished the targets for boring. Now, after several days of false starts, the actual machining can begin. Can anything else possibly crop up to complicate this job?

***

Our trips Friday went relatively smoothly after all, with a brisk wind in the morning and temperatures still cold enough to cause freezing of spray on deck. By early afternoon the velocity of wind had eased and the trips became easier.

***

Tully is on the roof of the Pizza building again, today. It's darn cold, our coldest yet this winter. I don't wish to join him, but I sure wish I had the health and stamina to do so. A trip to the clinic yesterday resulted in some new medicine from Patti to combat what could be an onset of bronchitis, on top of the viral flu that I seemed to be slowly getting over. For the week, I haven't had much energy and the confinement to indoor activities can only last so long.

***

There are many Ferry Line "irons in the fire." Most of them are based on a continued, strong, tourism business. Small steps will be taken to promote steady island growth, stabilize fuel costs, and find solutions to fluctuating water levels. We are planning new ramping systems, and dredging.

We think we see light at the end of a legal tunnel in settling our differences with the State of Wisconsin Department of Natural Resources over a permit for dock construction. We believe our legal position is strong, with an historical record of doing the right thing for the island, for our customers, which ultimately brings stability to our business. In the end, we want results that will support excellent service and necessary improvements.

The month of November ends with as many future questions and uncertainties as any in the recent past. Are we poised for a recession, a continued decline in the economy, or will we see a strengthening in the coming months?

DECEMBER

Saturday, December 1 –

Not a bad morning for the beginning of December.

Tree branches are motionless. No leaves skip across our yard. The air temperature is 15 degrees, and it will climb through the day as a warm front approaches, southerly air riding over the cold air of the incoming high pressure. The early morning sky is fairly bright, almost as if, maybe, the weatherman could be wrong that a snowstorm is coming.

I spent the night avoiding coughing by remaining upright, sleeping against propped up pillows, and by taking a dose or two of cough suppressant medicine. While I slept quite well, all things considered, I awoke with a major headache that ran from my left eyebrow over the top of my head and ended at the base of my skull. I attribute that nasty side effect to the cough medicine.

***

There are a few hours in which to retrieve things from our yard and put them indoors before the snow falls. I moved my motorcycle from underneath a tarp, parked under the cedar trees to make room for more venison processing, and rolled it into a far corner of the garage. Two push mowers went from the garage to the barn. And from our utility room in our home I moved a folding worktable of Mary Jo's to her barn workshop.

While I moved these items about, Hoyt stopped with a pickup truck with trash bags overflowing the sides, headed for the dump. On the passenger side, in his car seat, tugging at the restraining straps, was a smiling Aidan. I hadn't seen him all week, not since Sunday evening when I came down with fever and chills. His warm, broad smile lit up his face, but his left eye had an ugly patch of red, bloodshot from a fall against one of his toys. The eye didn't seem to bother him, though, and as soon as his restraints were loosened, he popped out of his car seat, climbed down from the running board, and ran off to the garage to find my tools — any tools.

***

At the ferry dock things seemed very quiet between trips for a

Saturday. Janet is posted at the front desk, and at his desk Bill is finishing up payroll. No traffic is in line to leave the island at the moment.

A check on our website weather link showed snow in the forecast, up to six inches depending upon where the front moved and how warm the air would be. I printed out a few NOAA weather reports for Janet to refer to when calls come in. The news of a snowstorm or high winds brings calls concerned about Sunday's travel, and for Monday too, especially for those who have key appointments off the island. How to predict what will happen? What do we recommend? What would we do in their position?

There is little doubt we'll have either snow, sleet, or rain. It's only a matter of how much and where. By noon sharp, large flakes begin to fall. The wind is ESE, off the lake, increasing, bringing moist air perfect for snowfall accumulation. By 12:45 only the nearest portions of Detroit Island can be seen from our office windows, perhaps a quarter mile away. The rest of the scene over Detroit Harbor is white.

***

Hoyt reported progress machinists had made at the shipyard yesterday. The tool set-up was accomplished at last and boring has begun. The men will work in pairs around the clock, hoping to finish by late Sunday. A small plastic enclosure was built around the ferry stern on the dry dock floor where the shaft tube exits, to shield workers and their tools from the elements.

Hoyt and Rich stopped to see Mike Kahr at a jobsite near the Town Dock in Fish Creek. They emphasized our concerns for getting dredging done soon. He is nearly finished at Chambers Island. Regardless of other jobs pending, we think ours has priority. We're not happy about bringing a ferry back home with the chance of damaging skegs or wheels from low water.

I phoned Mike later in the day to reinforce our message and he reassured us he would get to our location late next week. The time of year and cold weather works against us, even when working in a well-protected harbor. Barge movement and the activity of dredging become more difficult. Temperatures in the lower digits will freeze the sodden material as its scooped onto a barge deck or reloaded in dump trucks, increasing handling time and cost.

***

Throughout the rest of Saturday afternoon and into darkness, wet snowflakes swirled and stacked into drifts, first in inches, later in foot-

high ridges. Hoyt drove in our lane with a pickup and plow shortly after dark. Unknown to us, Aidan was his front seat companion. They
had plowed at the ferry dock, then Arni's lane. Aidan enjoyed the ride,
the motion of the truck and action of the plow, and the mesmerizing
swirling snow in the headlights. According to Hoyt, he also liked holding the plow control, and with its buttons resembling a portable phone
he pretended to "call Gramma." His insistence on using the plow control interrupted the plowing routine, so the two sat in our driveway
and hashed it out before coming indoors. Shortly afterward, warming
up in our home, Aidan located his hammer, screwdriver and pliers and
set his mind to "fixing" our furniture.

***

When we headed upstairs to bed, past 10 o'clock, a string of car
lights slowly worked their way north on Main Road, headlight beams
bouncing off blowing snow. These were play-goers from the TPAC driving homeward.

The play put on with local cast members at the TPAC is *The Christmas Tree Ship*, a story about the *Rouse Simmons* and her captain, the
schooner with a load of trees for Chicago. It went down a century ago
with all hands and a load of Christmas trees during an early December
storm off Sheboygan, WI.

That the trees came from Upper Michigan, and that Captain
Schuenemann and his crew sailed the *Rouse Simmons* through passages near Washington Island, adds an interesting historical connection for local theater-goers. Without having seen the play, but having
read reviews from other, similar productions, I suspect a strong romantic twist is given to the story of the ship and its crew going down
with the Christmas trees. It has become a holiday tug-at-the-
heartstrings (the poor children of Chicago would go without trees this
Christmas…). But, it also has a genuineness going for it that perhaps
Charlie Brown's Christmas Tree or *How The Grinch Stole Christmas*
stories can't quite match. The version put on last night and again this
afternoon is a musical.

The story of *The Christmas Tree Ship* caused me to reflect on
another, perhaps less romantic version of a very similar story.

It was told to me on several occasions by Arni's older brother,
Paul, who enjoyed telling this story especially after he had a glass of
Early Times and water in hand. He was on his second or third — no
ice, just water and Early Times — when he got around to his story,
brought on by our conversation of impending ice conditions and late
season sailing difficulties.

Paul and Arni had the notion they could make extra money by loading up an idled ferry with trees to sell in Chicago. While the *Griffin* kept the regular ferry schedule with Arni staying home as captain, the wooden-hulled *North Shore* was loaded for the delivery to Chicago. Trees cut from the Stonington Peninsula were loaded first. Then, at Washington Island the *North Shore* made another port call and the crew topped off their load with island trees. These were not good quality trees, Paul said, but local balsams cut by an island farmer and museum caretaker. But they loaded the island trees anyway, filling the cargo hold below decks and the rest of the main deck, before casting off for Chicago to make their fortune. Lucien Boshka was at the wheel, and Paul Richter and John Jessen were crew. Lucien was a seasoned ferry captain who worked year around for the Ferry Line. John was an engineer who sailed aboard Great Lakes ore freighters. He had recently returned home to his family at the close of the shipping season.

For the first two days the *North Shore* moored along the Chicago River not far from Montgomery Ward and cash sales went well. But success ended abruptly when a trainload of trees from somewhere out west flooded the Chicago tree market, Paul said. With too many trees on corner lots they couldn't sell a single one from the ferry's deck. Besides, temperatures had plunged and living aboard without proper cooking or bathing or sleeping facilities or decent heat to keep them warm had taken its toll. They decided to sail back to the island.

When they stuck their nose out of the Chicago breakwater, an inkling of what was to come hit them. Winds were out of the north, directly on the bow, and while they each considered themselves capable sailors, the next 16 hours were as rough and uncomfortable as any they cared to experience. The *North Shore* pitched her way slowly past the lights of the northern shore suburbs, toward Waukegan and Kenosha, with progress slowed by the head seas. The Christmas trees on board were now useless deck ornaments, and so Paul and John busied themselves by pitching the unsold trees over the side of the ferry. Late that evening, after taking a pounding complete with spray that froze on deck, they had had enough. The *North Shore* pulled into Milwaukee's harbor where the crew could rest. John Jessen departed early the next morning by bus to be with his wife and daughters. That left the remaining crew, Paul and Lucien, to bring the ferry back home.

That same morning while walking along the pier, Paul encountered a Coast Guardsman seeking information on a small vessel that had pulled in during the night. Either he wouldn't believe anyone would be out on the lake in such weather, or the Coast Guard had gotten word of trees being tossed overboard, Paul wasn't sure. "Did any of youse see the bums who brought this thing in?" he asked. Paul and Lucien shrugged their shoulders, not giving anything away. The rest of the day they laid low before casting off as soon as winds abated.

Paul's return home was marked by a soothing, hot bath, and he recalled how his mother used a brush to scrub the dirt and pitch from his back and neck. Paul implied that of the many Christmas trees rolling around the lake bottom, tangled occasionally in fishermen's nets, not all might have been from the wreck of the *Rouse Simmons* years before.

Sunday, December 2 –

A calm and beautiful morning followed the snowstorm. Winds during the night drifted the snow and a steady howling was heard through the trees in our yard and around our eaves. But during the early morning hours winds slackened and temperatures increased to 35 degrees. As a result, each shovel of snow was wet and heavy.

Our crew was out extra early to the ferry dock, some of them shortly after 5 a.m., to clean off the ferry decks. There is plenty of plowing to be done with trucks, but also lots of hand shoveling to clean ferry decks, steps, ramps and walks leading to the docks. After I completed my own sidewalks at home, I drove out to the dock and found the surfaces there already shoveled. A large pond from melted snow covered the lane near the ticket booth, and I worked to uncover and open up drains.

***

When I headed down Main Road toward the ferry dock this morning, I ran into a small cattle drive. A slight fog hovered in patches above the ground where warm air glided over cold snow the night before. In the haze at the intersection near the Community Center, I encountered Martin Andersen's pickup pulling a cattle trailer onto the Main Road. Calves were inside his trailer and two cows anxiously followed behind at the trailer's rear. Winding up the procession was Rich Ellefson in his pickup with plow. The parade was headed to Martin's farm, having recently come from pastureland to the east of school where the cattle had been feeding prior to the snowstorm. They would rejoin the rest of the herd in pasture near the barn on Main Road.

***

For a change this day, I felt healthy enough to engage in a few outdoor tasks, and the mild temperatures with little-to-no-wind cooperated. I pounded in several guide stakes for snow plowing. The ground still held only a small amount of frost. Then, working through drifts behind the barn that varied from ankle to knee deep, I dragged out the plow unit for my four-wheeler. The plow will be ready for the next snowfall.

Monday, December 3 –

Around 2 a.m. winds picked up again. We went to bed with temperatures at 31 degrees, still mild, but at 7 a.m. our thermometer read 21 degrees, and the wind speed was well over 30 mph.

When I pulled the living room curtains aside this morning I was greeted by a spot of bright red against the white snow. A male cardinal sat at our sunflower feeder facing my window, indifferent to the cold air and pleased to have the feeder to himself.

***

Gale warnings were posted today for the near shore into early afternoon with winds in the range of 35 mph. I called Hoyt early at home to discuss the weather. Shortly afterward, Rich called me from the dock. We decided to delay morning ferry trips at least until midday to see if the wind would ease as predicted.

As it happens, today is also our first day with reduced ferry trips, the schedule having been cut back from six to four daily round trips. Instead of the earliest ferry leaving the island at 7 a.m., the first one now leaves at 8 a.m.

***

The only trip we'll make today will be at 3:30 p.m. from the island, 4:30 from Northport. There is going to be a full, or nearly full load of vehicles. As conditions improved through the afternoon, calls were placed with customers who were anxious to leave the island, or get back to the island from the mainland.

Tuesday, December 4 –

My goal this morning as I leave home is to catch the extra-early ferry, one that is headed over to Northport to pick up two tankers for Hansen Oil. I plan to deliver Christmas wreaths along the way to, and on the way back from, Sturgeon Bay. One of my stops will be at Bay Ship to check progress on the *Arni J. Richter*.

It's dark out when I head to my truck at 6:50 a.m. A heavy frosting of thick snowflakes is stuck to the windshield glass. At the ferry dock aboard the *Washington*, Joel Gunnlaugsson, Tully Ellefson and Bill Crance are prepared to load. I picked up a few last-minute items from the office, including the shipyard pass to hang from my truck mirror, and Ferry Line stickers for the wreath boxes, before driving down the dock to board.

The 7:15 a.m. crossing is gray with a few snowflakes falling, errant flakes from low hanging clouds. The water is gray, too, dark in contrast with the strip of white snow that outlines Detroit, Plum, and Pilot. Above the white shoreline strip is a dark band, the tree line, almost black in the early morning light. A slight sea pushes the *Washington* about, but nothing to be concerned about as far as hauling tankers will go. In fact, this morning's as near perfect as it gets for hauling tankers in December.

As we pull in to Northport one LP tanker and one gasoline tanker are waiting in line. A short string of early-starters, including me, begins the drive down the peninsula. My stops before getting to the shipyard will include northern Door homes, then on to Sturgeon Bay for a half dozen more stops, and finally, Bay Shipbuilding.

When I arrived at the Bay Ship main office building, I presented our wreath. Pat O'Hern, company president, was at his desk with piles of thick brown files at his elbows. His desk is huge, yet nearly every square inch is covered in paperwork resulting from, as we soon discuss, many contracts.

It's actually a boom-time at Bay Shipbuilding. The yard has been building new barges like crazy and the good news is, they're six months ahead of schedule on the most recent delivery, with other contracts still backlogged. The most recently completed barge, Pat tells me, is at this moment being towed past the stone quarry at the west entrance to Sturgeon Bay, on the first leg of its route to the east coast. It will be put into immediate service when it arrives and will transport oil products for the northeast. This tow is escaping the Great Lakes and the Welland Canal just prior to the winter freeze up.

New tanker barges are in demand, and Pat also has several clients in the talking stages who Bay Ship is eager to sign. The shipyard, currently busy as probably it ever has been with new construction, anticipates the arrival of 18 lake freighters for winter lay up and repair. It's a good time to be company president, Pat assured me.

We exchanged a few pleasantries about Arni, and about his own father, and finally, about our ferry in dry dock. He admits he hasn't kept up on the *Arni J.'s* repair details. We wished each other Happy

Holidays, shook hands, and I began walking through the building in the direction of the dry dock.

To measure progress on the *Arni J.,* I first walked down the steps to the bottom of the dry dock. The new shaft was inserted three-quarters of its length, slipped inside the new Thordon stern bearing. This material is ceramic and machined carefully to fit the newly machined stern tube bore. The fit is good, tight. Nearby, the starboard wheel dangled from nylon straps attached to chain falls, the chain fall hooks, in turn, coupled to hooks welded to the underside plating of the ferry's stern. As soon as assembly work is completed within the engine room, the shaft will be connected to the gear, and the propeller slid over the key on the shaft taper. Two brass propeller nuts, weighing 15 pounds or so apiece, sat on a board nearby along with a stainless strap that will be welded as a keeper over the two nuts as a safety measure.

I heard tapping from inside the hull and voices of the machinists working there.

I climbed out of the dry dock, steps covered thick with compacted snow, met machinist supervisor Steve Krauel, and we headed toward the engine room. We found three machinists huddled over the starboard shaft alley. One man was on his knees wedged between the frames, cleaning out new boltholes by running a tap. The stuffing box would bolt up to the flange at that point. There was hardly room for onlookers at the base of the engine room ladder. I didn't stay long.

This machining work and the work just completed by the shaft boring crew is critical to the well being of the alignment. If properly done, the shaft center will be within a few thousandths of perfect, an amount small enough that shaft motion will be undetectable. That's been our goal all along.

If this machining job is completed today, then the shaft can be reconnected, Steve said. Following that and the fine-tuning of reduction gear hold-down bolts, an orange epoxy resin material known as Chock Fast will be poured in the morning, once hold-down bolts were checked for alignment. This particular epoxy will not shrink as it sets, and it will serve the same purpose as a carefully honed steel shim, filling the gap between gear mounts and engine rails.

If all goes well, the box may be flooded Friday morning. Following start-up and trials, perhaps Friday afternoon, the *AJR* will be sailed home.

✻✻✻

Having the *Arni J.* ready again for service brought up another detail: what water depths will we find at the island? Hoyt and I reviewed soundings taken at the end of August, and after adjustment for the continued drop over the past several months, it looks as though we won't have water enough to safely operate the *AJR* unless we dredge.

With water depths on my mind, I stopped at Fish Creek on my return to Northport to look up Mike Kahr. I was given a tip by a worker on the waterfront that Mike and his crew might be having lunch at the Bayside. That's where I headed. After I apologized for interrupting their lunch, we talked. Mike understood, I believe, our dire need to dredge soon. As we parted, I promised to send him a copy of our August soundings to reinforce our concerns about how shallow it has become.

One more wreath stop before I headed home: Hedy Eller's at Northport. I hadn't visited with Hedy for several weeks and this afternoon I have the extra time to sit down with her. She is delighted to get our wreath and she described a shop that she worked in nearly 40 years ago at a farm near what is now Newport State Park. Between 15 and 20 workers assembled wreaths there in the weeks prior to Christmas and shipped them off in semi trucks. The shop was located in an old chicken coop where pine needles accumulated several inches thick on the floor. The single exit door was, more or less, blocked by piles of pine boughs stacked on the ground outside, awaiting trimming into smaller pieces. Ernst, her husband, said finally, "That's enough. No more working in that fire trap!"

Before leaving Hedy's home, I hung her new wreath and fed her birds. At 92, and with deep snow, feeding the birds can be a challenging task.

The ferry is in and over at the freight garage our crew is loading packages onto carts.

Wednesday, December 5 –

A serene sky at sunset, actually a few minutes before 3 p.m., belies the fact it is cold outdoors. And the temperature is dropping, 18 degrees now. Except for the first few morning hours, sun appeared most of the day and the northerly winds were moderate. In the distance at mid-morning, looking toward the south end of Plum Island, we watched as the red-hulled Coast Guard cutter *Mackinaw* worked the Waverly Shoal buoy. They replaced a lit buoy with a smaller can, so that moving ice will slide over it in winter. This buoy is stationed over a 9-foot shoal located a mile southeast of Northport, partway between Pilot and Plum Islands. It marks a bottom feature all lake freighters need to steer away from as they swing through the Door.

Our four ferry round trips are down to the basics: hauling freight, mail, trucks, cars, and the passengers who have things to do, either on the island side or the mainland. Few travelers board the ferry as a means of recreation these days, unless their frivolity includes shopping or a movie on the mainland.

Our ferries are the island's only transportation link. And this time of year, that's the only reason we go!

***

Our reply brief to the DNR's response brief arrived this morning by email.

It required a significant block of time to read and digest. It's a well-written and well-reasoned document and I think the Administrative Law Judge ought to be quite impressed by the arguments. On the other hand, I'm not certain this Administrative Law Judge will be swayed by any legal arguments that require him to pass Summary Judgment, that is, forgo the public hearing with testimony, and rule solely on legal issues.

The other side of our approach is that a review court, in a later appeal, may look with greater favor upon our brief and agree with us.

Except for a very few minor corrections, the document will be smoothed and sent to the Administrative Law Judge by day's end.

***

Setting that aside, then, I began drafting our 2008 tariff, the document that outlines what our ferry charges will be and the appropriate categories to which charges are assigned. Over the years this document has grown and changed only slightly. We've tried to keep it simple and understandable, leaving little room for contradiction.

Fairness, comprehensiveness, simplicity, and the need to have sufficient operating revenues — all play into the question of what categories should be tweaked, what ones do we leave alone? The general economy of the island, plus our own business needs, must be considered. Can we afford not to raise? If we raise a rate category, what is a fair amount?

We review our rates just once each year, then go to press with 115,000 brochures, and we post the basic rates on our website where people from all over can plan business and vacation costs. An error at this juncture, such as not raising or not raising enough, can also come back to haunt us, especially if traffic or the economy tanks in the next 12 months.

***

It is that time of year when it is not only dark early in the day, but the land is covered in snow and the pavement in ice. Walking at dusk, whether in the yard, driveway, or anywhere outdoors, is made difficult and risky. A result is that our lives become more sedentary in winter unless we push to find new ways of getting exercise.

***

I passed Barry McNulty this noon as I drove north and he walked south, along Main Road between Dave's Garage and the Community Center. Barry's route took him closer to the centerline of the road than the side of the road, and as I prepared to pass him, a flatbed semi truck headed toward me in the opposite lane. No sidewalks on the island, just snowy ditches and icy shoulders. I slowed to ease around Barry after the truck passed.

Thursday, December 6 –

Island electrical power was out last night for approximately 30 minutes. First, lights flickered over a 10-minute period of time, then power went dead altogether around 11 p.m. The REA's standby diesels were soon started, with multiple attempts to bring the power up, each attempt with a 15-minute service delay in between. Finally, the power was restored and stable, and I wondered what tavern owners did in such circumstances? Maybe bar patrons who prefer it dark enjoy drinking in the dark, or by candlelight? The TV sports channel is out; card playing, difficult. Electricity to pump water to flush toilets would be a problem. But a drink poured in the dark may be to the patron's advantage.

***

It's 14 degrees this morning, and sunrise over the golf course behind our home showed a clear sky to the east. Snow is in the forecast again, maybe up to four inches of fluffy new snow, with warming temperatures through the day.

The traffic line for the 8 o'clock ferry this morning is long. There's nearly a load by 7:40 a.m. with 20 minutes yet to departure. Maybe the fact it's forecast to snow this evening encourages more people to get off the island. A second crew started a second ferry in response, the *Washington*, and they will load the remaining traffic. Then, from Northport the *Washington* will also haul the Veolia trash semi with empty bins back to the island. Later, our regular crew will use the *Washington* to haul the same truck with bins full of garbage back to the mainland, on its journey to Brown County's landfill.

***

The *Arni J.* has been missed in terms of its hauling capacity, but results of our internal discussions within the past 24 hours favor keeping it sidelined until we are more comfortable with depths around our docks.

How to get our dredging done sooner? A contractor has his own time clock, it seems, and we're not about to experiment dragging the bottom of a ferry recently out of dry dock. We consider leaving the *Arni J.* at Bay Ship for a few more days, or mooring it at the Potato Dock where water depths are deeper.

***

Looking toward the south end of Plum Island this morning, the returning ferry stands tall, exaggerated by mirage to appear twice the height it really is. A temperature inversion of cool air over warm water is just the right combination to magnify the image. In years past, especially in fall, I've observed ore boats on the horizon with an inverted, mirror image on top of the normal image.

The shore crew, guys who made the extra trip this morning, is engaged in pumping the poop tank on the *Washington*. With no heat source in the forward compartment, the remaining effluent needs to be pumped dry, the tank flushed, and the pump itself drained to avoid damage. Our portable waste tank is then towed a few hundred feet up the dock to a dumpsite near our office. There, the contents are gravity dropped by hose into our shore side sanitary system. Eventually, effluent captured while underway on a ferry is pumped to the woods behind the Welcome Center.

Other ferry holding tanks should be pumped, too, while the equipment is out and in use, so that we're not caught short in a cold stretch for sewage capacity. Among the worst aspects of being a late season ferry captain: dealing with exposed waste lines that are plugged and frozen solid with sewage.

Once again, the *Arni J.* is best suited for below-freezing weather because it has internal waste and water line systems that are insulated and protected from the cold. Since putting the *Arni J.* into service we haven't had a single waste line or toilet freeze-up.

Friday, December 7 –

My stops in Sturgeon Bay prior to the shipyard included dropping off a pair of land disturbance permits at the Planning Office for Kay Miller. The application is for temporarily placing dredge spoils on our property.

When I arrived at the shipyard it was already noon. The *AJR* had been floated and backed out of the box, and Rich and Hoyt were in the process of breaking six-inch plate ice in the slip near where they would moor. I waited in my truck on the pier, observing their progress. Winds were from the west, and this pier was fully exposed to the cold drafts. Knee deep snowdrifts had formed inside the pier wall where plows didn't make a pass, and pieces of steel, wooden boxes, and other shipyard items lay half-buried in the drifts, potential ankle twisters. The noon sun was out in full force and clouds were gone from the sky.

The shipyard workers were on lunch break, so we waited for the whistle to blow, for machinists to join us with a dial indicator, so that we could conduct sea trials.

In minutes the whistle had blown, and Terry Gunnlaugsson and another machinist set up their instrument over the shaft in the engine room, and we got underway. A dial indicator measures in thousandths, and it mounts with a magnet so that it can be placed at various locations to read shaft run-out. We cast off and headed through the ice toward Hill's Point and Potawatomi Park with Hoyt at the wheel.

The shaft readings looked good. That is, the most movement we detected was just forward of the stuffing box, and it ranged from .005 to .007 thousandths. This movement was imperceptible to the eye, and I couldn't feel any vibration on my hand as I placed my palm alongside the stuffing box. All other readings were even less than that, meaning, we had achieved the results we had hoped for.

From time to time, the shaft packing gland was tightened, squeezing the collar down on the rings of packing, slowing the drip of water entering the engine room. We repeated this process as the packing wore in from shaft rotation. The packing material is manufactured of flax and impregnated with bees' wax, an old-school style of packing. We've tried the newer Teflon packing, but not with success. It requires much more attentiveness because it easily overheats, melts, and can grab the shaft, creating scorch marks. The objective is to tighten the packing gradually, allowing a few drips per minute. If this is done, the gland runs cool and the shaft turns with acceptable resistance.

Since we were witnessing the results we hoped for, instead of keeping the ferry at the yard a few more days we decided to sail it home. But first, we had one more short sea trial, this time with Coast Guard Marine Safety inspectors onboard to witness the machinery in operation. The reduction gear, generator and major propulsion components had been disconnected and reassembled, and it's good practice to assure they are back in working order prior to carrying passengers once again.

A portable yard crane lifted our old shaft, packed in a crate, onto the *AJR* foredeck. Other spare parts, including spare stern bearings and a distorted output flange from the gear, were loaded in my pickup truck. Rich made a quick run for food (he and Hoyt hadn't eaten lunch) and by 2:45 p.m. the *Arni J.* departed Bay Shipbuilding for the island. I watched from the pier as our ferry sailed from the yard, past a freighter on blocks in the 1200-foot graving dock, and through sunlit ice toward Washington Island. Wind and sea conditions in the bay were excellent for getting the ferry home that afternoon.

I stopped briefly in the office to see Todd, General Manager, to let him know the sea trials went well and that we were taking the ferry home. When the dust settles on the long work list, we'll get together to complete the paperwork portion of this project, to determine division of financial responsibilities. "We may never know which one of the five or six things we did solved the problem," Todd smiled. Such things are never totally black and white, but there will be more discussion, to be sure.

***

At 7 p.m., following a phone call from Hoyt, I learned the *AJR* was beyond Door Bluff on its final course home. I headed to the Potato Dock to help them moor. The night was clear, and Orion's belt tilted low over Detroit Island to the east. In the west, the red port running light and white masthead light of the *Arni J.* could be seen in the distance, still 15 minutes or more away. I parked to illuminate the pier edge and pilings with my headlights. A second truck left there earlier by our crew was parked in a similar fashion.

Hoyt eased the *Arni J.* alongside the steel wall, within a foot or so of the tires, and Rich passed over the first mooring line eye. Then, we passed lines back and forth for the next 10 minutes, until we were satisfied we had the ferry safely situated. One wrinkle turned up: the *AJR* shore cord was too short to reach the outlet. So, I drove to where the *Eyrarbakki* was moored and swapped shore cords, and this extra length worked. With shore power on, engine room heaters working, we closed up and headed home.

***

The *Arni J.*'s return should help to quell recent island rumors. Just last evening, Town Supervisor Ron Overdahl had called me.

He forwarded information he'd heard up town or at Mann's Store, or wherever, to the effect that the *Arni J.* either couldn't or wouldn't be fixed, and that as a result we wouldn't be bringing it back to the island for the winter. Such craziness, I thought. "Do these sources think we're going to sell it for scrap?" I asked.

That such rumors even get started, and that people who hear them take them seriously means they haven't had the proper information. I told Ron about the short piece I wrote in the Passenger Cabin News that came out earlier in the day, and I hoped my article would explain the difficulties we'd been having with repairs. I went on to explain the additional hurdles we still faced with low water, our need to dredge, and the wait to get our contractor on site.

Saturday, December 8 –

This morning is colder than any so far, with 12 degrees showing on my home thermometer at 6 a.m. But we're still warmer than inland locations, where they've had minus and single figures regularly during this past week. Any temperature below 32 degrees will freeze water, eventually, and we're seeing that happen before our eyes as Detroit Harbor is now almost completely frozen over. It would be good skating, thick ice in the shallows near Holiday Inn and Snake Island, if it weren't for the very crusty cover of snow.

Near the ferry dock, patches of skim ice have formed. Not ice you would ever dare walk on, but the beginning of surface ice that will eventually become larger patches, sometimes resembling pancakes, little disks of ice mush frozen together. Overnight they'll knit and form the first sheet of solid ice around the ferries. This process may be somewhat early this year, but then again, we might hit a mild stretch that could temporarily reverse the process. For the near term, temperatures will continue to stay cold, meteorologists tell us.

The traffic is again "about right," that is, we take care of all cars in line. No one is disappointed. On the other hand, it's not a full load of cars.

Jim Hanson is both ticket seller and boat crew today. He does this by helping get the ferry ready before manning the island ticket booth. Then, he rides across with his cash box and when the ferry is unloaded, he opens up the Northport ticket booth and sells to customers there. It's superior to selling tickets on board when there are but two daily round trips and few customers.

***

The engine room ambient temperatures are good on the *Noble* and *Eyrarbakki*. Later, I'll check the *Arni J.* to make sure the electric heaters are working in her engine room. Not only would the engines be impossible to start in a freezing engine room, but there is added danger of freezing pipes, split valves, and unforeseen (and maybe out of sight) damage.

In the past, we've had just about everything happen, from hot water boilers blowing antifreeze through relief valves all over the engine room, to a furnace backfiring and sooting up a fresh paint job, to shore power going out and engine room temperatures plummeting.

Over the past several years, we've methodically replaced temperamental and messy oil-fired boilers with electric heaters. Because electric heaters make the meters spin, when we're moored in port we turn off all unnecessary heaters for a savings. Underway, our ship's generator produces excess KW's so that the supply of electrical power for all heaters — cabin, heads and pilot house — is readily available. Lack of insulation on our 'summer ferries' makes them cold and unpleasant on early winter days, especially during early morning hours, until the heaters have had a chance to catch up.

Sunday, December 9 –

It's 18 degrees this morning, a warming trend! Clear, with little to no wind. The snow predicted earlier in the week hasn't materialized, and so we may see only a few light flurries as a result. "Snow flurries" are the operational words to describe our weather most recently, having replaced "blustery winds." But, instead of blustery we could simply say the winds were "damn cold."

It's nearing the middle of this month, and I have a few corporate reports to complete, shareholder communications to write, crew bonus considerations, a Christmas party in 10 days at Karly's to plan, and projects to wind down before weather proves more difficult.

Monday, December 10 –

The air is a cold 12 degrees, but there is no wind at all and outdoors it seems quite pleasant. The sun is up and the day is bright. No clouds clutter the sky — only pure blue. Our snow hasn't settled much and hasn't melted either, although a slow evaporation process has helped to clear the pavement and sidewalks.

***

Skim ice, flat, smooth new ice nearly half an inch thick, extends in a solid sheet past the ferries and out the channel to the Detroit Harbor entrance buoy.

By 7:40 a.m., Rich had moved the *Robert Noble* from an inside slip near the old office to the south side of the service dock. Step one in preparation for lay up is to drain down the piping, shut off machinery, and turn off the electric heat. It's that time of year when kilowatts fly through the uninsulated steel hull to the outside atmosphere with very little benefit other than helping to keep equipment operational. The *Washington* and *Eyrarbakki*, each with greater freeboard than the *Noble* (and therefore better for loading, and less prone to deck icing), will still be available to make trips, at least until the ice thickens.

Out at the Potato Dock onboard the *Arni J.,* Joel, Ken and Bill Crance will work on cleaning up the engine room and reseating the engine room soft patch, the opening through which the gear and generator were passed at the shipyard. This hatch still leaks, maybe the result of the yard putting it back together without first cleaning ice and dirt from around the rubber gasket material. Our crew will lift the patch, clean it, and carefully reset it before retightening the bolts, hoping for watertight results. Rich proposed a bead of a rubberized caulk to insure a successful job.

***

The *Robert Noble* is now, more or less, put to bed for the winter.

There are few days as pleasant as a sunny winter day without wind, with snow covering the ground and temperatures in the low 30s. The going is excellent for our ferry in such conditions, although ice sheets are presently growing outward from shore, signaling a cooling of the bay waters. Our West Channel route at day's end was cleared of ice by wind and current, and by ferry activity. The late winter afternoon skies have soft light like no other.

***

Several bills have arrived by mail, for legal services rendered regarding the Northport south ramp WDNR permit, and they represent a significant cost, but it's the tip of the iceberg, in some respects. Legal runs toward $6,000 for our activity with the State of Wisconsin to sustain our rights as property owner, lease holder and ferry operator.

We're also starting to receive a few of the bills associated with the *Arni J. Richter* project. The arbor machined by Metso for the propeller balancing was $5000. That is the arbor only, not including balancing done by Badger Roll. And so it goes.

Our company must start the winter and the new year with a sizeable bank account, knowing it will dwindle as the months go by. Recent repair efforts will result in a much smaller cash position as we enter our least profitable months of the year. We may resort to short term borrowing on our good looks and reputation.

Tuesday, December 11 –

The overcast morning has the look of snow, and it will snow to our south according to the weather map. The morning temperature was 28 degrees, a good 14 degrees warmer than the past few days, with a moderate 15 mph wind from the WSW. Ferry travel will be good today.

I called Dr. Tom Wilson and reported a troublesome tooth, upper left. He asked me questions over the phone: "Is this the one we worked on last spring? Is there pressure?"

Tom consulted my charts which he happened to have handy in his canvas briefcase, part of a collection of "active" patient files and suggested a root canal may be in order when he gets to the island. Could I give him a ride to the clinic and be his first patient? It's Tom's Tuesday for island office hours, and I am appreciative of his concern.

Two patients were already waiting for Tom when he arrived at the clinic. I was #3. He escorted patient #1 to his office and "numbed up" her jaw. She came right back out to the waiting room as patient #2 entered. She returned to the waiting room inside of five minutes, and then it was my turn. In my pocket I carried the crown of porcelain and gold that had come unglued weeks before, and in a matter of minutes Tom had applied glue and filled the vacant slot in an upper left tooth. Then, Tom probed the area surrounding the suspect tooth. Believing the worst was already over for me, given the normal trend of a dying tooth, Tom prescribed antibiotics as a way to borrow more time until we can arrange for a root canal.

Jack Hagen entered the clinic waiting room as I was about to depart. On the shelf near the reception window, Janet's CD player broadcast sounds of the Hagen Family Christmas album. "That's you," I said, pointing to the CD player. "Your family's music."

"Yes," Jack replied, "they just played the other night at a church in Green Bay and there were over 200 people. I'm very blessed to have such a family. They always give me a hug when we say good-bye and tell me they love me. What more could I ask for?"

***

The load of daily UPS packages has noticeably increased of late.

On this island there are many things now ordered through the internet and shipped the following day, with arrival the day after that. Our postal packages and number of mail sacks has also increased.

Wednesday, December 12 –

Very little breeze and 21 degrees, with blue skies and sunshine at 8 a.m. Snow banks have settled and more bare patches are appearing on pavement and lawn.

Given the good weather, Rich and Tully and Ken are working to complete the rafter and eave alignment, and hang plywood on the roof and walls, essentially closing in the Island Pizza structure. Joel is working on the *Arni J.* to complete cleaning of the engine room and will hang a metal cabinet in the main deck head.

* * *

Ray Hansen was in to set up a special trip for tankers, only to learn the supply of LP and gasoline is in short supply at the terminal. That's the word received from Schuh Transport, the company that trucks Ray's product to the island. We'll try for early next week. While the mild weather is holding, it's too bad we couldn't have hauled in a few truckloads. The temperature is supposed to turn quite cold again on the weekend.

* * *

This day was beautiful and productive. Temperatures hit 28 degrees at one o'clock and ice melted on the dark pavement.

Joel Gunnlaugsson freshened up the *Arni J's* engine room, cleaning out sand, lost tools, bolts in the bilge, not to mention cigarette butts, peanut shells, sunflower seed hulls and other trash left behind by the work crew at Bay Ship. It's hard to keep a boat clean when the shipyard grounds are muddy and dirt gets tracked in on boot soles, but it's also hard to fathom the housekeeping habits of workers who are, in manner of speaking, onboard guests.

* * *

I completed the editing of our revised Employee Handbook, a task that had been at the bottom of the pile on my desk for quite some time. In the end, much of the work had already been done, and it was primarily a final edit before passing it along for proofing. My goal was to make the whole handbook read more easily, be less convoluted and less negative, listing desired positive traits and attributes, eliminating negative examples and shortening up paragraphs.

***

Harvey Koyen brought out six medium whitefish for Tully who will smoke them for our crew Christmas party next Wednesday. Fish pieces are soaked a day or two in brine before they're placed in the smoker. Tully's a master at it, but he prefers salmon. "Whitefish?" he questioned, as if this choice was a strange request. "Do you like smoked whitefish?" Of course we do!

***

A silver crescent, the moon a sliver against a southwest twilight of orange, pink, and aquamarine, hangs over Dave's Garage on Main Road. Extremes in colors come with the serenity of an early winter sky. Exactly like no other sunset or moonrise, but yet a timeless scene. Then, with darkness setting in, sets of headlamps pass Dave's moving south. Minutes later, a string of 10 headlight pairs travel north. A short interval, then 10 minutes later, stragglers, two more sets of headlights. The last ferry of the day has landed and island travelers are headed home, followed by the crew.

***

Basement projects become a pleasure this time of year, especially wood carving. My chisels and a partly completed project, one of the St. Andrew's crosses from the interior of the stavkirke, await me, with a pile of wood chips still on the cement floor from late March. A Norman Rockwell calendar hangs from a nail, compliments of Baylake Bank, and shows March 2007. What happened to spring, summer and fall? I may as well change the calendar to 2008 as soon as the bank gives out a new one. Or, should I leave the old one up? What's the difference? The projects will wait for me.

Thursday, December 13 –

Lake effect snowflakes float lazily to earth like light, frozen wafers. The air is moist, conditions perfect for a few inches of fresh snow cover.

In the lunchroom refrigerator are three Racine Danish Kringles, and on the training board is written, "kringles compliments of the Northport red squirrels." The previous afternoon, a shipment of the finely made, nationally-famous ovals of pastry, dozens of boxes of them, were off-loaded at our Northport garage. They were intended for island school children, pre-sold as a school fundraiser. A neighborhood red squirrel found the kringles in the garage and chewed through corner packaging to sample the bakery items.

This sort of thing has happened before, especially in late fall, and it seems the high-end bakery is preferred. The squirrels often select the most expensive donuts, leaving loaves of bread untouched. Maybe the sugar. Since the Northport freight garage door is generally left open during the daytime, it's a short trip from a nearby tree to the food source.

Hoyt packed a .22 with bird shot this morning when he rode across to Northport to meet with Mike Kahr. He claimed later to have bagged a fifteen-pounder as it came out of the garage. The red squirrel had been sitting on top of the UPS cart, looking at him, awaiting another kringle shipment. When Hoyt approached, it ran its last steps with full belly toward the nearest tree.

Now three kringles, with the chewed corners trimmed off, await human consumption, purchased by the Ferry Line as damaged goods.

***

Halfway across the Door this morning, I pointed out to Erik Foss, captain on the *Washington*, what I thought might be the yellow backhoe of Mike Kahr's on the dock. Shortly after that, a white puff of smoke arose as the excavator's cold diesel turned over.

"He's going to start digging from the dock, as far as he can reach, until the barge gets here," I said.

"He's missed some good weather to bring it around," was Erik's reply.

I went down to the main deck and stood in the bow, peering at the bottom over the rail as we approached the north ramp. Ahead of us, through the clear 12 to 15 feet of water, I saw scattered stones, loose and easy to scoop, it appeared. But then there were patches of flat rock with huge crevices, the tough limestone strata that would have to be busted up before it could be dug.

"It looks like the top of the Niagra escarpment," Jim Hanson said.

***

When we returned to Northport in late afternoon it was nearly dark, and we pulled in behind 15 other vehicles, all in line for the last ferry of the day. At the end of the dock was a set of dump truck headlights, and Mike's excavator was busy digging and loading the truck. I walked out to see how the work was coming along.

Mike Brown, a veteran employee of Mike's, told me he had already hauled 14 loads of material off the pier to a temporary upland site in our west parking lot. This bottom material consisted of sand, gravel, and a small amount of muck or clay. Already the water dripping from the excavator bucket and oozing from the tailgate of the dump truck had begun to freeze in a buildup of muddy ice on the dock surface. It would only get worse from hereon, given the fact temperatures today were nearly 32 degrees.

In the morning, according to Mike, they will attach the hydraulic breaker point, also known as a "pecker point," to the arm of the excavator in order to start breaking up the solid strata of limestone. The reach from the pier is limited to approximately 20 feet. Until his barge arrives, now with an ETA of late Sunday or Monday morning, that is all we can hope will be accomplished.

* * *

Our ferry course home took us under the mainland in the lee of the peninsula's tip, then we turned smartly for the entrance buoy to Detroit Harbor, taking a few deep rolls as we maneuvered. It was all in the dark of early evening, with only our deck lights and a few house lights visible on the shore behind us. The SW winds had created enough sea so that when we arrived at the island dock, the *Eyrarbakki* was dancing, tugging at its mooring lines in the confines of protected Detroit Harbor. Although it was only 5:05 p.m., it was dark except for the ferry office lights up the pier.

Saturday, December 15 –

By 10:30 a.m., large snowflakes began falling. The precipitation has increased over the past hour, although significant accumulation isn't in the forecast until evening.

Our two afternoon ferry trips went routinely.

A notable scene on our final return trip after dark was a fractional moon that pierced a thin shower of snowflakes. You would not even have known it was snowing except for seeing minute sparkles in our spotlight beam as we coasted up the channel. With temperatures dropping and the evening air calm, surface waters near the docks resembled a grease skim on a pot of cooling soup. The dock lights played across the expanse of the two slips. The harbor's still waters will be frozen by morning with a light ice cover.

It's time to fasten the lines, plug in the shore power cord, and head for home.

Sunday, December 16 –

Early morning temperatures were in the low 20s, with bright sun and a brisk NW wind. A light snow fell just after dark Saturday, and flakes lay exactly where they fell, not yet whisked about by the winds.

The *Washington* this morning at 8 a.m. had a nearly full load. The 10 a.m. ferry will have, maybe, half a load of vehicles. While the *Washington* is able to back in, stern first, to the island dock, making easy loading for the crew and easy driving aboard for customers, there are late-season drawbacks that are hard to resolve. For one, the restrooms are not functioning. Given cold weather, toilet piping was drained, including the waste holding tank below decks. Then, the commodes were pulled from the deck. In anticipation of laying up the ferry, half of the cabin benches were removed to the shop for maintenance. Electric heaters warm up the cabin pretty well after the first half hour or so, but the initial cold is hard to counter when there's been a freezing cold night. The pilothouse heater does not work well. Those are just some of the undesirable deficiencies for cold weather operation, and if it were to get down to the single digits, it would be difficult to operate this ferry.

***

There are six ice shanties out on the harbor. A few were set out the middle of last week. As soon as ice sets, fishermen follow, and they will fish as long as the ice supports them in the spring. Snowmobiles rather than pickup trucks are the vehicles of choice so far.

Is it the novelty and freedom of fishing from new ice, or do the fish come into the harbor in greater numbers after the ice has set, making fishing irresistible to fishermen? I observed a lone fishermen Thursday afternoon at the Sister Bay Village Marina preparing his ice drill, bucket and tip ups. It was impossible not to note the expanse of open water just beyond the marina break wall, and I wondered, how thick and secure was the ice cover within the harbor?

Detroit Harbor almost always has currents running back and forth past the northern points of Detroit Island, between the East-to-West Channels, varying with wind direction. Even after a stretch of extremely cold weather, an expansion crack may develop and stay open, perhaps covered over lightly with snow. Crossing that point when ice hasn't thickened to a foot or more is an invitation to put a vehicle or a leg through the ice.

Monday, December 17 –

It's slightly colder this morning at 19 degrees, but we're told daily highs will approach 30 degrees each of the next several days, a mild air flow closer to the normal temperatures this time of year. Heavy snows skipped our area but covered Milwaukee Saturday, and then pelted the east coast Sunday.

Our marine contractor, Mike Kahr, is due to arrive with his work barge within the hour at Northport. On past dredging projects, in isolated spots Mike has been able to pry the teeth of his bucket under the limestone and peel away at the edge, sometimes pulling off large pieces. The water is clear to begin with, but once the first bucket is scooped, the water is muddy and all work from then on is by feel and experience.

***

Winter's official start and our reservation book coincide. We require ferry reservations for vehicles beginning December 20th. At that same time, winter truck and freight rates also take effect. The premium on deck space and difficulty of making trips and maintaining equipment is the reason for the higher rates placed on large vehicles. With limitations of side-loading the *C.G. Richter*, it was previously impossible to carry a truck longer than 25 feet (although sometimes long pieces of lumber hung beyond the ferry rail). Each winter with the *AJR* we've hauled several dozen semis, plus many long trailers and straight trucks.

Calls come to our front desk frequently, customers asking to reserve vehicle spaces for winter travel. Most callers will plan their travels for the upcoming holidays, and some plan even further ahead for appointments and vacations. Ferry reservations are taken on a first-come, first-served basis.

Tuesday, December 18 –

December may not give us another day so perfect. Winds at 8 a.m. were nonexistent. The temperature was in the mid-20s with sunshine. By noon it should reach the low 30s.

Looking at our video cam at Northport at 11:30 a.m., I saw Mike had moved his construction barge to a position nearer the north ramp and began dredging loose material. A part of depth loss there is due to the accumulation of zebra mussels brought into the harbor by storms and currents, along with loose stones and sand. He should successfully sweep the north side for loose material today, and after repairs are made, begin the breaking of rock tomorrow.

Wednesday, December 19 –

We're into a window of mild weather today, an air mass flowing west-to-east from the Pacific. Nighttime temperatures are near-thawing now, and day temperatures are slightly warmer.

Two tankers this morning came in by special ferry, one carrying gasoline, one with LP. It's a perfect morning to haul them, with only a light breeze. The special ferry for flammables arrived back at the island and unloaded in time to take the 8 a.m. regular traffic.

***

Mary Jo rode with me to the landfill, her main purpose being to thank attendants John and Jeff for all of their help during the year. She really does appreciate their help in allowing her to sift through cast-offs, and also for their help in occasionally spotting and setting aside a piece with potential. It's always surprising what some people throw away. John and Jeff are most often the first ones to spot a piece of junk and recognize its value!

On our drive to the Island Exchange with a brief stop at the bank, I had the impression everyone had left town. There wasn't a single car at the bank, Mann's Mercantile, K.K. Fiske, or the several bars, other than the owner/operator vehicles. The first sign of active commerce was at Mann's Store where a few grocery shoppers had parked.

***

Tomorrow we'll fuel the *Arni J.* and the *Washington* by splitting a tanker between the two ferries at Northport. All fueling will take place on the south side of the pier while Mike Kahr dredges with his barge on the north side.

Thursday, December 20 –

The temperature at 8 a.m. was 34 degrees, indicating thawing took place during the entire evening. Today's forecast is for mild weather and overcast, with a chance of slight precipitation in isolated areas.

Our Christmas party was a success last night, and all but a few of our employees and their spouses attended. The bar was open and food was plentiful. Old Fashioned drinks were most popular, a Midwest and Wisconsin favorite, a mix of brandy with a dash of bitters, sweet mix, and a cherry or orange slice for flavor and color. Tim Jessen was behind the bar and Lois, his wife, prepared an outstanding spread of food that might be classed as "heavy appetizers." Many local favorites were among them: pickled whitefish; fried, fresh lawyers; deep fried whitefish livers; smoked whitefish; and beef tip open sandwiches on toast. The deep fried lawyers, a bottom feeding fish related to the cod, were most popular. It was a casual affair with conversation and visiting, with no planned program, games or speeches. We were home by 9 p.m.

One bit of news learned from Joel and Krista Gunnlaugsson, expecting their first child any day, is that they arranged with Krista's' doctor to leave the island today so that they could attend the party last night. They'll stay at Aurora Bay Care in Green Bay, with a planned delivery sometime the following day. Everyone is pleased and happy for them, expecting good news in a day or two.

***

The *Arni J. Richter* and the *Washington*, both in need of fuel, are fueling this morning at Northport. We're also bringing in a fuel semi for Hansen Oil at 11 a.m. The *Washington* will take on 5,000 gallons, an amount that will top off her 8800-gallon tank for the winter. The balance of 2500 gallons will be dropped into the *Arni J.'s* fuel tank, enough to carry us through January, perhaps into February. Rack fuel price from Green Bay plus the transport charge is $2.65 per gallon.

Hoyt reported Mike was working on his equipment as they were fueling, and that he expects him to resume digging soon. So far, he's been able to continue to peel or rip pieces of stone with his bucket, rather than switch to the breaker point.

Friday, December 21 –

My calendar book indicates tomorrow, Saturday, is the first official day of winter. Mary Jo and I awoke early, and by 5 a.m. were in our kitchen completing a few last Christmas cards and having breakfast. The thermometer outside our kitchen window read 35 degrees. For two days and two nights snow has been melting, and large patches of green show once again.

The forecast calls for light drizzle into Saturday, then the picture changes. From temperatures in the mid-thirties Saturday fed by a southerly airflow, the winds are forecast to shift to the west at gale force, dropping to the lower 20s.

For all ferry travelers Sunday, including our family members trying to return home to the island, crossing will be questionable. Up to
six inches of snow are forecast late Saturday in parts of the state. A
good thing, as a covering of white always makes the holiday more
enjoyable. It's the potential 35-40 mph winds with colder temperatures that may throw a wrench into Sunday's ferries. The ferry reservation book, according to Rich, holds the names of quite a few people
coming to the island for Christmas, and a nearly equal number headed
off the island.

We're committed to traveling to Mom's in Sturgeon Bay Saturday,
with no choice other than to see what transpires.

***

I spent half an hour on the phone with Todd at Bay Ship to discuss various invoiced charges from our recent yard visit with the *Arni
J. Richter*. Out of a total of $152,000, we are willing to pick up perhaps
a third of that amount, based on work done that may not have been a
result of misalignment. As a practical matter, we will likely settle this
amicably somewhere in between. As a regular Bay Ship customer with
the number of ferries we have, the Ferry Line wants continued good
relationships going forward, and so the negotiated result must be fair
to both parties.

***

Rich Ellefson drove a pickup with trailer to Badger Roll in Green
Bay this morning, delivering the old *AJR* starboard shaft and the old
gear output flange. Our intent is to have each of these pieces accurately measured for trueness, and hold them as spares.

On his way through Sturgeon Bay, Rich stopped at Marine Travelift
to visit with Bob Larson, Senior Engineer who had begun the engineering and design for our new ramp at the end of Northport Pier. Two options were posed, one being a continuous, 40-foot ramp structure, and
the other was made up of two sections, more or less 20-ft. each, hinged
together. Advantages with an articulated ramp are mainly with support
beams that are not as deep, and with smaller sections to transport and
assemble. We'd prefer keeping the depth of the ramp shallow. Cost
estimate for engineering and design for such a ramp and hydraulics
engineering included was $15,000.

Saturday, December 22 –

We greet the first official day of winter with fog and low visibility, mild air (37 degrees) and drizzle. This pattern will continue, with the air temperatures actually rising until the two lows converge and a cold air high pressure system brings wind and snow, perhaps tonight.

Mary Jo and I boarded the *Washington* at 8 a.m., ours being one of six vehicles including the Ferry Line mail van. We were headed to Sturgeon Bay to spend the rest of the day with Gramma P. If the forecast proves accurate, we just might end up spending a second day with her. Gale force winds from midnight Saturday through Sunday are coming our way, with blowing snow and falling temperatures. A rather unusual pair of lows, one moving northward from Illinois, the other stationed more or less over the UP, will converge, and the result being a deep low pressure system situated over northeastern Wisconsin. Instead of an east-to-west front it will run north and south, creating the converging isobars that indicate heavy snow production along the lake shore, as cold air pushes in from the west.

This morning our visibility is 1/2 mile and the going is good, and the seas moderate with no ice. Somewhere through the fog that reaches from horizon to horizon, the mainland lies hidden. Off to the side of the channel are several dozen swans.

Old-timer ferry captain, Alvin Cornell, used the expression, "December's fog can kill a dog." Today's weather is a prime example, because dampness will go right through you, making you wish for colder, drier air. How did natives centuries ago manage to survive wearing animal skins and living in bark lodges where smoky air competed with cold dampness?

As we drove off the ferry at Northport, Ken Berggren informed us Joel and Krista were parents of a 9 lb. 4 oz. girl, Gretta Jean, their first child. Congratulations!

***

Our arrival at Mom's home several hours after leaving the island found her waiting at the door dressed in a red Christmas sweater. After greetings, Mary Jo and I carried decorations down from the attic and set them out.

The entire afternoon and evening remained foggy. Midwest air and highway travel are hampered by the low visibility.

Sunday, December 23 –

We awoke in our motel room at the Maritime Inn, knowing it was warm outside, hoping we could take the 9 a.m. ferry home before the storm hit and winds picked up. But that didn't happen.

Although temperatures reached a balmy 42 degrees at 10 p.m. Saturday evening, we knew the temperature would fall. Shortly after 7 a.m. I spoke with Rich Ellefson. He and Erik Foss had driven to the Potato Dock where they could better read wind conditions on the water. Near the Detroit Harbor entrance, seas from the south were already building. Across the Door, Inland Steel's ore carrier, *Ryerson*, had dropped anchor in Hedgehog Harbor behind the Door Bluff headlands. Her captain anticipated wind velocities would increase and was avoiding the open lake.

Based on current conditions and predicted winds, Erik and Rich cancelled all of Sunday's ferry trips. By 8 a.m., Rich phoned me back. He was confident they had made the right call. Winds were estimated at 50 mph with higher gusts near the harbor entrance, and snow had started falling. We also noticed the dramatic change in Sturgeon Bay. In a matter of 15 minutes winds had whipped into a gale and snow flew in blizzard-like conditions.

I spoke with Rich several times that morning. After calling off the day's trips, Rich and Erik checked on the *Arni J. Richter* and found it surging back and forth at the Potato Dock with mooring lines stretched to the limit. Rich was concerned the lines might part under the strain. Main engines were started with propellers churning slowly in forward to counteract the seas that smacked against the transom. Tops of waves were being blown off, and the fine spray coated the car deck and pier with ice. Extra lines were set, and two crew stayed with the *Arni J.* to monitor the ferry's situation.

Further inside the harbor at the main ferry dock, Erik checked the *Eyrarbakki* and found two stern lines that had ridden up and over the top of mooring pipes, a vertical movement of over four feet during bouncing and surging. He refastened these lines, doubling the eyes over the pipe for added friction.

The strong southerly winds had pushed water into the northern Lake Michigan, including Detroit Harbor's waters. I was later told the level rose one foot in Detroit Harbor, flooding the ice and floating ice shanties, which then sailed downwind to the nearest shoreline. Eric DeJardin waded into waist deep water to retrieve his ice fishing gear and secure his shanty.

Monday, December 24 –

The overnight forecast called for storm winds to subside during the evening. We turned in to bed at the Maritime Inn Sunday evening confident that Monday's ferries would run. Our names were among the many from Sunday's reservation list, and there was a small backlog to catch up on, in addition to Monday's vehicle list. During breakfast at the Maritime Inn, I met at least five other parties also headed to the island.

***

Mike Kahr was in his excavator, hammering at the rock bottom on the north side of Northport Pier when we arrived at 8:30 a.m. He had switched out the breaker point for the bucket earlier that morning, and he was hammering away with the 18-inch steel point under water, and pressing downward with the excavator arm. The point penetrated the rock quite easily, and Mike guessed he'd be able to finish hammering the high spots on the north side today, then shift back to the bucket and clean up the broken rock. He would sweep the area once more to find loose hunks of stone that could be struck by the propeller.

I'm very pleased with the effort Mike's made to advance our dredging, understanding it was difficult for him to be on site at an earlier date. I also know he had pressure to complete other jobs. We're not wearing his work boots, and we don't know what decisions he makes to stay in business and make a profit. I also know Mike and his crew have put in many long days of late, one after the other, and that routine alone takes its toll. Loss of sleep, long days of physical work outdoors in all kinds of weather, maybe improper diet...all can affect health and stamina, and it may also impact a safe work place. I saw Mike wore just two fleece layers, no jacket, and a Santa's hat for good cheer, the only clothing barriers between his skin and the damp 28-degree air. He prefers to work with his excavator cab door wide open.

***

Many island institutions are closed Christmas Eve, such as the island post office, branch bank, and Mann's Mercantile. By 2 p.m. I had loaded my truck with trash from the dock, from Arni's, and from my place. I had forgotten to stop at Hoyt's where several plastic sacks with fermenting diapers filled a can in their garage. I was concerned the dump might be closed, too, this Christmas Eve, but when we arrived, the entry gate was open and John and Jeff were smiling and ready to help, as always. "What else have we got to do?" John said with a smile, as I tossed the bulging, 60-gallon, black plastic trash bags into the compactor.

Tuesday, December 25 – Christmas Day

The morning is a mild one at 28 degrees, with light winds.

* * *

We had gathered as a family Christmas Eve, first at Arni's home, then at ours. Our intent was to spend time with Arni by taking turns, giving opportunity for our children and grandchildren to see him.

We recalled a Christmas in the past when our children ran the length of the Richter living room in front of the fireplace, so warm they stripped down to underwear and diapers because the fireplace logs put out so much heat. Everyone felt over-dressed in sweaters and wool clothing. Reduced to skimpy attire, our children stood on the hearth and sang Christmas carols. But on this day, there was no fire in the fireplace, and the living room lighting was minimal, subdued, easier on Arni's sensitive eyes. Most of Arni's waking hours now are spent in his recliner in the small room off the kitchen, a space that's warm and comfortable, and more suited to visiting.

* * *

Grandson Atlas awoke at six and joined us in our bedroom. He announced he had good dreams last night, and afterwards, he awoke and made his bed! He wished to impress upon us how good and deserving a boy he was. We dressed and followed him downstairs to see what Santa had brought him.

There's no excitement like that of a young child, and as Atlas ripped opened his gifts from Santa, he filled the room with exclamations like, "This is the best ever...." A medieval castle with knights and horses, catapult and swords are what capture his interest these days, and that was just the first gift opened.

Monday, December 26 –

The morning is beautiful with soft, pinkish lighting through moist, hazy air. The temperature is 28 degrees, and my truck windshield has a layer of mushy frost. To our south, in Sturgeon Bay, WDOR reported fog, but on the island the air is clear and still.

Chad, Evy, Atlas and Thor all leave today for their respective homes. We'll see them again this coming New Year's weekend. Their visit has been great fun, and we capped it off with a poker game last evening after our grandchildren went to bed.

***

Despite mild temperatures, skim ice has formed in the calm waters surrounding the ferry docks. A really cold night would be enough to set the ice up an inch or two in thickness. If we can continue with the *Washington* and *Eyrarbakki*, it will allow us more time before we're forced to use the icebreaker *Arni J. Richter*.

Ken Berggren reported Mike Kahr should have Northport cleared of broken stone today, giving us a working depth of nearly 14 feet.

***

Harbor waters near the ferries in late afternoon were dead calm. This has been a surprisingly excellent several days of weather following the last storm. Nearly all the snow that fell has already melted, and green grass is showing once again across the lawns. Winter is arriving in fits and starts as it does most years, not a defined time when snow, ice and cold are required to begin. For our marine contractor Mike Kahr, this is weather made to order, and as a result he's made great progress at Northport.

Thursday, December 27 –

During the evening, a soft wet snow fell. Tree limbs and yard objects were lightly outlined in frozen ermine. Shoveling was easy, and each pass left a distinct swipe 24 inches wide on the pavement. At the ferry dock near open water, temperatures might have been slightly warmer, but overall, the island was a basic 32 degrees, the melt-freeze point. More light snow is on the way.

An early ferry with Jim Hanson, captain, and Bill Crance, crew, left just before sunup to pick up a single gasoline tanker for Mann's Mercantile. The regular ferry at 8 a.m. was the *Washington*, and it carried a full load of cars, as it will on the return trip, also.

***

I had a note on my office door that Arni had called for me. I phoned him back and he picked up after a series of rings. It was hard for Arni to understand that the voice was mine, despite my working to be heard and understood.

"Are you going away on a trip on a yacht?" he asked.

"No," I responded. "Just to visit Evy and Chad for the New Year's weekend."

I used too many words and the sentence was too long for him to hear and comprehend.

"I didn't get that. Did you say you were going south on a yacht?"
"No," I replied. "Not me. I'm staying here." He still hadn't understood me.
"Well, I read your letter, but I think I lost it. Do you have another copy?"
Was it our Christmas card letter he referred to? Then, I remembered he had received an email sent to the Ferry Line a week or so ago from his nephew, Dick, who lives in Florida, who occasionally sends Arni email messages through our office. Bill Schutz later verified that Dick Schumann had written and was indeed going on a cruise. Bill would try to locate the old email message and print out another copy for Arni.

Friday, December 28 –

Thursday's mid-afternoon sky cleared, and we enjoyed a beautiful sunset and evening. More snow is in the works for the eastern part of Wisconsin, less snow in the north, greater amounts for Milwaukee and south.

We're headed south, Mary Jo and I, to spend the weekend through Tuesday, New Year's Day, with Chad, Evy and Atlas at their home. Youngest son Thor will fly from the Pellston, MI, airport north of Charlevoix, and pass through Detroit before flying west to Milwaukee.

***

We boarded the *Washington* at 8 a.m. on the first leg of our trip to Brookfield, a western suburb of Milwaukee. Conditions were moderate with a slight wind, small sea, and gray skies, but with a forecast that predicted up to eight inches of snow as we headed south.

Following the customary half-dozen stops in Sturgeon Bay and Green Bay, we entered a twilight zone of snow as we motored south on I-43. Between Denmark and Manitowoc, snow obliterated the highway stripes. Ahead of us, providing me with a target to steer by, were two large trucks with hazard lights flashing, traveling at half the posted 65 mph speed, attempting to stay centered in the right hand lane. Despite the poor visibility and slippery going, impatient drivers passed us in the left lane doing 45 or 50 mph. We observed several dozen cars in the ditch as we continued on toward Milwaukee, drivers with cell phones to their ears calling for towing assistance. We continued in the wake of big trucks.

During our two hours in the white tunnel, where the only objects to focus on were the truck lights ahead of us, we were comfortable and warm. We listened to Wisconsin Public Radio's Ira Flatow, and his subject was science. An asteroid would soon, possibly, strike Mars. A new and powerful telescope had been built in Antarctica, and it had begun to help advance our knowledge of the universe. Flatow interviewed human subjects who participated in highly unusual science experiments. Surrounded by intense highway activity, most of which we saw very little of, we were transported by radio waves to distant realms of thought.

As we neared Milwaukee, even though the snow had fallen longer there and with greater accumulation, driving became suddenly easier. For one thing, I now had objects to focus my eyes on, and the road surfaces seemed in better condition. The air temperature was a degree or two warmer, too, and the plows had been out, plowing and salting. We were thankful, later, to be safely in familiar surroundings in Brookfield, truck and bodies intact, but we also missed the rest of the public radio program as our drive ended.

Saturday, December 29 –

Chad, Atlas and I met Thor as he arrived at Milwaukee's Mitchell Field, while Mary Jo and Evy post-Christmas shopped, the art of bargain hunting. Our chosen afternoon project, amid snow-covered trees in a windless, mild winter environment, was to build a tree fort, a solid platform five feet off the ground from which Atlas could float his imagination and have fun. We sawed, screwed and were instructed by Atlas on how to proceed for several hours. Work finally done, he scrambled up the ladder and surveyed the results. We had strung a zip-wire as an extra touch, a "T" handle slide with nylon rollers that ran along a 70-foot cable. It would take Atlas from tree house to ground in a sweep of seconds.

***

I write my journal entries this day from an oak dining room table that has four matching chairs. This same table anchored our island home living room for over 30 years, used for family gatherings, school projects, sewing, games, and for meetings. Arni's 91st birthday party and his retirement were celebrated on the same day around this table. At various times each of our children took refuge beneath this table to escape the adult world.

Before we had this table, it was in Clara Jessen's home, and her daughters at one time refinished the top, giving the solid oak a clear, lasting luster that displayed the beauty of the oak grain. Clara offered it to us in 1977, shortly after we moved into our Main Road home. She and husband John had received the table and four pieces of the six-chair set from Maggie and Carl Richter, Mary Jo's grandparents. Mary Jo already had the two end chairs with arms and needlepoint seat covers, given to her by her grandmother. Maggie and Carl had received this table and chairs, Mary Jo thought, as a wedding gift from the Nichols' family. The Nichols, Arni and Mary Richter told us years ago, were the original owners. This set had been purchased from Milwaukee and was manufactured in North Carolina, according to markings on the underside of the chairs. Had they been delivered to the island by ferry, or by Goodrich steamer, or were the pieces carried across the ice?

This table is again useful, primarily as a dining table, but it's also used for games, projects, and in my case today, writing. It is heavy, sturdily constructed, with two unusual end pieces that pull out and upward, locking in place to expand from a six- to an eight-place setting. Its value exceeds that of an antique.

***

Atlas joined us in bed this morning at 6 a.m. to talk about science. He's interested in volcanoes, gravity, tornadoes, hurricanes, and he exhausts our knowledge in those departments quickly. He criticized my interest in watching end-of-year bowl games on TV as not having any learning value. I admit he's right, and arguing differently rings hollow.

Monday, December 31 –

It is one more day's vacation at Chad and Evy's in Brookfield, WI, while preparing in a low-key way for the coming New Year. An evening highlight will be "Party Time" with Atlas, who likes to direct us in games such as Hide and Seek. He'll go to bed early, 7 p.m., and we'll play board games afterward on the dining room table.

While away from home, end-of-year ferry business activities continue. Major considerations face this company, about to enter three months with bleak income. Saturday Bill did payroll for the last time this year. The total payroll came to $28,000. Bill just paid our last fuel bill for the *Washington* and *Arni J. Richter*, just over $20,000. The ongoing dredging will be paid in the coming year, when it is completed, and we can only guess at this time what those costs may be. Our bill for Bay Shipbuilding will be settled by phone with General Manager Todd Thayse Thursday morning.

How quickly our winter reserves will dwindle.

***

Being away from the island as the year's final hours pass gives me a bit of perspective. The year has handed out lumps and bruises, but there are polished high points, too. I have a special fondness for this place I call home, where my talents are needed and bonds are strong.

This passage filled with water separating the Door Peninsula from Washington Island that we call Death's Door requires ferry service and people to run the ferries. This is what we do. The water and our ferries define our community, and to a great extent, who I am.

More than just the physical island, Washington Island is also a community and a state of mind that follows wherever we go.

Words on Water Photos

Page 4   cars leaving ferry in winter

Page 24   door, winter

Page 37   cloudline

Page 38   stone fence in winter

Page 56   Stavkirke roof

Page 79   Bethel Church, Washington Island

Page 108   ship's bell

Page 132   fishing tug, Jackson Harbor

Page 159   *Washington Island Observer* building

Page 160   gulls over water

Page 196   Stavkirke ceiling with boat

Page 207   rocking chair in lighthouse

Page 231   *A. J. Richter* crew (L–R):

                Al Stelter, Kim Hansen, Erik Foss, Bill Jorgenson,
                Bill Crance, Joel Gunnlaugsson, Hoyt Purinton, Rich
                Ellefson, Jason Carr, Ken Berggren, Carol Meyer,
                Fred Hankwitz

Page 232   ice along the shore

Page 267   ferry in winter

Page 303   Richard Purinton, author

Patrons of WORDS ON WATER:
A Ferryman's Journal, Washington Island, WI
and Cross+Roads Press

Anonymous G.E.B.

Anonymous E.R.B.

Anonymous N.F.R.

Nancy Akerly

Tom & Judy Amberg

Sharon Auberle

Mariana Beck

Evy Beneda

Christopher & Antonia Blei

Eric Bonow

Gary Busha / **WOLFSONG PUBLICATIONS**

Charles Calkins / **THE BADGER BIBLIOPHILE, BOOKS & MAPS**

Carl T. Carlson

Bill & Carol Crance

Dan Cummings / **Attorney at Law**

Alice D'Alessio

Henry Denander / **KAMINI PRESS**

Bob DeNoto

Ann Eddy

Barbara Ellefson

Hedy Eller

John & Bonnie Evans

Patricia Fittante

David M. Foss

Gary Frommelt

Barbara Fuhrmann

Jude Genereaux

Adam Gessert

Renee Glos-Block

Ruth & Mary Gunnerson

Nathan Gunnlaugsson

R. Chris Halla / **SHAGBARK PRESS**

Frederick Hankwitz

Jeannette Hanlin

Susan Hannus

Kim Hansen

William & Mary Hartman

Laurel Hauser

Ken & Linda Henning

Allan J. Hiller

Suzanne & Cal Holvenstot

Catherine Hovis

Charles Imig

Emmett Johns / **EMMETT JOHNS GALLERY**

Fred Johnson / **THE DRAGONS-BREATH PRESS**

Charlotte Johnston

Lawrence T. Kieck

Capt. Donald Kilpela / **ISLE ROYALE LINE**

Kate Knutson

Lowell B. Komie / Attorney at Law, **SWORDFISH CHICAGO PRESS**

Paula Kosin

Bobbie Krinsky

William G. Ladewig / **Attorney at Law**

Barbara Luhring / **3W DESIGN GROUP**

Gretchen & John Maring

Scott McFarlane

Robert E. McMahon Jr. / **PINNACLE MARINE CORP.**

Shaun & Sue Melarvie

Jan & Bruce Mielke/ **NEGATIVE SPACE STUDIO**

Carol Meyer

Chuck Moser

Ralph Murre / **LITTLE EAGLE PRESS**

– continued

Patrons, continued

John Nelson
Susan O'Leary & James Roseberry
Ginger O'Leary
William H. Olson / **JACKSON HARBOR PRESS**
Maggie Perry
Susan and Charles Peterson
John Plume
Elizabeth Pochron / **CASSANDRA, Charts & Consultation**
Hoyt Purinton
Thor Purinton
Ralph Rausch
Estelle Richter
Dudley and Mickey Riggle
Allen & Helen Roberts
Paul Schroeder
David & Rachel Schwandt
Steve & Karen Schwandt
Marie Skrobot / **Lucha of Arcadia**
Richard R. Spaete

Kenneth F. Stein III / **SAYVILLE FERRY SERVICE**
C.T. Stone Jr.
Dorothy Terry
Kristin Thacher / **MOUNTAIN WORKSHOP**
Pete Thelen / **BLUES TODAY**
Robin Trinko-Russell / **MADELINE ISLAND FERRY**
Barbara Vroman / **PEARL-WIN PRESS**
Capt. Jeff Whitaker / **HUDSON RIVER CRUISES**
Judith Wiker
John & Treiva Wilterding
Jeff Winke
Dave Wright
Larry & Jeanie Young
Sherry Young
Robert M. Zoschke

John and Marilyn Hanson
Carol Holder

Cross+Roads Press List

#1. AN EVENING ON MILDRED STREET, poetry, Mariann Ritzer

#2. THE THOUGHT MUSEUM, poetry, Paul Schroeder

#3. I WANT TO TALK ABOUT YOU, poetry, Dave Etter

#4. EYE DEA, The Autobiography of An Invisible Artist, Bill Stipe

#5. A FIRE ON THE WATERS OF DOUBT, poetry, Pedro D. Villarreal

#6. I THOUGHT YOU WERE THE PICTURE, Artist's Journal, Emmett Johns

#7. ONCE I LOVED HIM MADLY, short fictions, Mariann Ritzer

#8. FINDING THE LOST WOMAN, A Poet's Journal, DyAnne Korda

#9. THE JAMES DEAN JACKET STORY and Other Stories, Don Skiles

#10. THE LAST HOUSEWIFE IN AMERICA, poetry, Donna Balfe

#11. BLUE ISLAND, poetry, Phillip Bryant

#12. TANGLETOWN, poetry, Mike Koehler

#13. Ben Zen, THE OX OF PARADOX, poetry, Tom Montag

#14. WHITE SHOULDERS, poetry, Jackie Langetieg

#15. BACK BEAT, poetry/prose, Albert DeGenova and Charles Rossiter

#16. PRACTICE, The Here & Now, poetry/prose, Edith Nash

#17. BLACK BODY PARTS, poetry, Monique Semoné Ferrell

#18. OUR LADY OF SEVEN SORROWS and Other Stories, prose,
      D. L. Snyder

#19. THE BLUFF, prose, Sue Wentz

#20. A BUTTERFLY SLEEPS ON THE TEMPLE BELL, prose/poetry,
      Don Olsen

#21. A BLESSING OF TREES, poetry, Alice D'Alessio

#22. CIGARETTE LOVE SONGS AND NICOTINE KISSES, poetry,
      Emily Rose

#23. BREATH TAKING, poetry, Susan O'Leary

#24. THE FATHER POEMS, poetry, David Pichaske

#25. THE RAIN BARREL, prose/poetry, Frances May

#26. A GLEAM ACROSS THE WAVE, biography, Arthur and Evelyn Knudsen

#27. SALUD, selected writings, Curt Johnson

Cross+Roads Press List – continued

#28. CRUDE RED BOAT, poetry, Ralph Murre

#29. OTHER VOICES: Works in Progress, anthology; Norbert Blei, editor

#30. THE ELEPHANTS AND EVERYBODY ELSE, poetry, Ronald Baatz

#31. SATURDAY NIGHTS AT THE CRYSTAL BALL, poetry, Sharon Auberle

#32. WORDS ON WATER; A Ferryman's Journal, Washington Island, WI,
      Richard Purinton

Broadsides

Broadside Beat #1: LITTLE BITS OF TRUTH, Women in the Beat,
      Susan O'Leary

Broadside Beat #2: ON EROTIC WRITING, Mariann Ritzer

Broadside Beat #3: OBSCURITY, Don Skiles

Broadside Beat #4: SMOKEY THE BEAR SUTRA, Gary Snyder

Broadside Beat #5: CALL AND ANSWER, Robert Bly

Broadside Beat #6: CROW, Chris Halla

Broadside Beat #7: DRAWING STORIES, Barbara Luhring